Data Analysis with Python

Introducing NumPy, Pandas, Matplotlib, and Essential Elements of Python Programming

Rituraj Dixit

bpb

www.bpbonline.com

Copyright © 2023 BPB Online

All rights reserved. No part of this book may be reproduced, stored in a retrieval system, or transmitted in any form or by any means, without the prior written permission of the publisher, except in the case of brief quotations embedded in critical articles or reviews.

Every effort has been made in the preparation of this book to ensure the accuracy of the information presented. However, the information contained in this book is sold without warranty, either express or implied. Neither the author, nor BPB Online or its dealers and distributors, will be held liable for any damages caused or alleged to have been caused directly or indirectly by this book.

BPB Online has endeavored to provide trademark information about all of the companies and products mentioned in this book by the appropriate use of capitals. However, BPB Online cannot guarantee the accuracy of this information.

Group Product Manager: Marianne Conor
Publishing Product Manager: Eva Brawn
Senior Editor: Connell
Content Development Editor: Melissa Monroe
Technical Editor: Anne Stokes
Copy Editor: Joe Austin
Language Support Editor: Justin Baldwin
Project Coordinator: Tyler Horan
Proofreader: Khloe Styles
Indexer: V. Krishnamurthy
Production Designer: Malcolm D'Souza
Marketing Coordinator: Kristen Kramer

First published: 2023

Published by BPB Online
WeWork, 119 Marylebone Road
London NW1 5PU

UK | UAE | INDIA | SINGAPORE

ISBN 978-93-55510-655

www.bpbonline.com

Dedicated to

My beloved Parents:
Mrs. Indra Dixit
Mr. Sudesh Kumar Dixit
&
My fiancée **Sachi** *and my* **sisters**

About the Author

- **Rituraj Dixit** is a seasoned software engineer who has been actively involved with developing solutions and architecting in the ETL, DWH, Big Data, Data on Cloud, and Data Science space for over a decade. He has worked with global clients and successfully delivered projects involving cutting-edge technologies such as Big Data, Data Science, Machine Learning, AI, and others.

  He is passionate about sharing his experience and knowledge and has trained newcomers and professionals across the globe. Currently, he is Associated as a Technical Lead with Cognizant Technology Solutions, Singapore.

About the Reviewer

❖ **Vikash Chandra** is a data scientist and software developer having industry experience in executing and implementing projects in the area of predictive analytics and machine learning across domains. Experienced in handling and tweeting large volumes of structured and unstructured data. He enjoys teaching Python and Data Science, leveraging Python's power & awesomeness in projects at scale.

Specialties: Predictive modeling, Forecasting, Machine learning, Artificial Intelligence, Deep Learning, Data mining, Business Analytics, Text Mining, NLP, Statistics, SAS, R, Python, TensorFlow.

Acknowledgement

○ I want to thank a few people for their ongoing support during the writing of this book. First and foremost, I'd like to thank my parents for constantly encouraging me to write the book — I could never have finished it without their support.

I am grateful to the course and the companies which supported me throughout the learning process. Thank you for all the direct or indirect support provided.

A special thanks go out to Team at BPB Publications for being so accommodating in providing the time I needed to finish the book and for letting me publish it.

Preface

Data is the fuel in the current information age. Data analysis is quickly becoming a popular topic due to the rapid growth and collection of data. To comprehend data insights and uncover hidden patterns, we require a data analyst who can collect, understand, and analyze data that helps make data-driven decisions.

This book is the first step in learning data analysis for students. This book lays the groundwork for an absolute beginner in the field of Python Data Analysis. Because Python is the language of choice for data analysts and data scientists, this book covers the essential Python tools for data analysis. For each topic, there are various hands-on examples in this book. This book's content covers the fundamentals of core Python programming, as well as Python's widely used data analysis libraries such as Pandas and NumPy, and the data visualization library matplotlib. It also includes the fundamental concepts and process flow of Data Analysis, as well as a real-time use case to give you an idea of how to solve real-time Data analysis problems.

This book is divided into **12 chapters**. They will cover Python basics, Data Analysis, and Python Libraries for Data Analysis. Following are the details of the chapter's content.

Chapter 1 covers the introduction to Python; in this chapter, we will get information about the history of Python and its evaluation. Also, learn Python's various features and versions 1. x, 2. x, and 3. x. We discussed the real-time use cases of Python.

Chapter 2 covers the installation of Python and other Data Analysis Libraries in order to set up a Data Analysis environment.

Chapter 3 starts with the Python programming building blocks such as Variable in Python, Operators, Number, String, Boolean data types, Lists, Tuples, Sets, and Dictionaries. All the programing concepts have been explained with hands-on examples.

Chapter 4 will explore another essential programming construct, how to write conditional statements in Python. In this chapter, we will learn how to write the conditional instructions in Python using if...else, elif, and nested if. All the programing concepts have been explained with hands-on examples.

Chapter 5 covers the concepts of loops in Python. This chapter has a good explanation with appropriate hands-on examples for the while loop, for loop, and nested loops.

Chapter 6 will have content about the functions and modules in Python. It explained how to write the functions in Python and how to use them. Also, this chapter has information about the Python modules and other essential concepts of functional programming like lambda function, map(), reduce(), and filter() functions.

Chapter 7 will cover how to work with file I/O in Python. How to read and write on the external files with various modes and to save the data on file. All concepts have been explained with hands-on examples.

Chapter 8 covers the Introduction to Data Analysis fundamental concepts. This chapter discusses the data analysis concepts, why we need that, and the steps involved in performing a data analysis task. This chapter covers all the basic foundations we need to understand the real-time data analysis problem and the steps to solve the data analysis problem.

Chapter 9 covers the introduction to Pandas Library, a famous and vastly used Data Analysis Library. This chapter has a detailed explanation of features and methods provided by this Library with rich hands-on examples.

Chapter 10 covers the introduction to NumPy Library, a famous and vastly used Numerical Data Analysis Library. This chapter has a detailed explanation of features and methods provided by this Library with rich hands-on examples.

Chapter 11 covers the introduction to Matplotlib Library, a famous and vastly used Data Visualization Library. Data Visualization is a significant part of the Data Analysis process; it is always important to present the Data Analysis results or summaries with an appropriate visual graph or plot. This chapter has a detailed explanation of features and methods provided by this Library with rich hands-on examples of various types of graph plots.

Chapter 12 includes a data analysis use case with a given data set. This chapter has explained one data analysis problem statement and performed an end-to-end data analysis task with a step-by-step explanation to answer the questions mentioned in the problem statement so that learners can clearly understand how to analyze data in real-time.

Coloured Images

Please follow the link to download the
Coloured Images of the book:

https://rebrand.ly/1xbft5b

We have code bundles from our rich catalogue of books and videos available at **https://github.com/bpbpublications**. Check them out!

Errata

We take immense pride in our work at BPB Publications and follow best practices to ensure the accuracy of our content to provide with an indulging reading experience to our subscribers. Our readers are our mirrors, and we use their inputs to reflect and improve upon human errors, if any, that may have occurred during the publishing processes involved. To let us maintain the quality and help us reach out to any readers who might be having difficulties due to any unforeseen errors, please write to us at :

errata@bpbonline.com

Your support, suggestions and feedbacks are highly appreciated by the BPB Publications' Family.

Did you know that BPB offers eBook versions of every book published, with PDF and ePub files available? You can upgrade to the eBook version at www.bpbonline.com and as a print book customer, you are entitled to a discount on the eBook copy. Get in touch with us at :

business@bpbonline.com for more details.

At **www.bpbonline.com**, you can also read a collection of free technical articles, sign up for a range of free newsletters, and receive exclusive discounts and offers on BPB books and eBooks.

Piracy

If you come across any illegal copies of our works in any form on the internet, we would be grateful if you would provide us with the location address or website name. Please contact us at **business@bpbonline.com** with a link to the material.

If you are interested in becoming an author

If there is a topic that you have expertise in, and you are interested in either writing or contributing to a book, please visit **www.bpbonline.com**. We have worked with thousands of developers and tech professionals, just like you, to help them share their insights with the global tech community. You can make a general application, apply for a specific hot topic that we are recruiting an author for, or submit your own idea.

Reviews

Please leave a review. Once you have read and used this book, why not leave a review on the site that you purchased it from? Potential readers can then see and use your unbiased opinion to make purchase decisions. We at BPB can understand what you think about our products, and our authors can see your feedback on their book. Thank you!

For more information about BPB, please visit **www.bpbonline.com**.

Table of Contents

1. Introducing Python 1
Structure 1
Objectives 2
A brief history of Python 2
Versions of Python 2
Features of Python 3
    General purpose 3
    Interpreted 3
    High level 4
    Multiparadigm 4
    Open source 4
    Portable 4
    Extensible 4
    Embeddable/Integrated 4
    Interactive 4
    Dynamically typed 5
Python use cases 5
    Automation 5
    Web scraping 5
    Healthcare 5
    Finance and banking 6
    Data analytics 6
    AI/ML 6
Conclusion 6
Questions 6
Points to remember 7

2. Environment Setup for Development 9
Structure 9
Objectives 10
Downloading and installing the Anaconda package 10
Testing the installation 17
    Testing Python in interactive shell 17
    Running and testing Jupyter Notebook 18
Conclusion 21
Questions 21

3. Operators and Built-in Data Types 23
Structure 23
Objectives 24
Variables in Python? 24
Rules for defining a variable name in Python 24
Operators in Python 24
    Arithmetic operators 24
        Coding example(s) 25
    Relational operators 26
    Assignment operator 28
    Logical operators 30
    Bitwise operators 31
    Membership operators 32
    Identity operators 33
Built-in data types in Python 34
    Numeric type 34
    Type conversion or type casting 36
String 38
    Accessing string components 39

  String concatenation 40
  String operations and built-in methods 40
 List 41
 Tuples 48
 Sets 52
 Dictionaries 57
 Conclusion 61
 Questions 61

4. Conditional Expressions in Python 63
 Structure 63
 Objectives 64
 Indentation in Python 64
 Conditional expressions in Python 64
  'If' statement 64
  If…else statement 65
  Nested if (if..elif or if…if statements) 67
  AND/OR condition with IF statements 69
 Conclusion 71
 Questions 71

5. Loops in Python 73
 Structure 73
 Objectives 74
 Loop construct in Python 74
 Types of loops in Python 74
 Else clause with loops 78
 Loop control statements 79
 Conclusion 81
 Questions 81

6. Functions and Modules in Python 83
Structure 83
Objectives 84
Defining a function 84
    Parameter(s) and argument(s) in a function 85
        Types of arguments 85
Lambda function/anonyms function in Python 88
The map(), filter(), and reduce() functions in Python 89
Python modules 91
How to create and use Python modules 91
    Creating a Python module 91
Conclusion 94
Questions 94

7. Working with Files I/O in Python 95
Structure 95
Objectives 95
Opening a file in Python 96
Closing a file in Python 97
Reading the content of a file in Python 99
Writing the content into a file in Python 101
Conclusion 102
Questions 103

8. Introducing Data Analysis 105
Structure 105
Objectives 106
What is data analysis 106
Data analysis versus data analytics 106
Why data analysis? 107

- Types of data analysis 107
  - *Descriptive data analysis* 107
  - *Diagnostic data analysis – (Why something happened in the past?)* 108
  - *Predictive data analysis – (What can happen in the future?)* 108
  - *Prescriptive data analysis – (What actions should I take?)* 108
- Process flow of data analysis 108
  - *Requirements: gathering and planning* 109
  - *Data collection* 109
  - *Data cleaning* 110
  - *Data preparation* 110
  - *Data analysis* 110
  - *Data interpretation and result summarization* 110
  - *Data visualization* 110
- Type of data 111
  - *Structured data* 111
  - *Semi-structured data* 111
  - *Unstructured data* 111
  - *Tools for data analysis in Python* 111
  - *IPython* 111
  - *Pandas* 111
  - *NumPy* 112
  - *Matplotlib* 112
- Conclusion 112
- Questions 112

9. Introducing Pandas 113
- Structure 113
- Objectives 114
- Defining pandas library 115
- Why do we need pandas library? 115

Pandas data structure 117
    Loading data from external files into DataFrame 119
Exploring the data of a DataFrame 124
Selecting data from DataFrame 128
Data cleaning in pandas DataFrame 131
Grouping and aggregation 141
    Grouping 141
    Aggregation 142
Sorting and ranking 143
Adding row into DataFrame 146
Adding column into DataFrame 148
Dropping the row/column from DataFrame 152
Concatenating the dataframes 154
Merging/joining the dataframes 157
The merge() function 157
The join() function 162
Writing the DataFrame to external files 165
Conclusion 169
Questions 169

10. Introduction to NumPy 171
Structure 171
Objectives 172
What is NumPy? 172
    NumPy array object 173
    Creating the NumPy array 173
Creating NumPy arrays using the Python list and tuple 176
Creating the array using numeric range series 177
Indexing and slicing in NumPy array 178

Data types in NumPy 181

NumPy array shape manipulation 186

Inserting and deleting array element(s) 188

Joining and splitting NumPy arrays 191

Statistical functions in NumPy 195

Numeric operations in NumPy 199

Sorting in NumPy 202

Writing data into files 204

Reading data from files 206

Conclusion 207

Questions 208

11. Introduction to Matplotlib 209

Structure 209

Objectives 210

What is data visualization 210

What is Matplotlib? 211

Getting started with Matplotlib 211

Simple line plot using Matplotlib 212

Object-oriented API in matplotlib 213

The subplot() function in matplotlib 214

Example#1 (1 by 2 subplot) 214

Example#2 (2 by 2 subplot) 215

Customizing the plot 216

Some basic types of plots in matplotlib 227

Export the plot into a file 231

Conclusion 233

Questions 233

12. Connecting Dots – Step-by-step Data Analysis and Hands-on Use Case.... 235
　　Structure... 235
　　Objectives... 236
　　Understanding the Dataset 236
　　Problem statement 236
　　Step by step example to perform the data analysis on a given dataset..... 237
　　Conclusion 251

Index 253-258

CHAPTER 1
Introducing Python

These days Python is getting more attention among developers, especially from data scientists, data analysts, and AI/ML practitioners. In this chapter, we will discuss the history, evaluation, and features of Python, due to which it is one of the most popular programming languages today.

According to the latest **TIOBE Programming Community Index** (**https://www.tiobe.com/tiobe-index/**), Python is ranked first among the most popular programming languages of 2022.

Structure

In this chapter, we will discuss the following topics:

- A brief history of Python
- Different versions of Python
- Features of Python
- Use cases of Python

Objectives

After studying this chapter, you should be able to:

- get information about the creator of Python
- get information about the evaluation of Python
- discuss the feature and use cases of Python

A brief history of Python

Python is a general-purpose and high-level programming language; it supports the programming's procedural, object-oriented, and functional paradigms.

Python was conceived by *Guido van Rossum* in the late 1980s at **Centrum Wiskunde & Informatica** (**CWI**) in Nederland as a successor of the ABC language. Python was initially released in 1991.

Python was named after the BBC TV show *Monty Python's Flying Circus*, as Guido liked this show very much.

Versions of Python

Python version 1.0 was released in 1994; in 2000, it introduced Python 2.0, and Python 3.0 (also called "Python 3000" or "Py3K") was released in 2008. Most of the projects in the industry now use Python 3.x. For this book, we are using Python 3.8:

Python Version	Release Date
0.9	2/20/1991
1	1/26/1994
1.1	10/11/1994
1.2	4/13/1995
1.3	10/13/1995
1.4	10/25/1996
1.5	1/3/1998
1.6	9/5/2000
2	10/16/2000
2.1	4/15/2001
2.2	12/21/2001
2.3	6/29/2003

Python Version	Release Date
2.4	11/30/2004
2.5	9/19/2006
2.6	10/1/2008
2.7	7/3/2010
3	12/3/2008
3.1	6/27/2009
3.2	2/20/2011
3.3	9/29/2012
3.4	3/16/2014
3.5	9/13/2015
3.6	12/23/2016
3.7	6/27/2018
3.8	10/14/2019
3.9	10/5/2020
3.10	10/4/2021

Table 1.1: *Different versions of Python (Source: https://en.wikipedia.org)*

Note: Official support for Python 2 ended in Jan 2020.

Features of Python

Here, we will see the various properties/features of Python, which make Python more popular among all other programming languages.

General purpose

A programming language, which can develop the various applications of domains, not restrict within the specific use of the area, is known as the general-purpose programming language. Python is a general-purpose programming language as we can develop web applications, desktop applications, scientific applications, data analytics, AI/ML applications, and many more applications of various domains.

Interpreted

Python is an interpreted programming language, which means it executes the code line by line.

High level

Python is a high-level programming language like C, C++, and Java. A high-level programming language is more readable and easier to understand for humans as it abstracts to machine languages, which is close to the machine, less human-readable.

Multiparadigm

Python programming language supports multiple programming paradigms; this made Python more powerful and flexible in developing the solution for complex problems. Python supports procedural programming, but it has object-oriented programming, functional programming, and aspect-oriented programming features.

Open source

Python is open source and has excellent developer community support. It has a rich list of standard libraries developed by the Python community, which supports rapid development.

Portable

Python is a portable programming language; Portable means we can execute the same code on multiple platforms without making any code changes. If we write any code in the mac machine and want to run it on the Windows computer, we can execute it without making any code change.

Extensible

Python provides the interface to extend the Python code with other programming languages like C, C++, and so on. In Python, various libraries and modules are built using C and C++.

Embeddable/Integrated

Unlike the extensible, embeddable means, we can call Python code from other programming languages, which means we can easily integrate Python with other programming languages.

Interactive

Interactive Python Shell mode provides the **Read, Eval Print, and Loop (REPL)** feature, which gives instant interactive feedback to the user. It is one of the features that offers Python more popularity among data analysts and data scientists.

The steps in the REPL process are as follows:
- **Read**: takes user input.
- **Eval**: evaluates the input.
- **Print**: exposes the output to the user.
- **Loop**: repeat.

Due to this REPL feature, prototyping in Python is easier than other programming languages like C, C++, and Java.

Dynamically typed

Python is a dynamically typed programming language, unlike C, C++, and Java. Programming languages for which type checking occurred at run-time are known as dynamically typed.

Garbage collected: Python automatically takes care of the allocation and deallocation of memory. The programmer doesn't need to allocate or deallocate memory in Python as it does in C and C++.

Python use cases

Python is one of the fastest evolving and most popular programming languages today. Python is used from automation of day-to-day manual works to AI implementations. In this section of the chapter, we discuss how Python is used to solve our business problems and the applications of Python.

Automation

For automation, Python is widely used to write automation scripts, utilities, and tools. For example, in automation testing, various Python frameworks are used by the developers.

Web scraping

Collecting a large amount of data or information from the web pages is a tedious and manual task, but Python has various efficient libraries like Beautiful Soup, Scrapy, and so on, for web scraping

Healthcare

Advanced Machine Learning solutions are used in medical diagnostics systems and disease prognosis predictions. Developed system is capable of disease diagnosis by analyzing MRI and CT scan images.

Finance and banking

Finance and banking fields are widely using Python in analyzing and visualizing finance datasets. Applications for risk management and fraud detection is developed using Python and then used by many Banking organizations.

Weather forecasting: We can forecast or predict the weather conditions by analyzing the weather sensor data and applying machine learning.

Data analytics

Data analytics is one of the most famous use cases of Python, and we have many powerful tools and libraries in Python for data analysis and data interpretation, using the various visualizations methods. *Pandas, NumPy, Matplotlib,* seaborn many more libraries are available for data analytics and data visualization. We can analyze the multi nature of data using Python and can explore new insights. We will focus on this use case in this book.

AI/ML

Artificial Intelligence and Machine Learning give more popularity to Python; Python is one of the best suited programming languages for AI and ML. There are many libraries like *SciPy, Scikit-learn, PyTorch, TensorFlow, Keras,* and so on, available in Python for AI and ML.

Conclusion

In this chapter, we have learned that Python is an open-source, high-level, interpreted programming language, which supports the programming's procedural, object-oriented, and functional paradigms. It is used to develop various applications (Scripting, Web application, desktop GUI applications, Command Line utilities, and tools). We get information on how the Python programming language gets developed and evolved over years and years.

After completing this chapter, you can clearly understand the programming language's nature and where we can use this.

In the next chapter, we will learn how to set up and configure Python and its developmental environment to learn Python and data analysis.

Questions

1. What is Python, and why is it so popular?
2. Who has developed the Python programming language?

3. Does Python support Object Oriented programming?
4. List some use cases where we can use Python programming
5. What are the different ways to run the Python program?
6. What are the features of Python programming?

Points to remember

- Guido van Rossum developed Python, and in 1991 it was released publicly.
- Python is a high level, interpreted, dynamically typed programming language.
- Python is a multiparadigm programming language.
- Due to interactive REPEL, future prototyping is easy with Python.
- Python is easy to learn but takes time to master.

CHAPTER 2
Environment Setup for Development

This chapter will demonstrate step by step how to install the Anaconda package manager and Jupyter Notebook for Python development on Windows machine for a data science project.

Like any other programming language, we need the Python software for installation; also, we need to install many other libraries specific to the task. For data analysis and data science, the project Anaconda is quite popular, as it is easy to install and use.

Anaconda is a robust package manager that has many pre-installed open-source essential packages (*Pandas*, *NumPy*, *Matplotlib*, and so on). We will use Python Version 3.8 and Jupyter Notebook throughout this book.

Structure

In this chapter, we will discuss the following topics:

- Environment setup for Python development
- Installing Anaconda
- Setting up Jupyter IPython Notebook
- Testing the environment

Objectives

After studying this chapter, you should be able to:

- Set up Python development environment on the local machine
- Work with Jupyter Notebook
- Execute Python code to test the installation

Downloading and installing the Anaconda package

Here, we have the Anaconda installation steps on the Microsoft Windows 10 machine.

Step 1: Go to the https://www.anaconda.com/distribution/#download-section, you will get the screen as shown below, and click on the **Download** button.

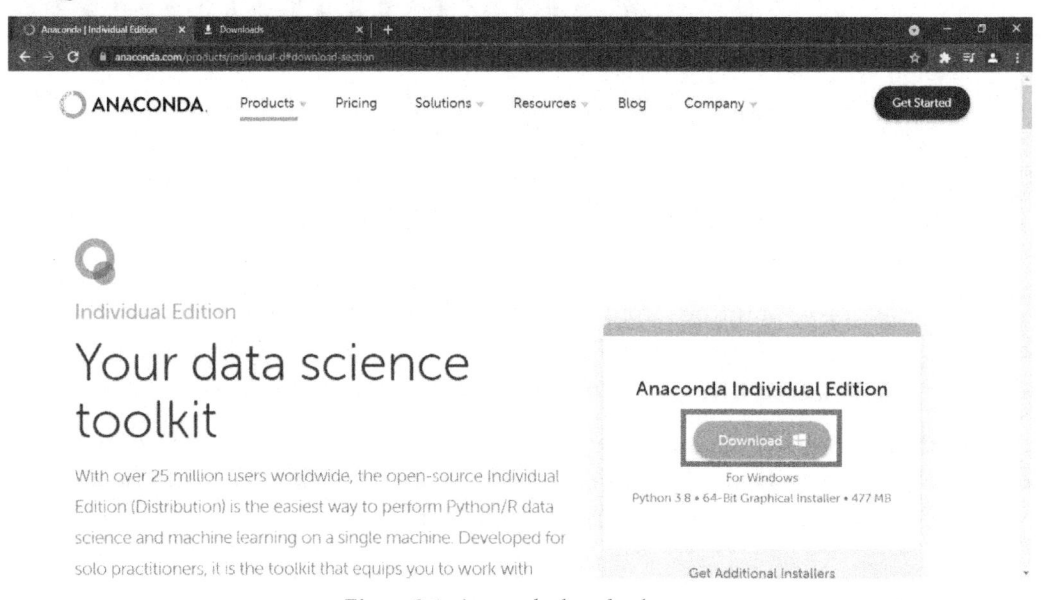

Figure 2.1: Anaconda download page

Step 2: Once you click on the download page, it will start downloading the installation exe file (**Anaconda3-2021.05-Windows-x86_64.exe**).

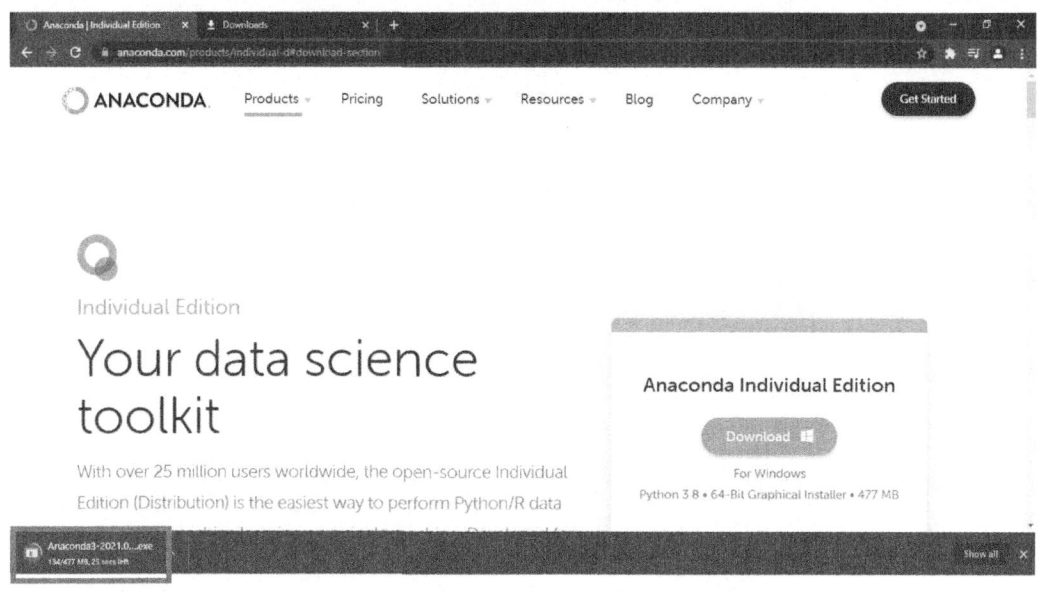

Figure 2.2: Anaconda downloading in progress

In the screenshot above, you can see the download start for the Anaconda exe.

Step 3: Once the download is completed, right-click on the installation file (**Anaconda3-2021.05-Windows-x86_64.exe**) and select `Run as Administrator`.

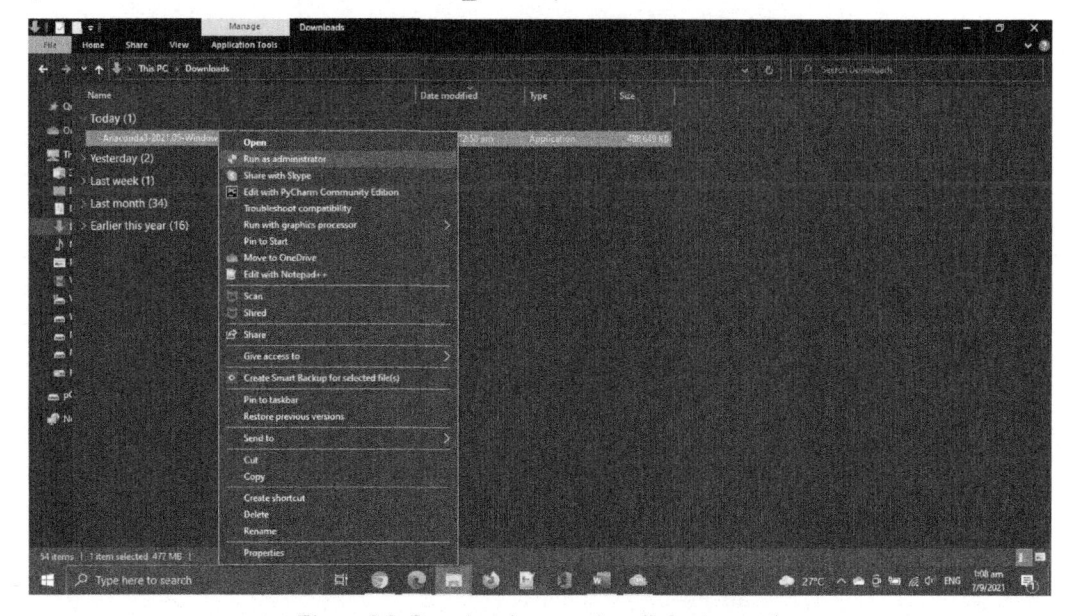

Figure 2.3: Running the exe to install the Anaconda

Step 4: Click on the **Next** button, as shown in following screenshot:

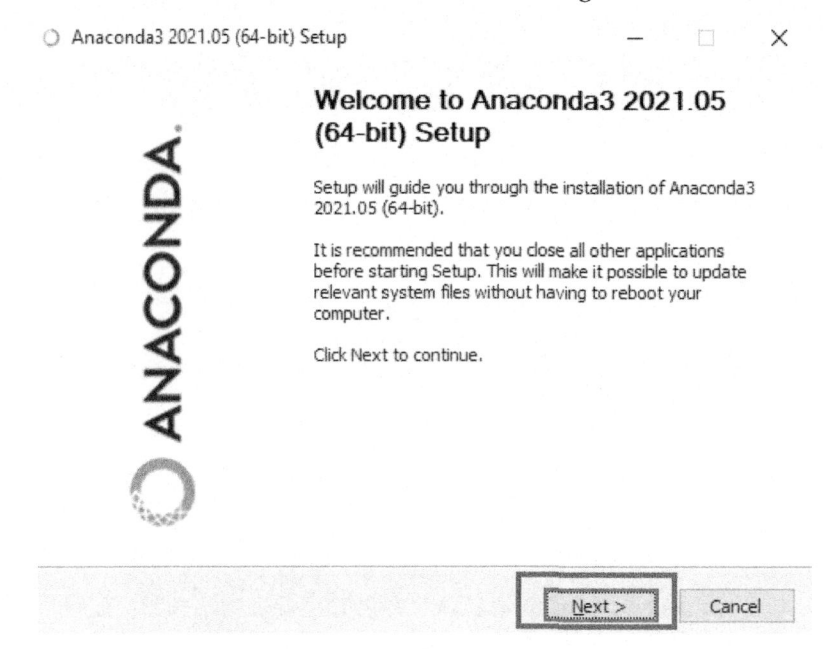

Figure 2.4: Anaconda installation – Welcome screen

Step 5: Click on the **I Agree** button after reading the **License Agreement**.

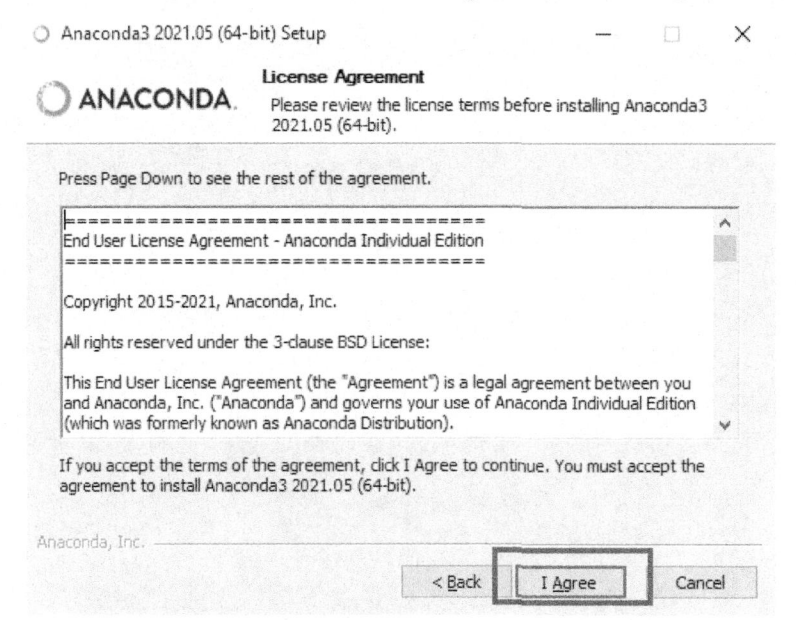

Figure 2.5: Anaconda installation – License Agreement screen

Step 6: Click on the **Next** button after choosing the `Just me`/`All users` radio button, as shown below. In this case, it is `All Users`.

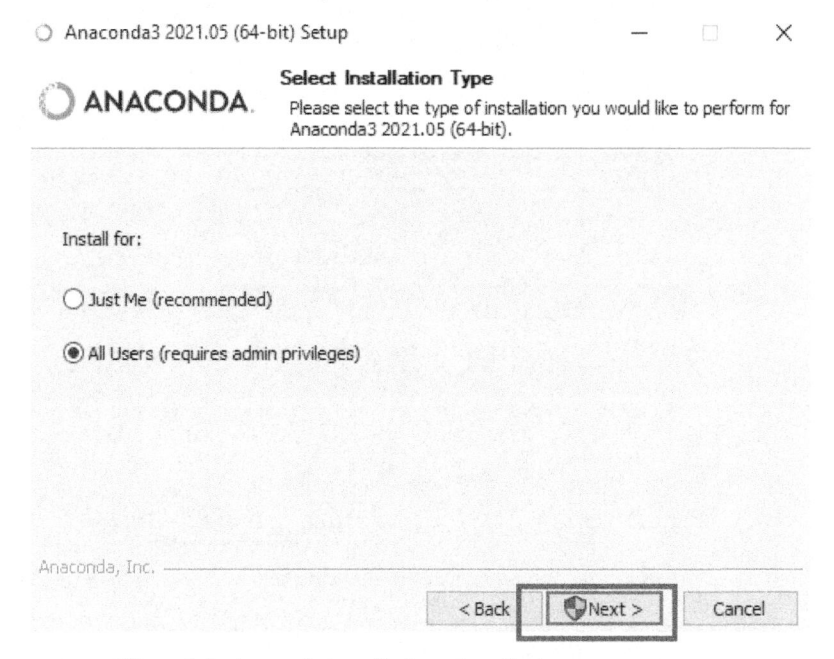

Figure 2.6: Anaconda installation – Installation type screen

Step 7: Now, specify the installation folder path and click on the **Next** button.

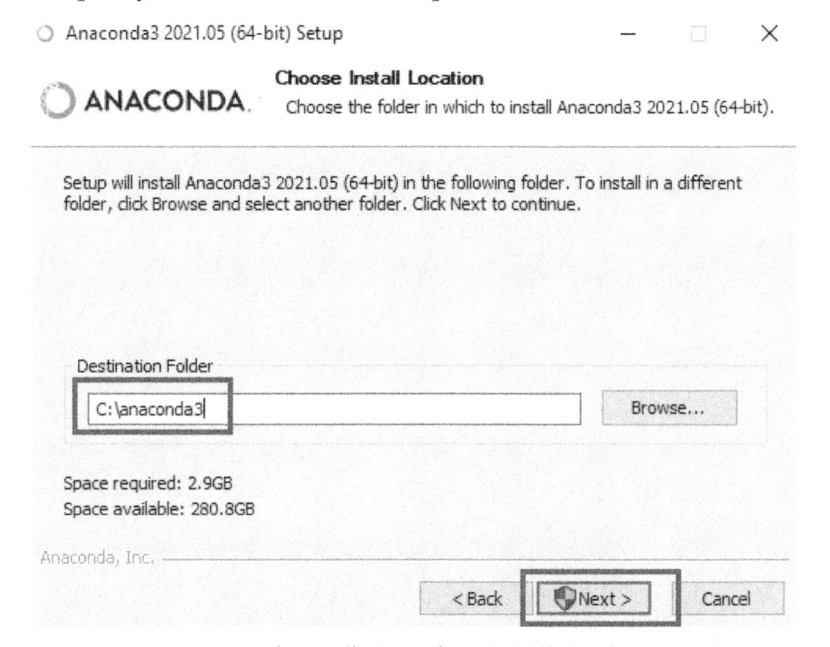

Figure 2.7: Anaconda installation – choose installation location screen

Step 8: Now, check both the checkboxes and click on the **Install** button.

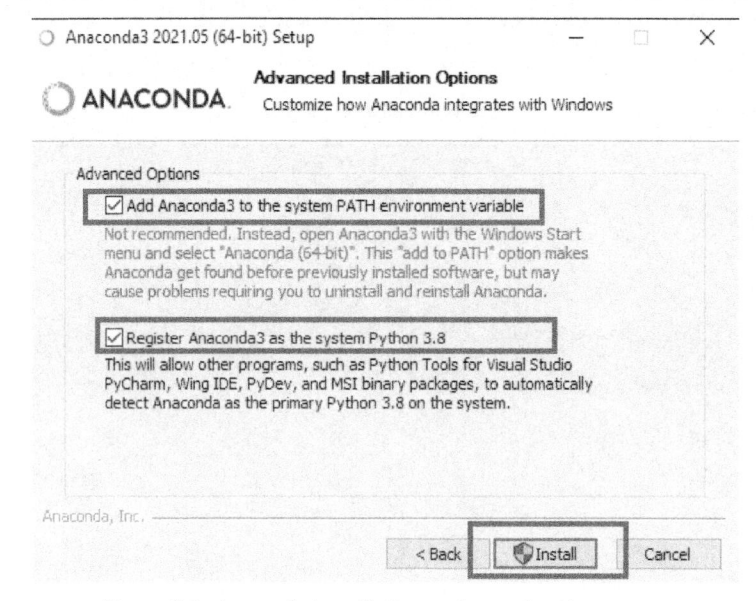

Figure 2.8: Anaconda installation – advanced options screen

Step 9: After clicking the **Install** button, it will start installing. You will get the following screens; wait until installation is complete:

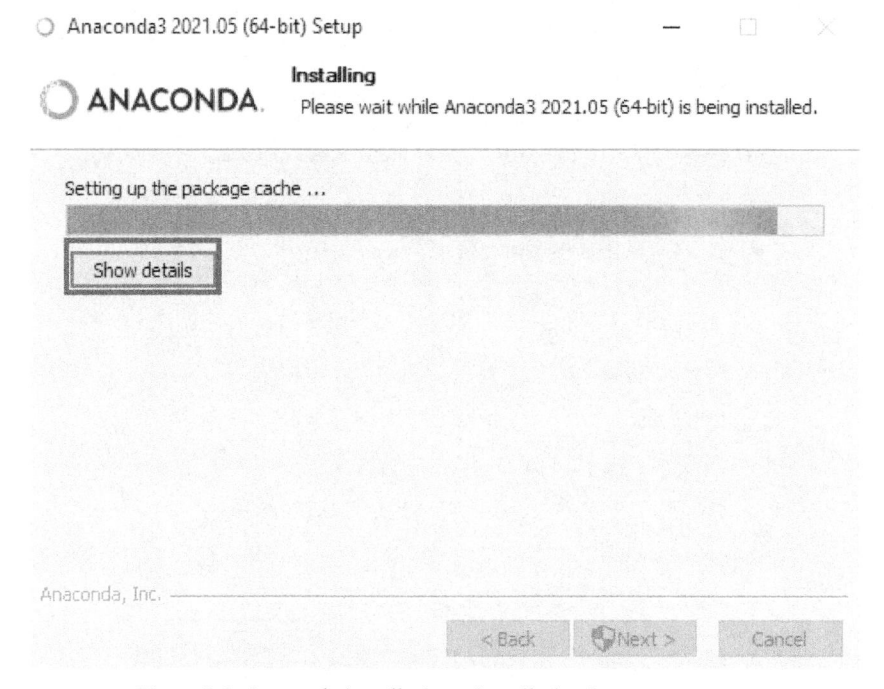

Figure 2.9: Anaconda installation – installation in progress screen

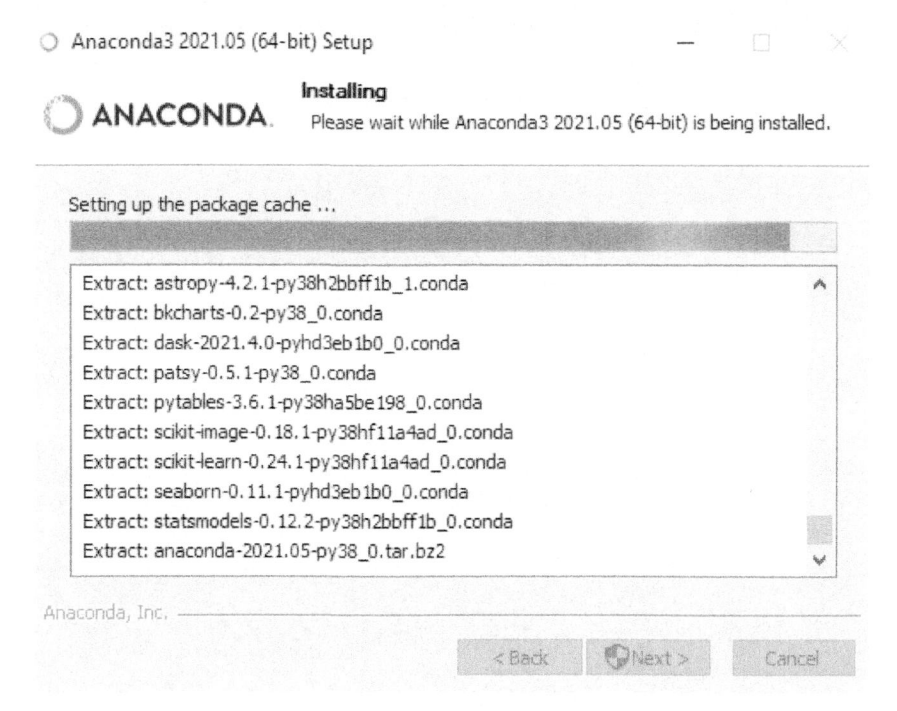

Figure 2.10: Anaconda installation – installation in progress with detailed information screen

Step 10: Once it is complete, click on the **Next** button.

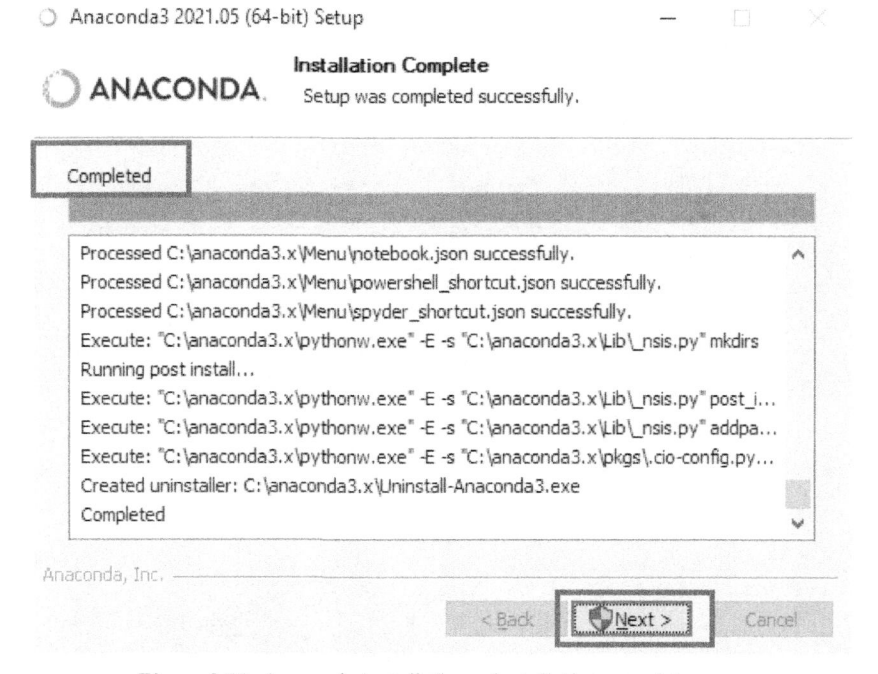

Figure 2.11: Anaconda installation – installation complete screen

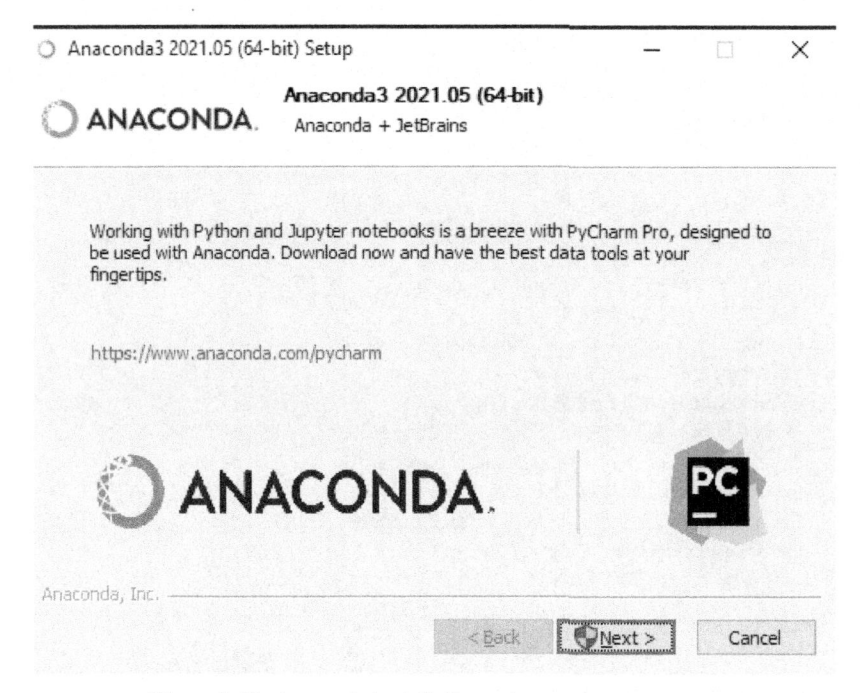

Figure 2.12: *Anaconda installation – Anaconda setup screen*

Step 11: Click on the `Finish` button on the new screen. Now, Anaconda is installed successfully.

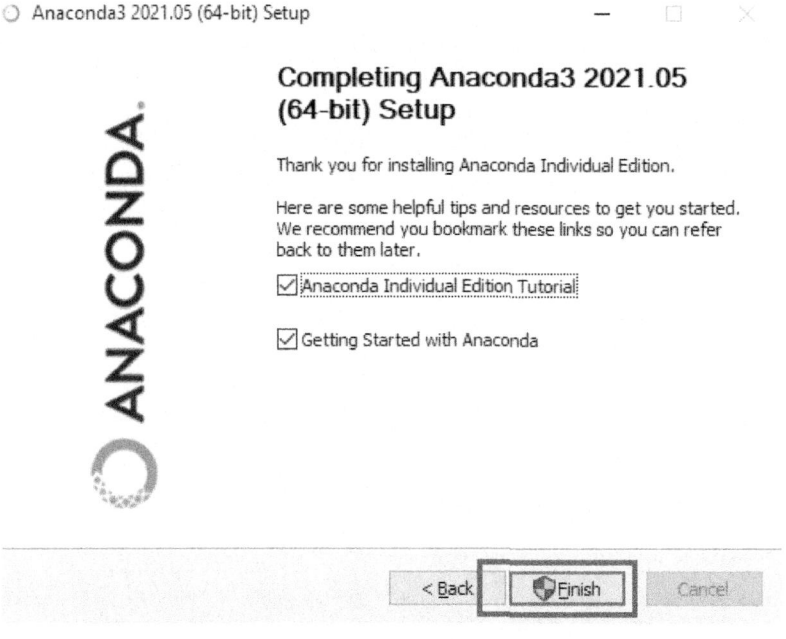

Figure 2.13: *Anaconda installation – Installation finish screen*

Once you click on the **Finish** button, it will open up a web page on the browser for more information related to the Anaconda product, which you can ignore. At this stage, we have completed our Anaconda installation. Now, time to test our installation and understand the Python and anaconda development environment.

Testing the installation

After completing the Anaconda installation, we will check our setup of Python and Jupyter Notebook; are they successfully installed or not? To verify our installation, you need to perform the following steps:

Testing Python in interactive shell

Step 1: Press *Windows + R* **to open the Run box** and hit enter after typing **cmd** inside the prompt.

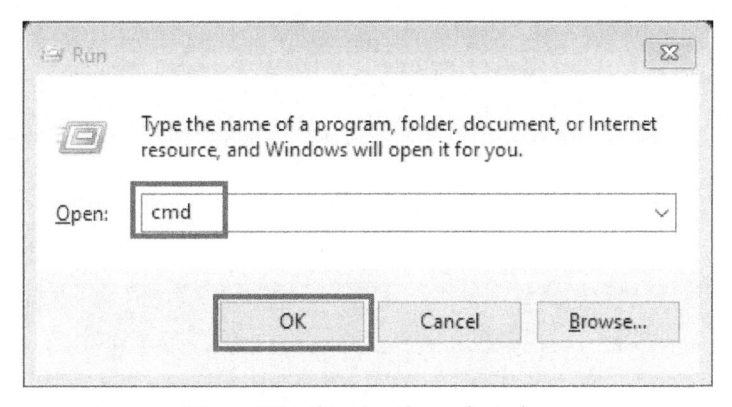

Figure 2.14: Opening the cmd window

Step 2: To check if Python is installed or not, type **Python -version** in command prompt and hit *Enter*. If you get output like the following screenshot, it means Python got installed successfully:

Figure 2.15: Checking the installed Python version

Step 3: Now, type Python and hit *Enter* to initialize the Interactive Python Shell. You will get output like the following screenshot:

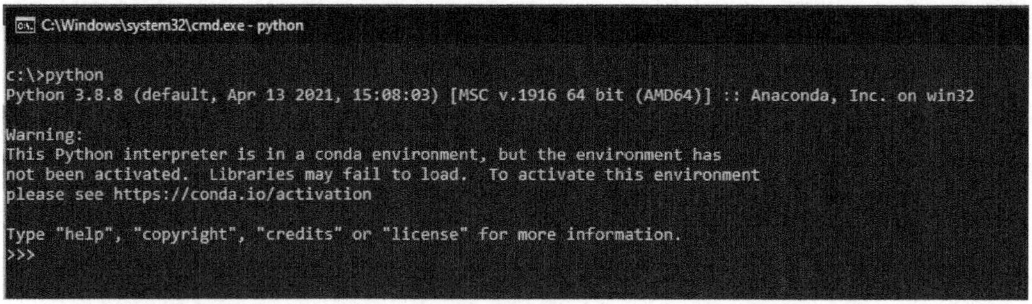

Figure 2.16: Opening the Python interactive shell

Step 4: Now type **print("Data Analysis with Python")** and enter to execute this print instruction. If the installation was successful, you would get output like the following screenshot:

Figure 2.17: Testing the print function with Python interactive shell

Step 4: To get out from the Interactive Python Shell, type **quit()** and hit *Enter*.

Figure 2.18: Closing the Python Interactive shell

Now, we have seen how to run the Python code using the Python interactive shell. Let's see how we can use Jupiter Notebook to run the Python code.

Running and testing Jupyter Notebook

Jupyter Notebook is a popular platform for writing and executing Python code among data scientists and data analysts.

This section of the chapter will demonstrate how to run the Jupyter Notebook and how to execute the Python code.

Step 1: First, let's create a working directory (simple windows folder) by typing the following command on cmd:

mkdir Data_Analysis_with_python

Environment Setup for Development ■ 19

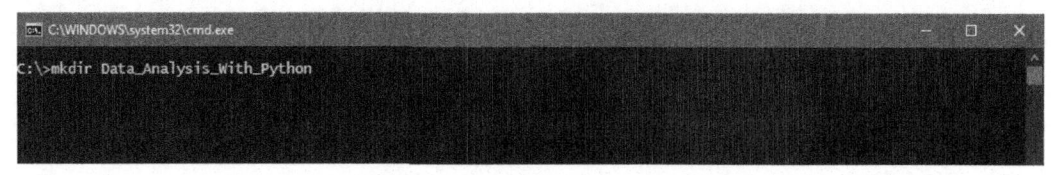

Figure 2.19: Creating the project directory

Step 2: Then, change the directory.

Figure 2.20: Change the current directory to a specified directory

Step 3: Now, **type** Jupyter Notebook in cmd and hit *Enter*.

Figure 2.21: Running the command to launch the Jupyter Notebook

It will start the local server, and you will get a Jupyter Notebook web page as shown below.

Figure 2.22: Starting up the Jupyter notebook local server

20 ■ Data Analysis with Python

You will have a Jupyter Notebook webpage like the following screenshot:

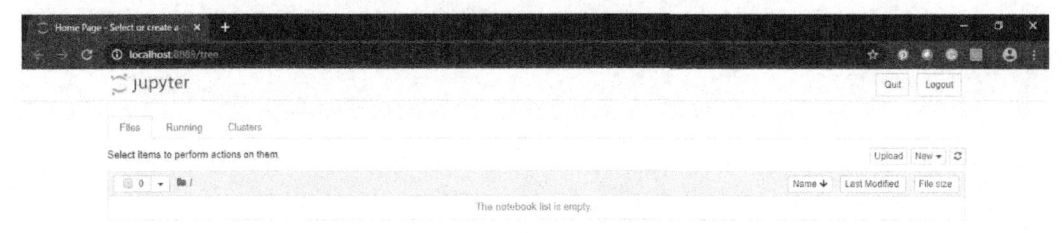

Figure 2.23: Jupyter Notebook home page

Step 2: Change the click on the new drop-down button on the upper right side and select **Python3**.

Figure 2.24: Selecting the Python3 and opening the new notebook Page

Step 3: You will get a page like the following screenshot, where each row is called a cell. We can add and remove the cell by using the option mentioned in the **File** menu.

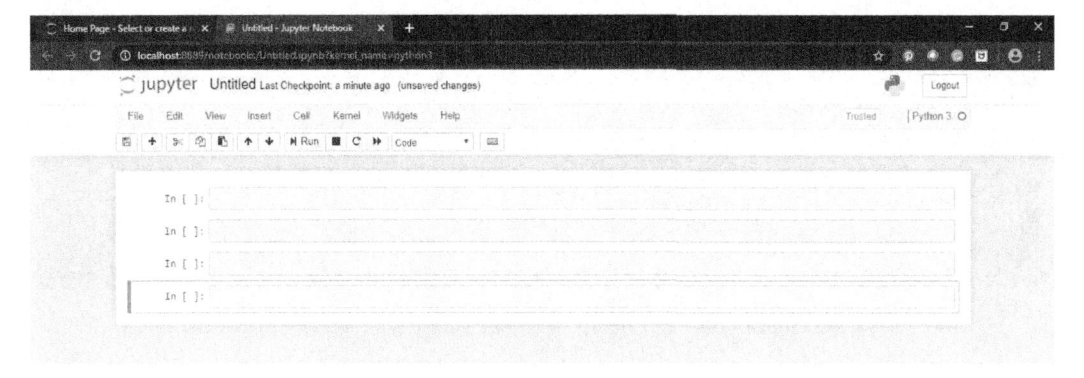

Figure 2.25: New Jupyter notebook page

Step 4: Now, we will write and execute the python print instruction. First, write the Python code given below into the cell, and to execute it press **Shift+Enter** (**or** use the menu option); it will run the code, and you will get the following:

```
print("Welcome to Data Analysis with Python Course")
```

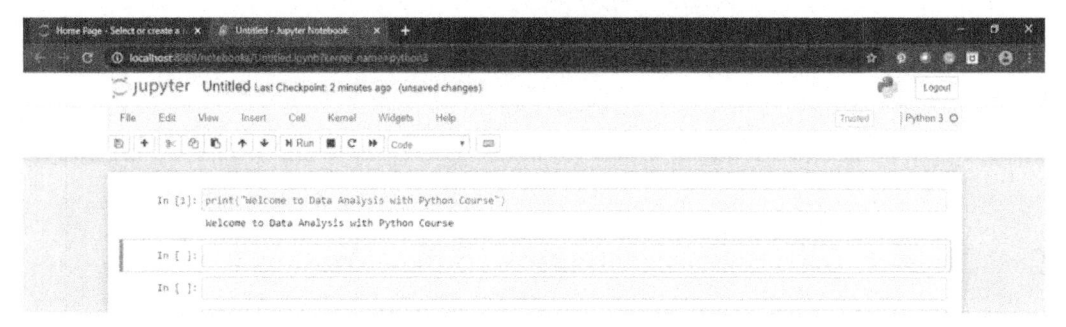

Figure 2.26: Testing the print function in Notebook

If all steps, as mentioned earlier, have been completed successfully by you, it means you have successfully installed the Anaconda package for Python development.

Conclusion

In this chapter, we installed and tested the Anaconda-Python development environment. There are many IDEs available for Python Development in the marketplace. It is totally up to the developer to choose the IDEs; it depends on the developer's convenience and choice. In general, most data scientists and analysts use Jupyter Notebook for their initial development.

In the next chapter, we will learn the basics of Python programming with hands-on coding examples.

Questions

1. What is Anaconda?
2. List some pre-installed Packages/Libraries in Anaconda.
3. How to check the installed Python version?
4. How to open Python interactive shell?
5. What is Jupyter Notebook, and how can it be launched through cmd?

CHAPTER 3
Operators and Built-in Data Types

In the last chapter, we demonstrated how to install and run Anaconda and Jupyter notebook to develop and execute a Python program. In this chapter, we are going to learn about operators and built-in data types in Python. Operators and data types are necessary elements of any programming language. Data types are essential to store and retrieve the values in a program.

Structure

In this chapter, we will discuss the following topics:

- Variables in Python
- Operators in Python
- Built-in data types in Python
- Lists
- Tuples
- Sets
- Dictionaries

Objectives

After studying this chapter, you will be able to:

- Define a variable in Python
- Use appropriate data types in the Python program
- Work with a list, a tuple, sets, and a dictionary in Python

Variables in Python?

A variable is the name of a reserved memory location that holds some value.

For example: Let's take a = 10. Here, 'a' is the variable name, the equal sign (=) is an assignment operator, and 10 is the value or literal. So, by using an assignment operator (=) in Python, we can reserve memory for value without explicitly declaring it.

Rules for defining a variable name in Python

- A variable name must begin with a letter or underscore (_); it cannot start with a number.
- It can contain only (A-Z, a-z, 0-9, and _).
- In Python, variable names are case-sensitive.

Operators in Python

To perform operations, we need operators, which are the function of the operation, and operands are the input to that operation. For example, 10+6 = 16; here, in this expression, 10 and 6 are the operands, and + is the operator.

Various types of operators in Python are depicted with their implementation in Python as follows.

Arithmetic operators

Arithmetic operators are required to perform arithmetic operations like addition, subtraction, multiplication, division, and so on. The following table is the list of arithmetic operators in Python:

Operator name	Operator symbol	Description	Example
addition	+	Add the two operands	a+b
subtraction	-	Subtract the right operands from the left operand	a-b
multiplication	*	Multiply the two operands	a*b
division or float division	/	Left operand divide by the right operand and gives the float value as a result	a/b
floor division	//	Left operand divide by the right operand and gives the floor value of division as a result	a//b
exponent	**	Raised the left operand to the power of right	a**b (3**2 means 3 to the power of 2)
modules	%	Gives the remainder of the division of the left operand by the right operand	a%b

Table 3.1: Arithmetic operators in Python

The following are some codes where we used arithmetic operators on the variables a and b:

Coding example(s)

```
a = 10
b = 8

# Addition (+)
addition =  a + b
print('addition        => a + b  =',addition)

# Subtraction (-)
Subtraction =  a - b
print('Subtraction     => a - b  =',Subtraction)

# Multiplication (*)
multiplication =  a * b
print('Multiplication  => a * b  =',multiplication)
```

```
# Division or float division (/)
division_float =  a / b
print('division_float =>  a / b  =',division_float)

# Floor Division (//)
division_floor =  a // b
print('division_floor =>  a // b =',division_floor)

# Modulus (%)
modulus =  a % b
print('modulus          =>  a % b  =',modulus)

# exponent (**)
exponent = a**2
print('exponent         =>  a**2   =',exponent)
```

Output:

```
addition        =>  a + b  = 18
Subtraction     =>  a - b  = 2
Multiplication  =>  a * b  = 80
division_float  =>  a / b  = 1.25
division_floor  =>  a // b = 1
modulus         =>  a % b  = 2
exponent        =>  a**2   = 100
```

Relational operators

Relational operators are used for checking the relation between operand and to compare the values. According to the condition, these operators return 'True' or 'False' as a result. Please go through the relational operators in Python listed as follows:

Operator name	Operator symbol	Description	Example
equal to	==	compare if the value of the left operand is equal to the value of the right operand	a==b

not equal to	!=	compare if the value of the left operand is not equal to the value of the right operand	a!=b
less than	<	compare if the value of the left operand is less than the value of the right operand	a<b
greater than	>	compare if the value of the left operand is greater than the value of the right operand	a>b
less than or equal to	<=	compare the value of the left operand is less than or equal to the value of the right operand	a<=b
greater than or equal to	>=	compare the value of the left operand is greater than or equal to the value of the right operand	a>=b

Table 3.2: Relational operators in Python

The following codes depict the use of relational operators on the variables a and b:

Coding example(s)

```
a = 10
b = 8

# equal to relation (==)
print("equal to relation => (a==b) is", a==b)

# not equal to relation (!=)
print("not equal to relation => (a!=b) is", a!=b)

# less than relation (<)
print("less than relation => (a < b) is", a < b)

# greater than relation (>)
print("greater than relation => (a > b) is", a > b)

# less than or equal to relation (<=)
print("less than relation => (a <= b) is", a <= b)

# greater than or equal to relation (>=)
print("greater than relation => (a >= b) is", a >= b)
```

Output

```
equal to relation => (a==b) is False
not equal to relation => (a!=b) is True
less than relation => (a < b) is False
greater than relation => (a > b) is True
less than relation => (a <= b) is False
greater than relation => (a >= b) is True
```

Assignment operator

For assigning the value to a variable, we use assignment operators. The following is a list of assignment operators in Python:

Operator name	Operator symbol	Description	Example
Assign	=	Assign the value of the right operand to the left operand	a=b
Addition and Assign	+=	Add the value of the right operand to the left and assign the result to the left operand	a+=10 (a = a+10)
Subtract and Assign	-=	Subtract the value of right operand to the left and assign the result to the left operand	a-=10 (a = a-20)
Multiply and Assign	*=	Multiply the value of right operand to the left and assign the result to the left operand	a*=10 (a = a*5)
Divide and Assign	/=	Divide the value of right operand to the left and assign the result to left operand	a/=2 (a = a/2)
Floor Divide and Assign	//=	Floor divide the value of the right operand to the left and assign the result to the left operand	a//=9 (a = a//9)
Modulus and Assign	%=	Perform the modulus by the value of the right operand on the left and assign the result to the left operand	a%=3 (a = a%3)
Exponent and Assign	**=	Perform the exponent of operands and assign the result to the left operand	a**=2 (a = a**2)

Table 3.3: Assignment Operators in Python

Let us show how assignment operators work on variables a and b:

Coding example(s)
```
# Assign (=) --Assign  value to left variable
a = 15
print("Assign(a=15) => ",a)
b =  8
print("Assign(b=8) =>",b)

# Addition and Assign (+=) --
a+=10
print ("Addition and Assign(a +=10) =>",a)

# Subtract  and Assign (-=)
a-=10
print("Subtract  and Assign (a -=10) =>",a)

# Multiply  and Assign (*=)
a*=10
print("Multiply  and Assign (a*=10) =>",a)

# Divide  and Assign (/=)
a/=10
print("Divide  and Assign(a/=10) =>",a)

# Floor-Divide and Assign (//=)
b//=3
print("Floor-Divide and Assign(a//=4) =>",b)

# Modulus and Assign (%=)
b%=3
print("Modulus and Assign(b%=3) =>",b)

# exponent and Assign (**=)
b**=3
print("exponent and Assign(b**=2) =>",b)
```

Output

```
Assign(a=15) =>  15
Assign(b=8) => 8
Addition and Assign(a +=10) => 25
Subtract  and Assign (a -=10) => 15
Multiply  and Assign (a*=10) => 150
Divide  and Assign(a/=10) => 15.0
Floor-Divide and Assign(a//=4) => 2
Modulus and Assign(b%=3) => 2
exponent and Assign(b**=2) => 8
```

Logical operators

These operators are used to combine conditional expressions in Python.

The following table has the complete information on logical operators in Python.

Operator name	Operator symbol	Description	Example
Logical AND	and	It gives 'True' as a result if both operands are 'True' and 'False' otherwise.	a and b
Logical OR	or	It gives 'True' as a result if any one of operands is 'True' and 'False' otherwise.	a or b
Logical NOT	not	It gives 'True' as a result if an operand is 'False' and 'True' if an operand is 'True'.	not a

Table 3.4: Logical Operators in Python

In the following example, we see how logical operators work:

Coding Example(s)

```
a= False
b= True
# Logical AND operator (and)
print(" Logical AND => a and b is ", a and b)
# Logical OR operator (or)
print(" Logical OR => a or b is ", a or b)
# Logical NOT operator (not)
print(" Logical  NOT => not b is ", not b)
```

Output

```
Logical AND => a and b is  False
Logical OR => a or b is  True
Logical  NOT => not b is  False
```

Bitwise operators

Bitwise operators are used to perform bit-by-bit operations on integers in Python. First, they convert the Python integer value of operands into binary; then, they execute the mentioned Bitwise operation after getting the binary result. They translate the final value back into an integer, and return that integer value as a result.

Various Bitwise operators in Python have been depicted as follows:

Operator name	Operator symbol	Description	Example
Bitwise AND	&	performs bit by bit AND operation on the bits of binary value left and right operands	a & b
Bitwise OR	|	perform bit by bit OR operation on the bits of binary value left and right operands	a | b
Bitwise NOT	~	one's complement in Python means it gives – (binary value of operand +1) in decimal	~a means –(binary value of a+1)
Bitwise XOR	^	perform bit by bit XOR operation on the bits of binary value left and right operands	a ^ b
Bitwise right shift	>>	left operand shifted towards the right by the bits mentioned in the right operand	a>>1
Bitwise left shift	<<	left operand shifted towards left by the bits mentioned in right operand	a<<1

Table 3.5: Bitwise Operators in Python

Now, we will see how the bitwise operators can be applied on variables a and b:

Coding Example(s)

```
a = 10   # 1010
b = 8    #1000
```

```
#Bitwise AND (&)
print("Bitwise AND (&) => a & b ->",a & b)
#Bitwise OR (|)
print("Bitwise OR (|) => a | b ->",a | b)
#Bitwise NOT (~)
print("Bitwise NOT (~) =>  ~ b ->", ~ b)   # -(1000+1) = -(1001) = -(9)
#Bitwise XOR (^)
print("Bitwise XOR (^) => a ^ b ->",a ^ b)
#Bitwise right shift (>>)
print("Bitwise right shift by one bit (>>) => a >> b ->",a >> 1)
#Bitwise left shift (<<)
print("Bitwise left shift by one bit (<<) => a << b ->",a << 1)
```

Output

```
Bitwise AND (&) => a & b -> 8
Bitwise OR (|) => a | b -> 10
Bitwise NOT (~) =>  ~ b -> -9
Bitwise XOR (^) => a ^ b -> 2
Bitwise right shift by one bit (>>) => a >> b -> 5
Bitwise left shift by one bit (<<) => a << b -> 20
```

Membership operators

These operators are used to check the membership with a sequence in Python (list, string, tuple, and so on). Please check the following table of membership operators in Python:

Operator name	Operator symbol	Description	Example
In	in	This operator will check if an element is present in a sequence.	'Data' in "Data Analysis with Python"
Not in	not in	This operator will check if an element is not present in a sequence.	'data' not in "Data Analysis with Python"

Table 3.6: Membership operators in Python

The following are the coding examples to demonstrate the membership operators.

Coding example(s)
```
fruits = ['apple', 'orange', 'banana']
astring = "Data Analysis with Python"

# in
print ("orange in fruits =>",'orange' in fruits)
print("Data in astring =>",'Data' in astring)

# not in
print ("mango not in fruits =>",'mango' not in fruits)
print("spark not in astring =>",'spark' not in astring)
```

Output

orange in fruits => True

Data in astring => True

mango not in fruits => True

spark not in astring => True

Identity operators

Identity operators are used for checking the identity of the two objects. If they are equal, i.e., they are identical, then they will share the exact memory locations, otherwise not. The following is a list of identity operators in Python:

Operator name	Operator symbol	Description	Example
Is	Is	This operator will check if an element is present in a sequence.	A is B
Is not	is not	This operator will check if an element is not present in a sequence.	A is not B

Table 3.7: Identity operators in Python

The following are the coding examples to demonstrate the identity opreateres:

Example (Python Code)

'apple' is 'mango'

Output

```
False
```

Example (Python Code)

```
'apple' is not 'mango'
```

Output

```
True
```

Built-in data types in Python

In this section of the chapter, we will discuss the built-in data types in Python. Important built-in data types are listed as follows:

Numeric type

Working with numbers, we need numeric data types. In Python, numbers are immutable. In Python 3.x, we have three numeric data types.

- **Int or Integer**: Integers are positive or negative whole numbers; that means, they have no decimal point.

    Example (Python code)

    ```
    # example of int data type
    a = 10 # positive Integer value
    a1 = -10 # Negative Integer value
    #printing the value
    print ("a = ",a)
    print ("a1 = ",a1)
    # check the type of variable a
    print("Type of variable a is :", type(a))
    print("Type of variable a1 is :", type(a1))
    ```

    Output

    ```
    a =  10
    a1 =  -10
    Type of variable a is : <class 'int'>
    Type of variable a1 is : <class 'int'>
    ```

- **Float**: These are floating numeric type values or real values; unlike the integers, the float has a decimal point.

Coding example(s)

```
# example for float data type
b = 10.5 # positive float value
b1 = -10.5 # Negative float value
#printing the value
print ("b = ",b)
print ("b1 = ",b1)
# check the type of variable a
print("Type of variable b is :", type(b))
print("Type of variable b1 is :", type(b1))
```

Output

```
b =  10.5
b1 =  -10.5
Type of variable b is : <class 'float'>
Type of variable b1 is : <class 'float'>
```

- **Complex**

Complex numbers can be expressed in the form a + bi, here, a is the real part and b is the imaginary part [a and b are the whole numbers but i is the imaginary number (square root of -1)].

Coding example(s)

```
# example for complex data type
c = 10+5j
d = 5j
e = 10-5j
f = -5j
#printing the value of a
print ("c = ",c)
# check the type of variable a
print("Type of variable c is :", type(c))
print("Type of variable d is :", type(d))
```

print("Type of variable d is :", type(e))

print("Type of variable d is :", type(f))

Output

```
c =  (10+5j)
Type of variable c is : <class 'complex'>
Type of variable d is : <class 'complex'>
Type of variable d is : <class 'complex'>
Type of variable d is : <class 'complex'>
```

Type conversion or type casting

In Python, we can convert the types from int to float or float to int or int to complex using **int ()**, **float ()**, and **complex ()** methods. We can check the type for any variable using the **type()** method. Also, we can cast an int or float to String using **str ()** or any numeric string to Int or float using **int()** and **float()** method.

Coding example(s)

```
# from int to float

a=10 # Integer type

print("\noriginal value and type : {} and {} ".format(a,type(a)))

a = float(a)

print("After casting to float from int value and type : {} and {} ".format(a,type(a)))


# from float to int


a=10.5 # Integer type

print("\noriginal value and type : {} and {} ".format(a,type(a)))

a = int(a)

print("cAfter casting to int from float value and type : {} and {} ".format(a,type(a)))


# from int to Complex


a=10 # Integer type

print("\noriginal value and type : {} and {} ".format(a,type(a)))

a = complex(a) # this will be the complex number with zero imaginary
```

part

print("After casting to complex type from int value and type : {} and {} ".format(a,type(a)))

let's take two integers a=10 and b =5 now let try to convert them into complex number

a = 11

b = 8

z= complex(a,b) # this will give non zero imaginary complex number

print("\nAfter casting to complex type from int value and type : {} and {} ".format(z,type(z)))

str to int

a= "10"   # string

print("\noriginal value and type : {} and {} ".format(a,type(a)))

a= int(a)   # use int() to cast string into int

print("After casting to int from string value and type : {} and {} ".format(a,type(a)))   # printing the type of a

str to float

a= "10.5" # string type

print("\noriginal value and type : {} and {} ".format(a,type(a)))

a= float(a)   # use float() to cast string into float

print("After casting to float from string value and type : {} and {} ".format(a,type(a)))   # printing the type of a

int to string

a= 10

print("\noriginal value and type : {} and {} ".format(a,type(a)))

a = str(a)   # casting a integer value into string

print("After casting to string from int value and type : {} and {} ".format(a,type(a)))

float to string

a= 11.8

print("\noriginal value and type : {} and {} ".format(a,type(a)))

```
a = str(a)    #  casting a integer value into string
print("After casting to string from float value and type : {} and {} ".format(a,type(a)))
```

Output

original value and type : 10 and <class 'int'>

After casting to float from int value and type : 10.0 and <class 'float'>

original value and type : 10.5 and <class 'float'>

After casting to int from float value and type : 10 and <class 'int'>

original value and type : 10 and <class 'int'>

After casting to complex type from int value and type : (10+0j) and <class 'complex'>

After casting to complex type from int value and type : (11+8j) and <class 'complex'>

original value and type : 10 and <class 'str'>

After casting to int from string value and type : 10 and <class 'int'>

original value and type : 10.5 and <class 'str'>

After casting to float from string value and type : 10.5 and <class 'float'>

original value and type : 10 and <class 'int'>

After casting to string from int value and type : 10 and <class 'str'>

original value and type : 11.8 and <class 'float'>

After casting to string from float value and type : 11.8 and <class 'str'>

String

Strings are a sequence of characters enclosed with single, double, or triple single quotes or triple double quotes. Single and double quotes are used to write a single line string, but triple quotes are used to write a multiline string.

Coding example(s)

```
str1 = 'This is a string enclosed with single quotes'
```

str2 = "This is a string enclosed with double quotes"

str3 = '''
Line one
Line two
Line Three''' # multiline string

print (str1)

print (str2)

print (str3)

Output

`This is a string enclosed with single quotes`

`This is a string enclosed with double quotes`

`Line one`

`Line two`

`Line Three`

Accessing string components

A string in Python is a sequence type, so it supports indexing. In Python, indexing starts from 0. For example, **language = "Python";** language [0] => P (this way, we can assess the first element of String). Similarly, language [1] => y, language [2] => t, and so on. Python also supports negative indexes, meaning -1, -2, and so on.; -1 index means the last element of a string, -2 means the second last character of a string, and so on. For example, language [-1] will give 'n' from a string.

Coding example(s)

language = "Python"

print("language[0] => ", language[0])
print("\nlanguage[-1] => ", language[-1])   # negative index start from -1 (last element of string)

Output

`language[0] => P`

`language[1] => y`

String concatenation

In Python, to concatenate the two strings, we use + operator. *String1 + String2*, gives a new concatenated string for string1 and string2.

Coding example(s)

```
# Concatenating two strings
str1 = "Hello"
str2 = "Python"
str3 = str1+str2 # Concatenating two string using + operator
print("Concatenated string is :",str3)
```

Output

`Concatenated string is: HelloPython`

String operations and built-in methods

We have rich built-in methods in Python to perform various operations with strings. The basis syntax is - **str.String_method()**. Some of the most important string methods are given as follows:

- **upper()**: It returns a string with upper-case.
- **lower()**: It returns a string with lower-case.
- **capitalize()**: It returns a string by making the first letter capital.
- **split()**: It splits a string based on a separator and returns a list. The default separator is white space.
- **strip ()**: It removes the leading and trailing characters from a string. In the default case, it will remove leading and trailing white space from a string.
- **rstrip()**: It removes the specified characters from the right side of a string. In the default case, it will remove white space from the right side of a string.
- **lstrip()**: It removes the specified characters from the left side of a string. In the default case, it will remove white space from the left side of a string.
- **len()**: It gives the length of a string.
- **replace()**: It replaces the substring in a string.
- **find()**: It finds the first occurrence of a specified substring in a string.
- **startswith()**: This method will check and return 'True' if a string starts with a specified substring.

- **endswith()**: This method will check and return 'True' if a string ends with a specified substring.
- **isdigit()**: This method will check and return 'True' if all string characters are digits.
- **isdecimal()**: This method will check and return 'True' if all string characters are decimals.
- **isalpha()**: This method will check and return 'True' if all characters in a string are alphabets.
- **islower()**: This method will check and return 'True' if the string is lower-case.
- **isupper()**: This method will check and return 'True' if the string is in upper-case.
- **isalnum()**: This method will check and return 'True' if all string characters are alphanumeric.

The following examples show the application of a few string methods:

Coding example(s)

```
# Converting all lower-case letters to upper-case
book_title = "Data Analysis with Python"
book_title_with_upper_case = book_title.upper() # upper() method will convert all lower-case letters to upper-case
print(book_title_with_upper_case)
```

Output

```
DATA ANALYSIS WITH PYTHON
```

List

A list is an ordered collection of elements. Lists are mutable, it means that we can update the list item at the index level. Though, a list is also a kind of sequence, so it supports indexing. To create the list, we need to put elements inside the square brackets ([]) by separating them with a comma. For example, **a = []**, represents an empty list and **num_list = [1,2,3,4,5]**. Here, **num_list** is a list of numbers from 1 to 5.

Coding example(s)

```
# creating a list in Python
number_list = [1,2,3,4,5]
```

```
fruits = ['apple','orange','mango']
print(number_list)
print(fruits)
```

Output

```
[1, 2, 3, 4, 5]
['apple', 'orange', 'mango']
```

Working with list

In this section, we will demonstrate the essential list of operations using the built-in functions and methods of Python list.

Accessing the list items

The list supports the indexing (starting from 0), so, to access the elements of a Python list, we will use the index of that element. The Python list also supports negative indexing (starting from -1, the last element of the Python list).

Coding Example(s)

```
list_demo = [1,2,3,4,'Five',6]

# first element of list @ index => [0]
print("1st element of list =",list_demo[0] )

print("1st element of list =",list_demo[1] )

# last element of list @ index => [-1], negative index
print("1st element of list =",list_demo[-1] )
```

Output

```
1st element of list = 1
1st element of list = 2
1st element of list = 6
```

Adding element(s) in list

To add value or element into the Python list, we have **append(value)** and **insert(index, value)** functions; **append ()** will add the value at the end of the Python list, but **insert()** will add value at the specified index of list.

Coding example(s)

```
# append()
# append() will add a new element in the specified list after last #index of initial list
list_demo = [1,2,3,4,'Five',6]
print("Initial list :",list_demo)
# used append() method to add a new item into the list
list_demo.append("new_element")
print("updated list by appending new element :",list_demo)

# insert()
# insert(index,value) will add the value or new item into the list # at specified index number.
list_demo = [1,2,3,4,'Five',6]
print("Initial list :",list_demo)
list_demo.insert(4,5)
print("updated list by appending new element :",list_demo)
```

Output

```
Initial list : [1, 2, 3, 4, 'Five', 6]
updated list by appending new element : [1, 2, 3, 4, 'Five', 6, 'new element']
Initial list : [1, 2, 3, 4, 'Five', 6]
updated list by appending new element : [1, 2, 3, 4, 5, 'Five', 6]
```

Concatenation and repetition

To concatenate two Python lists, we can use the "+" operator or **extend(sequence)** function.

Coding example(s)

```
# using + operator
even = [2,4,6,8,10]
odd = [1,3,5,7]

numbers = even+odd
print(numbers)
```

```
# extend(sequence)
odd.extend(even)
print(odd)
```

Output
```
[2, 4, 6, 8, 10, 1, 3, 5, 7]
[1, 3, 5, 7, 9, 2, 4, 6, 8, 10]
```

Updating the Python list

Using indexing, we can update the specified indexed value in a list.

Coding example(s)
```
numbers = [1,2,3,4,5,6]
numbers[1] = 22 # updating the value at index 1
print(numbers)
```

Output
```
[1, 22, 3, 4, 5, 6]
```

Removing an item from Python list

Python lists have functions **remove()** and **pop()** to remove an element from the list.

remove(value): It takes a value or list object as an argument and removes that item from the list.

pop(index): It takes index as an argument, removes, and returns the value at the given index. If we pass no index as an argument, it will remove and return the value from the last index of the list.

Coding example(s)
```
numbers = [1,2,3,4,5,6]
numbers.remove(6)
print(numbers)

# pop(index)
removed_value = numbers.pop(1)
print("\nremoved_value =",removed_value)
print(numbers)
```

Output

```
[1, 2, 3, 4, 5]

removed_value = 2
[1, 3, 4, 5]
```

Checking for membership of an element

By using the 'in' operator, we can check if any value is present in the list or not. If the value exists in the list, it will return 'True'.

Coding example(s)

```
fruits = ["Mango","Apple","Orange"]

print("Checking if mango in list :","Mango" in fruits)
print("Checking if Kiwi in list :","Kiwi" in fruits)
```

Output

```
Checking if mango in list : True
Checking if Kiwi in list : False
```

Sorting the list items

Using the **sort()** method, we can sort list items.

Coding example(s)

```
numbers = [11,45,2,1,40,20]
print("initial list :",numbers)
numbers.sort() # sort(), used to sort a list
print("sorted list :",numbers)
# By passing reverse = True we can sort a list in descending order, # by default it will sort list in ascending order.
numbers.sort(reverse = True)
print("sorted list in descending:",numbers)
```

Output

```
initial list : [11, 45, 2, 1, 40, 20]
sorted list : [1, 2, 11, 20, 40, 45]
sorted list in descending: [45, 40, 20, 11, 2, 1]
```

Length of a list and count of an element in the list

To get the length of any list (size of the list), we can use the **len()** function. And to get the count of how many occurrences of the specified item or element, we can use the **count()** function.

Coding example(s)

```
numbers = [11,45,2,1,20,2,1,2]
list_length = len(numbers)
print(list_length)
list_count = numbers.count(1)
print(list_count)
```

Output

8

2

List slicing

List slicing is a handy way to get the subset of a list or a slice of a list, and it is based on indexing.

Syntax: **list[start:stop:step]**

start: Slice object will start from this index.

stop: Slice object will stop at this index, which means the value at this index will not be included in a returned slice of the list.

step: Slicing step determines the increment from one index to another index. The default is 1.

Here is an example:

Coding example(s)

```
mylist = ["P","Y","T","H","O","N"]

# mylist[1:5] => gives a list slice from 1st  index till 5th index
print(mylist[1:5])

# if stop is not mentioned then it will give till the end of the # list
print(mylist[1:])

# if start is not mentioned then it will give till the end of
```

```
# list
print(mylist[:3])

# if neither start nor stop indexes mentioned then it returns    #
complete list as list slice
print(mylist[:])

# supports negative indexes as well
print(mylist[-3:-1])

# list slice with step=2
print(mylist[1:6:2])
```

Output
```
['Y', 'T', 'H', 'O']
['Y', 'T', 'H', 'O', 'N']
['P', 'Y', 'T']
['P', 'Y', 'T', 'H', 'O', 'N']
['H', 'O']
['Y', 'H', 'N']
```

> **Note: We can also do slicing with Python Strings and Python Tuples.**

Converting string and tuple into the list

Using the **list(seq)**, we can convert sequence (string, tuple) into list type.

Coding example(s)
```
astring = "PYTHON"
atuple = ("P","Y","T","H","O","N")
print("type of astring = {} is :{}".format(astring,type(astring)))
print("type of atuple= {} is :{}".format(atuple,type(atuple)))
print("Converting astring into a list :",list(astring))
print("Converting atuple into a list :",list(atuple))
```

Output
```
type of astring = PYTHON is :<class 'str'>
type of atuple= ('P', 'Y', 'T', 'H', 'O', 'N') is :<class 'tuple'>
```

```
Converting astring into a list : ['P', 'Y', 'T', 'H', 'O', 'N']
Converting atuple into a list : ['p', 'Y', 'T', 'H', 'o', 'N']
```

Tuples

A tuple is also an ordered collection of elements like a list, but tuples are immutable, i.e., we cannot change or modify the value of the elements in the tuple.

Coding example(s)

```python
# creating a list in Python
number_list = [1,2,3,4,5]
fruits = ['apple','orange','mango']
print(number_list)
print(fruits)
```

Output

```
[1, 2, 3, 4, 5]
['apple', 'orange', 'mango']
```

Working with list

In this section, we will demonstrate the essential Tuple operations by using the built-in functions and methods of Python tuple.

Accessing the Tuple items

Tuples also support indexing (starting from 0 in the positive index and -1 in the case of a negative index). We need to pass the index in square bracket ([]) to access the value of tuple (tuple[index]).

Coding example(s)

```python
tuple_demo = (1,2,3,4,'Five',6)

# first element of tuple @ index => [0]
print("1st element of tuple =",tuple_demo[0] )


print("1st element of tuple =",tuple_demo[1] )


# last element of tuple @ index => [-1], negative index
print("last  element of tuple =",tuple_demo[-1] )
```

Output

```
1st element of tuple = 1
1st element of tuple = 2
last  element of tuple = 6
```

Adding element(s) in tuple

As tuples are immutable, we cannot add or modify the existing tuple. But in another way, we can use the concatenation operator "+" and concatenate the new tuple with a single element in the existing one and create a new tuple reference.

Coding example(s)

```
t1 = (1,2,3) 3 # initial Tuple t1
print("tuple t1 =",t1)
# created new tuple t1 by adding (4,), tuple with single element in #
initial tuple t1
t1 = t1 + (4,)
print("tuple t1 =",t1)
```

Output

```
tuple t1 = (1, 2, 3)
tuple t1 = (1, 2, 3, 4)
```

Concatenation and repetition

To concatenate two Python tuples, we can use "+". We use the "*" operator with the int value (number of repeats) for repetition.

Coding example(s)

```
# Concatenation
t1 = (1,2,3)
t2 = ('one','two','three')
t3 = t1 +t2
print(t3)


#Repetition
t1 = (1,2,3) * 2
print(t1)
```

Output

(1, 2, 3, 'one', 'two', 'three')

(1, 2, 3, 1, 2, 3)

Checking for membership of an element

By using the **in** operator, we can check if any value is present in the tuple or not. If the value exists in the tuple, it will return 'True'.

Coding example(s)

```
fruits = ["Mango","Apple","Orange"]

print("Checking if mango in list :","Mango" in fruits)
print("Checking if Kiwi in list :","Kiwi" in fruits)
```

Output

```
Checking if mango is in list: True
Checking if Kiwi is in list: False
```

Tuple slicing

We can slice a tuple in a similar way to the list.

Syntax: **Tuple[start:stop:step]**

start: Slice object will start from this index.

stop: Slice object will stop at this index, which means the value at this index will not be included in a returned slice of the list.

step: Slicing step determines the increment from one index to another index. The default is 1.

Let's see the following example:

Coding example(s)

```
mytuple = ["P","Y","T","H","O","N"]
# mytuple[1:5] => gives a tuple slice from 1st  index till 5th     #index
print(mytuple[1:5])


# if stop is not mentioned then it will give till the end of the # tuple
print(mytuple[1:])
```

```
# if start is not mentioned then it will give till the end of
# tuple
print(mytuple[:3])

# if neither start nor stop indexes mentioned, then it returns   #
complete tuple as tuple slice
print(mytuple[:])

# supports negative indexes as well
print(mytuple[-3:-1])

# tuple slice with step=2
print(mytuple[1:6:2])
```

Output
['Y', 'T', 'H', 'O']
['Y', 'T', 'H', 'O', 'N']
['P', 'Y', 'T']
['P', 'Y', 'T', 'H', 'O', 'N']
['H', 'O']
['Y', 'H', 'N']

Converting string and list into the tuple

Using the tuple (seq), we can convert sequence (string or list) into tuple type.

Coding example(s)
```
astring = "PYTHON"
alist = ["p","Y","T","H","o","N"]
print("type of astring = {} is :{}".format(astring,type(astring)))
print("type of alist= {} is :{}".format(alist,type(alist)))
print("Converting astring into a tuple :",tuple(astring))
print("Converting alist into a tuple :",tuple(alist))
```

Output
type of astring = PYTHON is :<class 'str'>
type of alist= ['p', 'Y', 'T', 'H', 'o', 'N'] is :<class 'list'>
Converting astring into a tuple : ('P', 'Y', 'T', 'H', 'O', 'N')
Converting alist into a tuple : ('p', 'Y', 'T', 'H', 'o', 'N')

> Note: Tuples are immutable, so adding/deleting or updating at the index level is not allowed. This means we cannot add, delete, or update elements in the existing tuple reference.

Sets

Sets are unordered and un-indexed collections of unique elements. In Python, sets are represented by the curly braces {}; for example, **set_a = {1,2,3,4,5}**, here **set_a** is a set of numbers from 1 to 5.

Coding example(s)

```
# creating a Set in Python
set_a = {2,3,4,5,6,}
print("set_a = {} type=>{}".format(A,type(A)))
```

Output

```
set_a = {2, 3, 4, 5, 6, 7} type=><class 'set'>
```

Working with set

This section will demonstrate the essential set operations using the built-in Python set functions and methods.

Accessing the set items

As Python sets are unindexed, we cannot access the set by using an index like string, list, or tuple. We can iterate the set elements one by one through a loop.

Coding example(s)

```
set_a = {1,2,3}
for element in set_a:
    print(element)
```

Output

```
1
2
3
```

Adding element(s) in set

To add element(s) in set **add()** function can be used.

Coding example(s)

```
# add(value)
set_a = {2,3,4,5,6,}
print("initial set set_a = ",set_a)
set_a.add(7)
print("After adding 7 in initial set",set_a)
```

Output

```
initial set set_a =  {2, 3, 4, 5, 6}
After adding 7 in initial set {2, 3, 4, 5, 6, 7}

{1, 2, 3}
{1, 2, 3, 4}
{1, 2, 3, 4, 5}
{1, 2, 3, 4, 5, '7', '6', '5'}
```

Removing an item from Python set

Python sets have functions **remove()**, **discard()** and **pop()** to remove an element from the list.

- **remove(value)**: It takes a value or list object as an argument, removes that item from the list, and gives an error if the specified value is not in the set.
- **discard(value)**: It works like **remove()**, but it will not give an error in case value is not found in the set, instead of that, it returns 'None'.
- **pop()**: With set, pop works without an index. It removes and returns the random value from the set.

Here are the codes where the preceding functions are applied:

Coding example(s)

```
#remove()
set_a = {1,2,3,4}
print(set_a)
set_a.remove(3)
print(set_a)

# gives error in case value is not present in set
print(set_a.remove(8))
```

```
#discard()
set_a = {1,2,3,4}
print(set_a)
set_a.discard(3)
print(set_a)

# Return None if specified value is not in set
print(set_a.discard(8))

# pop()
set_a = {2,3,4}
print(set_a.pop())
```

Output

```
{1, 2, 3, 4}
{1, 2, 4}
```

```
KeyError Traceback (most recent call last)
<ipython-input-195-248aa3cbeebd> in <module>
      6
      7 # gives error in case value is not present in set
----> 8 print(set_a.remove(8))
      9
     10 #discard()

KeyError: 8
```

```
{1, 2, 3, 4}
{1, 2, 4}
None
2
```

Checking for membership of an element

By using the **in** operator, we can check if any value is present in the set or not. If the value exists in the set, it will return 'True'.

Coding example(s)

```
fruits = {"Mango","Apple","Orange}

print("Checking if mango in list :","Mango" in fruits)
print("Checking if Kiwi in list :","Kiwi" in fruits)
```

Output

```
Checking if mango in list : True
Checking if Kiwi in list : False
```

Set operations

Python set supports mathematic set operations like set union, set intersection, set difference, set symmetric-difference, and so on. Some of the essential set operations are demonstrated as follows:

- `Union()`: It returns a set of unique elements from both sets.
- `intersection()`: It returns a set of unique common elements from both sets.
- `difference()`: It returns a set of elements that are not present in another one.
- `symmetric_difference()`: It returns a set of elements that are not common in two specified sets.
- `issubset()`: It returns 'True' if another set is a subset.
- `issuperset()`: It returns 'True' if another set is a superset.
- `isdisjoint()`: It returns 'True' if there is no intersection between two sets.

Some examples are shown here using these operations:

Coding example(s)

```
set_a = {1,2,3,4}
set_b = {3,4,5}
set_c = {1,2}
set_d = {10,11,12}

### Union()
a_union_b = set_a.union(set_b)
print("\nUnion() => a_union_b :",a_union_b)
```

```
### intersection()
a_intersect_b = set_a.intersection(set_b)
print("\nintersection() => a_intersect_b :",a_intersect_b)

### difference()
a_diff_b = set_a.difference(set_b)
print("\ndifference() => a_diff_b :",a_diff_b)
b_diff_a = set_b.difference(set_a)
print("difference() => b_diff_a :",b_diff_a)

### symmetric_difference()
a_symm_diff_b = set_a.symmetric_difference(set_b)
print("\nsymmetric_difference() => a_diff_b :",a_symm_diff_b)

### issubset()
print("\nissubset() => is set b subset of set a :",set_b.issubset(set_a))
print("issubset() => is set c subset of set a :",set_c.issubset(set_a))

### issuperset()
print("\nissuperset() => is set a superset of set b :",set_a.issuperset(set_b))
print("issuperset() => is set a superset of set c :",set_a.issuperset(set_c))

### isdisjoint()
# True if there is no intersection between specified two sets
print("\nisdisjoint() => is set a and d are disjoint :",set_a.isdisjoint(set_d))
```

Output
Union() => a_union_b : {1, 2, 3, 4, 5}

intersection() => a_intersect_b : {3, 4}

difference() => a_diff_b : {1, 2}
difference() => b_diff_a : {5}

symmetric_difference() => a_diff_b : {1, 2, 5}

```
issubset() => is set b subset of set a : False
issubset() => is set c subset of set a : True

issuperset() => is set a superset of set b : False
issuperset() => is set a superset of set c : True

isdisjoint() => is set a and d are disjoint : True
```

Converting string, tuple, and list into the set

Using the Tuple (seq), we can convert sequence (String, Tuple) into list type.

Coding example(s)

```
astring = "Hello"
atuple = ("H","e","l","l","o")
alist = ["H","e","l","l","o"]
print("type of astring = {} is :{}".format(astring,type(astring)))
print("type of atuple= {} is :{}".format(atuple,type(atuple)))
print("type of alist= {} is :{}".format(alist,type(alist)))

print("\nConverting astring into a list :",set(astring))
print("Converting atuple into a list :",set(atuple))
print("Converting atuple into a list :",set(alist))
```

Output

```
type of astring = Hello is :<class 'str'>
type of atuple= ('H', 'e', 'l', 'l', 'o') is :<class 'tuple'>
type of alist= ['H', 'e', 'l', 'l', 'o'] is :<class 'list'>

Converting astring into a list : {'o', 'l', 'e', 'H'}
Converting atuple into a list : {'o', 'l', 'e', 'H'}
Converting atuple into a list : {'o', 'l', 'e', 'H'}
```

Dictionaries

Python dictionaries are the un-ordered collection key, value pairs.

dict_demo = {1:"60%",2:"50%",3:"30%"}, here **my_dict** is the dictionary with 3 key, value pairs.

Coding example(s)

```
# creating a Dictionary in Python
dict_demo = {1:"60%",2:"50%",3:"30%"}
print(dict_demo)
```

Output

```
{1: 'one', 2: 'two', 3: 'Three'}
```

Working with dictionaries

In this section, we will demonstrate the essential dictionary operations.

Accessing the dictionaries items

In the Python dictionary, we can access the value by specifying the key inside the square bracket([]) or pass the key as an argument in the **get()** method to obtain the value of a specified key.

If the specified key is not available in a dictionary, it will raise an error, but it will return 'None' with **get()** methods.

Coding example(s)

```
dict_demo = {1:"60%",2:"50%",3:"30%"}
# dict[key] => return the vaue for specified key
print("Value for Key 2 is ",dict_demo[2])

traffic_light = {"Red":"Stop","Yellow":" Ready to GO","Green": " Good to GO"}
print(traffic_light["Yellow"])

# using get()
print(my_dict.get(2))
```

Output

```
Value for Key 2 is   50%
Ready to GO
two
```

Adding element(s) in the dictionary

Using the key and passing the value, we can add a new key, value pair, in the dictionary. If a key is already present, then it will update the value for that key.

Coding example(s)

```
dict_demo = {1:"60%",2:"50%",3:"30%"}
print("Initial :",dict_demo)
dict_demo[4]="25%"
print("After adding an element  :",dict_demo)
```

Output

```
Initial : {1: '60%', 2: '50%', 3: '30%'}
After adding an element  : {1: '60%', 2: '50%', 3: '30%', 4: '25%'}
```

Removing an item from Python dictionary

We can delete the specified key's value from the dictionary by mentioning the key in the square bracket with the del keyword (**del dict[key]**). Another way is to use the **popitem()** method, but it will remove and return a random key, value pair, from a dictionary.

Coding example(s)

```
dict_demo = {1:"60%",2:"50%",3:"30%"}
print("Initial :",dict_demo)
del dict_demo[3]
print("Update dictionary after deleting element :",dict_demo)

# popitem(Key) Random
print(dict_demo.popitem())
```

Output

```
Initial : {1: '60%', 2: '50%', 3: '30%'}
Update dictionary after deleting element : {1: '60%', 2: '50%'}
(2, '50%')
```

Checking for membership of an element

By using the **in** operator, we can check if any value is present in the dictionary or not. If the value exists in the dictionary, it will return 'True'.

Coding example(s)

```
dict_demo = {1:"60%",2:"50%",3:"30%"}
print("Key 2 is in my_dict :",1 in dict_demo)
print("Key 8 is in my_dict :",8 in dict_demo)
```

Output
```
Key 2 is in dict_demo : True
Key 8 is in dict_demo : False
```

Getting the list of all keys of a dictionary

Method `dict.keys()` returns the list of all keys of a dictionary.

Coding Example(s)
```
dict_demo = {1:"60%",2:"50%",3:"30%"}
print(dict_demo.keys())
```

Output
```
dict_keys([1, 2, 3])
```

Getting the list of all values of a dictionary

Method `dict.values()` returns the list of all values of a dictionary.

Coding example(s)
```
dict_demo = {1:"60%",2:"50%",3:"30%"}
print(dict_demo.values())
```

Output
```
dict_values(['60%', '50%', '30%'])
```

Getting the list of key, value pair tuples

Method `dict.items()` returns the list of all keys or value tuples of a dictionary.

Coding example(s)
```
dict_demo = {1:"60%",2:"50%",3:"30%"}
print(dict_demo.items())
```

Output
```
dict_items([(1, '60%'), (2, '50%'), (3, '30%')])
```

Iterating a dictionary

By using for loop, we can iterate a dictionary.

Coding example(s)
```
dict_demo = {1:"60%",2:"50%",3:"30%"}
for k,v in dict_demo.items():
```

```
    print("Value for Key {} is {}".format(k,v))
```

Output

```
Value for Key 1 is 60%
Value for Key 2 is 50%
Value for Key 3 is 30%
```

Converting key, value iterable into dictionary

By passing the key or value iterable as an argument into function **dict()**, we can convert key or value iterable into a dictionary.

Coding example(s)

```
my_tuple = [(1,"60%"),(2,"50%"),(3,"30%")]
dict_demo = dict(my_tuple)
print(dict_demo)
```

Output

{1: '60%', 2: '50%', 3: '30%'}

Conclusion

In this chapter, we demonstrated various operators and data types in Python with hands-on examples. We know how to work with built-in data types like strings, numbers, lists, sets, and dictionaries in Python. Also, have a bright idea of what immutable and mutable data types are in Python.

In the next chapter, we will use these data types and operators with some other Python programming constructs.

Questions

1. Summarize the list of the built-in data types in Python.
2. What do you mean by immutable and mutable data types?
3. What is the difference between the tuple and the list data type in Python?
4. What is a dictionary in Python?
5. How to print the list of all keys of a dictionary?
6. How to print the list of all values of a dictionary?
7. Can we access the set using an index?

CHAPTER 4
Conditional Expressions in Python

In the last chapter, we have learned about Python operators and built-in data types and seen various hands-on examples in Python. In this chapter, we will explore another essential programming construct: how to write the conditional statements in Python? After completing this chapter, you can write a program that can execute or take predefined actions based on the outcome of a specified condition or expression.

Structure

In this chapter, we will discuss the following topics:

- Indentation in Python
- How to write conditional statements in Python
- 'If' condition statement
- 'If-else' condition statement
- 'elif' condition statement
- 'Nested if' conditional statement
- 'AND/OR' with 'if' statements

Objectives

After completing this chapter, you should be able to:

- Understand and write the Python code using the correct indentation
- Write conditional expressions in Python

Indentation in Python

To define a block of code, many programming languages like C, C++, and Java use curly braces {}. But Python uses Indentation to determine a code block (in general, it means the body of a function, loop, and so on). We used four spaces or a tab for Indentation, but spaces are preferred to tabs.

Code block starts with indentation followed by statement and end with first unintended line. A Python error can be caused by wrongly used indentation.

Conditional expressions in Python

Writing code for a conditional expression means we need to write a code that can take the decision (means can execute or process some specified action) against a given condition (or outcome of a conditional expression).

The following are the conditional statements in Python:

'If' statement

'If' is a conditional statement, which contains a condition or logical expression and executes the action if the condition or expression's result gets evaluated to 'True'.

Syntax:

```
if condition/expression:
    action/decision statement(s)
```

Coding example(s):

Example 1: Let us see the following example for a simple 'if' statement:

```
1  # if
2  traffic_light = "Red"
3  print("Output:")
4  if (traffic_light == "Red"):
5      print("Please Stop!")
6  
```

```
Output:
Please Stop!
```

Figure 4.1: *'If' statement with a passed case*

In the preceding example, in line 2, the string value "**Red**" has been assigned to the variables **traffic_light**, and in line 4, it checks if the variable has string value **Red** or not. If it is true, it will display the next **print()** statement; otherwise, it will not display anything in output.

Example 2:

Let's see the following example to see what happens if the condition fails:

```
1  # if
2  traffic_light = "Green"
3  print("Output:")
4  if (traffic_light == "Red"):
5      print("Please Stop!")
6
```

```
Output:
```

Figure 4.2: 'If' statement with a failed case

Let's discuss this example: at line 1, we can see that the variable **traffic_light** has been assigned the string value **Green**. Now, at line 4, if variable traffic light has the value **Red**, it will be returned as 'False', so it will not go to execute the **print()** function. That is why in the output, it will print nothing.

If...else statement

Now, it will be clear how the 'if' statement works. Still, the question remains, how to handle if any statements fail. This means, we have some situation where if some condition is passed, then do task1 otherwise do task2. In Python, we can achieve such a requirement using the 'if...else' statement.

In this, the 'if...else' statement, we have an else statement combined with the 'if' statement. The 'else' block contains the statement(s), which will be executed if the conditional expression is evaluated as 'False'.

Syntax:
```
if condition/expression:
    action/decision statement(s)
else:
    action/decision statement(s)
```

Coding Example(s):

Example 1: Let us see the following simple 'if...else' example:

```python
1  # if...else
2  a=101
3  print("Output:")
4  if a>101:
5      print("a is greater than 101")
6  else:
7      print(" a is not greater than 101")
```

```
Output:
 a is not greater than 101
```

Figure 4.3: 'If...else' with the failed case

Now, we need to check if this variable 'a' is greater than 101. If yes, then it'll print the message: **a is greater than 101**; otherwise, it'll print the message: **a is not greater than 101**. So, to achieve this, we have used the 'if...else' statement in the code. Here, in line 2 variable a is assigned with the value 101. At line 4, it will check the condition if variable a is greater than 101, though 101 is not greater than the value assigned to variable a (a=101).

The condition will be evaluated and returned as False; then the program control will skip line 5, fall under the 'else' part, and will execute the **print()** function at line 7.

Example 1: The following is an example when the 'else' part will not execute as paired if the condition is evaluated as 'True'.

```python
1  # if...else
2  a=103
3  print("Output:")
4  if a>101:
5      print("a is greater than 101")
6  else:
7      print("a is not greater than 101")
```

```
Output:
a is greater than 101
```

Figure 4.4: 'If...else' with the passed case

Let's understand the example: at line 1, variable a has been assigned the value 103. When it got evaluated at line 4 for the condition of greater than 101, it returned 'true'. The program control fell under the 'if' block of the program and executed the **print()** function mentioned in line 5.

Nested if (if..elif or if...if statements)

'Nested if' statement means one or more than 'if' or 'elif' or 'else' conditional statements inside an 'if' statement. In case we have multiple conditions and actions, we use this 'nested if'.

Syntax:

```
if condition1/expression1:
    action/decision statement(s)
if condition2/xpresssion2:
    action/decision statement(s)
else:
    action/decision statement(s)
            elif condition3/expression3:
                    action/decision statement(s)
                else:
                    action/decision statement(s)
```

We will understand the implementation of this with an example given in the following:

Example:

We have to give the grade to the students based on the number of the attempts they have taken and the percentage of marks obtained by the student, so the rules are as follows:

- If any student obtained 90% marks in their first attempt, then the grade awarded to a student will be A.
- Students who obtain 90% marks, but have taken two attempts will be awarded grade B.
- If any student is neither in the first or the second criteria, the grade will be C.

Let's see the following coding snippet, which has implemented the preceding requirement.

```
1  #CASE#1
2
3  obtained_marks_percentage =90
4  number_of_attempt = 1
5
6  print("Output:")
7
8  if obtained_marks_percentage>=90:
9      if number_of_attempt ==1:
10         print("Garde A")
11     elif number_of_attempt==2:
12         print("Garde B")
13 else:
14     print("Grade C")
15
16
```

```
Output:
Garde A
```

Figure 4.5: 'Nested if' case#1

In this coding snippet, we have two variables **obtained_marks_percentage** and **number_of_attempt**, and we have assigned value 90 as **obtained_marks_percentage** and 1 to **number_of_attempt**; now, we can see it has returned grade A as output, which is correct. Here, we can see how we use 'nested if' statements to fulfill this requirement.

If we change the value of variable **number_of_attempt** to 2, this will come under the second rule and it should be assigned grade B. Same has been evaluated by the following coding example:

```
1  #CASE#2
2  # nested if statement
3
4  obtained_marks_percentage =90
5  number_of_attempt = 2
6
7  print("Output:")
8
9  if obtained_marks_percentage>=90:
10     if number_of_attempt ==1:
11         print("Garde A")
12     elif number_of_attempt==2:
13         print("Garde B")
14 else:
15     print("Grade C")
16
17
```

```
Output:
Garde B
```

Figure 4.6: Nested if case#2

Similar to the preceding example, the following code demonstrates the third rule of grade-awarding logic:

```
1   #CASE#3
2
3   obtained_marks_percentage =70
4   number_of_attempt = 1
5
6   print("Output:")
7
8   if obtained_marks_percentage>=90:
9       if number_of_attempt ==1:
10          print("Garde A")
11      elif number_of_attempt==2:
12          print("Garde B")
13  else:
14      print("Grade C")
15
Output:
Grade C
```

Figure 4.7: 'Nested if' case#3

By going through the preceding coding examples, we have an excellent idea of using 'nested if' statements in Python.

AND/OR condition with IF statements

Sometimes, we have such a need to check two or more conditions simultaneously to execute some actions. For example, we have C1 and C2, and we have a task T1, now we have a case:

- In the first case, we need to perform task T1 if and only if both conditions C1 and C2 are fulfilled.

- The second case is that we have to perform task T1 if at least one condition of either C1 or C2 is fulfilled.

Let's understand the same with an example; suppose XYZ e-commerce site has offered a discount of 20%, if the user has spent Rs. 5000/- and held a Gold membership.

The following is the code snippet to demonstrate the preceding example:

```
1  bill_amt = 5000
2  # membership_type = "Platinum"
3  membership_type = "Gold"
4
5  print("output:")
6  if (bill_amt>=5000) and (membership_type=='Gold'):
7      print ("Discount = 20%")
8
```

output:
Discount = 20%

Figure 4.8: 'If' statement with 'and' condition

In the preceding code snippet, we have to check two conditions: first, the billed amount should be equal to or greater than 5k, and second, the membership type should be Gold; the only offered discount will be 20%. So, in such a case, we can use the AND logic if the same statement has been implemented at line 6 or above.

Now, to understand how to use OR with the if statement, let's consider that XYZ has another offer of a 20% discount. Still, the condition is like this – either the billed amount should be greater or equal to 10K, or the customer should be a Platinum member. So here, we can use the 'if' statement with OR logic. In the following snippet, the code demonstrates the same situation:

```
1  bill_amt = 10000
2  membership_type = "Platinum"
3
4  print("output:")
5  if (bill_amt>=10000) or (membership_type=='Gold'):
6      print ("Discount = 20%")
```

output:
Discount = 20%

Figure 4.9: 'If' statement with 'or' condition

In this example, we have two conditioned in If statement with OR, so if any one of them is true, it will be treated das Pass and execute the **print()** function, in above the first condition (billed amount >= 10000) got fulfilled, so it offered 20% discount.

Conclusion

In this chapter of this book, we have learned how to write conditional expressions or decision statements in Python using 'if', 'if...else', and 'nested if' constructs. In programming, we use these constructs very often.

In the next chapter, we will see how to write loops in Python to execute a block of code multiple times (not infinite); and the benefits of the loop construct.

Questions

1. Give an example of an 'if' statement.
2. What is the 'if...else' statement in Python? Give an example.
3. What do you mean by 'nested if' statements in Python? Explain with the help of an example.
4. Write a program in Python to check if the given number is even or odd.

CHAPTER 5
Loops in Python

In the last Chapter, we demonstrated how to write conditional expressions in Python. Now, in this chapter of the book, we will learn how to write loops in Python.

Loops are essential constructs of programming languages. Loops provide an excellent approach for executing a code block multiple times without writing the same code multiple times.

Structure

In this chapter, we will discuss the following topics:

- Loop construct in Python
- 'For' loop
- 'While' loop
- 'Nested' loop
- 'Else' statement with loop
- Loop control statements
    - break

- continue
- pass

Objectives

After studying this chapter, you should be able to:

- Understand and implement loop constructs in Python.
- Use 'for', 'while', and 'nested' loop programming constructs in Python.
- Work with loops control statements—break, continue, pass, and exit.

Loop construct in Python

When we must execute a block of code repeatedly fixed multiple times, we can use the Loop construct to avoid repeating the same code multiple times. For example, to print the title of this book, *Data Analysis with Python* ten times, one approach is to; use the print function ten times, but it is not an efficient way for this problem. So, instead of printing the print function ten times, we can use a looping construct here.

Types of loops in Python

The following are the types of loops in Python:

1. **'While' loop in Python**

    In a 'while' loop, the first/expression is evaluated, and then it executes the loop's body until the condition is True.

    Syntax:

    ```
    while expression or test condition:
        body of loop (statement(s))
    ```

    Example 1: The following snippet demonstrates a simple while loop to print the numbers from 1 to 5:

```
1  # using while loop
2  i=1
3  while i<= 5:
4      print(i)
5      i=i+1
```

```
1
2
3
4
5
```

Figure 5.1: *while loop example*

In the preceding example, we have four parts—the first one is the starting point of the loop (i.e., line#1 i=1), the second loop condition indicates how long we must repeat the loop for, the third part shows which action needs to be performed at each iteration of the loop, i.e., in the preceding example it is printing the value of variable i, and the fourth part is increasing/decreasing value of the loop variables, in the preceding example, we are increasing the value of i with 1 step forward. Thus, this while loop is executed and the number from 1 to 5 is printed.

Example 1: Let us see another example. In the following example, we need to tag even or odd for the numbers from 1 to 10:

```
1  # print the even and odd numbers from 1 to 10:
2
3  num = 1
4
5  print("Output:")
6  while num <=10:
7      if num%2==0:
8          print("{} is even number".format(num))
9      else:
10         print("{} is odd number".format(num))
11     num = num+1
```

```
Output:
1 is odd number
2 is even number
3 is odd number
4 is even number
5 is odd number
6 is even number
7 is odd number
8 is even number
9 is odd number
10 is even number
```

Figure 5.2: *The 'while' loop, tagging whether the number is even or odd*

In this example, we have initialized variable **num** with value one, and then put the while loop condition to repeat the loop till **num <=10**. In the action part, we have the logic to check whether the number is even or odd. So this way, we have printed the number 1 to 10 with a tag of even or odd.

2. **'For' loop in Python**

   Generally, the use of 'for' loop in Python is iterating over the sequences (List, Tuple, Set, Strings, and range ()). Like other programming languages, 'for' loop in Python is not as typical as it is in those. It will execute and the loop body (Python statement(s)) for each element of the Python sequence.

   Syntax:

   `for loop_var in Python_sequence:`

   `    body of loop (Python statement(s))`

   Let's see the following example that demonstrates the 'for' loop:

```
# print the even and odd numbers from the given list of numbers

num_list = [1,2,3,4,5,6,7,8,9,10]

print("Output :")
for num in num_list:
    if num%2==0:
        print("{} is even number".format(num))
    else:
        print("{} is odd number".format(num))
```

```
Output :
1 is odd number
2 is even number
3 is odd number
4 is even number
5 is odd number
6 is even number
7 is odd number
8 is even number
9 is odd number
10 is even number
```

Figure 5.3: An example of 'for' loop

Let's understand the preceding example. In this code, we have given a list of numbers from 1 to 10, now, we need to print all the numbers from this list with a tag, even or not. In line 6, we have used 'for' loop and 'traversed' over the list one by one using the **in** keyword. After that, we apply the action block to check whether the number present in the list is even or odd. So, this loop will be repeated until it traverses over all the elements of the list.

3. **'Nested' loop in Python**

   Writing a loop within another loop is known as a nested loop. The following are examples of the nested loop. We can write a 'while' loop inside another 'while' loop, 'for' loop inside another 'for' loop, 'while' loop inside another 'for' loop, or vice versa.

   It is recommended not to use more than 2-3 levels of the loop as that would be more difficult to read and to maintain the code.

   'Nested while' loop

   The 'while' loop executes a block of code repeatedly until the condition is TRUE, the following is the example for the same:

```
1  i=2
2  j=1
3
4  print("Output :")
5  while i<=2:
6      while j<=10:
7          print("{}*{} = {}".format(i,j,i*j))
8          j=j+1
9      i=i+1
```

```
Output :
2*1 = 2
2*2 = 4
2*3 = 6
2*4 = 8
2*5 = 10
2*6 = 12
2*7 = 14
2*8 = 16
2*9 = 18
2*10 = 20
```

Figure 5.4: Nested while loop example

The preceding coding snippet has demonstrated the 'nested while' loop here. We printed the table of 2 using the 'nested while' loop.

'Nested for' loop

The 'for' loop needs some iterable (a sequence object like Lists, tuples, dictionaries, sets, etc.). This way, it can help to iterate over the sequence and apply the compatible function over the elements of iterable. In the following example, we are adding each element of **numlist_1** to **numlist_2,** and printing the result.

```
1  # Add each element from numlist1 to each elemnts of numlist2 and print the result list.
2
3  numlist_1 = [1,2,3]
4  numlist_2 = [2,3,4]
5
6  result=[]
7  print("Output :")
8  for num1 in numlist_1:
9      temp=[]
10     for num2 in numlist_2:
11         temp.append(num1+num2)
12     result.append(temp)
13 print(result)
```

```
Output :
[[3, 4, 5], [4, 5, 6], [5, 6, 7]]
```

Figure 5.5: Nested for loop example

This coding snippet demonstrates the 'nested for' loop. The example above for a loop at line 10 is the inner 'for' loop of the 'for' loop mentioned at line 8.

Else clause with loops

In Python, we can use the else statement with loops. The else block will be executed once the loop is typically complete without a break.

```
1  # serching for Kiwi in fruits_basket
2
3  fruits_basket=['Mango','Apple','Orange','Grapes']
4
5  print("Output :")
6
7  for fruit in fruits_basket:
8      if fruit=='Kiwi':
9          break
10 else:
11     # will excute this block if loops complete normally
12     print("Kiwi is not in fruit's basket")
```

```
Output :
Kiwi is not in fruit's basket
```

Figure 5.6: An example of the 'else' clause with the 'while' loop

In this example, the kiwi is not in the fruits' basket and the loop completes typically, so this 'else' got executed. If we search for grapes and that can be found in the basket, it will break the loop and the else block will not be executed, see the following example:

```python
fruits_basket=['Mango','Apple','Orange','Grapes']

print("Output :")

for fruit in fruits_basket:
    if fruit=='Grapes':
        print("Grapes are in fruit's basket")
        break
else:
    # will excute this block if loops complete normally
    # here loop get break before it's completion so this else will not execute.
    print("Kiwi is not in fruit's basket")
```

```
Output :
Grapes are in fruit's basket
```

Figure 5.7: else clause with for loop example

In this example, this time loop is not completed typically (not exhausted completely; it breaks before completing), so, this time, the 'else' part is not executed. This way, it is clear that if we use 'else with' loop, that block will be executed only if the loop is exhausted completely.

Loop control statements

Loop control statements provide the facility to control the flow of a loop. For example, to terminate the loop or to skip the loop execution, and so on. Python has the following loop control statements:

1. **break**

    It is used to break or terminate the loop. It will end the loop's execution and pass the execution control to the following statement in the program:

    ```python
    fruits_basket=['Mango','Apple','Orange','Grapes']

    print("Output :")

    for fruit in fruits_basket:
        if fruit=='Apple':
            break
        print("fruit:",fruit)

    print("\nLoop got terminated")
    ```

    ```
    Output :
    fruit: Mango

    Loop got terminated
    ```

    Figure 5.8: Using 'break' with the loop

In this coding snippet, when the value for the fruit variable is updated with Apple, it immediately breaks the loop.

2. **continue**

   It is used to skip the current iteration. It ignores the loop's current iteration, gives the execution control to the very first line of loop construct, and continues from the next iteration of the loop.

   ```
   1  fruits_basket=['Mango','Apple','Orange','Grapes']
   2
   3  print("Output :")
   4
   5  for fruit in fruits_basket:
   6      if fruit=='Apple':
   7          continue
   8      print("fruit:",fruit)
   9
   10 print("\nApple got skipped")
   ```

   ```
   Output :
   fruit: Mango
   fruit: Orange
   fruit: Grapes

   Apple got skipped
   ```

   Figure 5.9: Using 'continue' with the loop

   In this coding snippet, when the value for the fruit variable was updated with Apple, it skipped the current state (not printed Apple), and continued with the next one (Orange).

3. **pass**

   In Python, the pass statement does nothing, while it is a valid logical statement. Whenever you need to write some logical statements but you want nothing to execute, use pass. Generally, the pass is used in some functions in the body, which we want to write in the future. Pass is not like a comment, as the interpreter ignores the comments while it is not incase of the **pass** keyword it means do nothing.

   ```
   1  fruits_basket=['Mango','Apple','Orange','Grapes']
   2
   3  print("Output :")
   4
   5  for fruit in fruits_basket:
   6      if fruit=='Apple':
   7          pass
   8      else:
   9          print("fruit:",fruit)
   ```

   ```
   Output :
   fruit: Mango
   fruit: Orange
   fruit: Grapes
   ```

   Figure 5.10: Pass keyword

The coding snippet shows that when the value for the **fruit** variable is updated with Apple, it activates the pass and does nothing; otherwise, it falls under 'else' block and executes the **print()** function.

Note: The pass can also be used in 'if...else' constructs in the function's body.

Conclusion

In this chapter, we learnt how to work with loops in Python. We also got familiar with the different types of loops (for and while) with the loop control statements—break, continue, and pass.

In the next chapter, we will demonstrate how to write and work with functions in Python, an essential construct of any programming language.

Questions

1. What is the benefit of loops in programming?
2. What is the difference between 'for' and 'while' loops?
3. What is range() function?
4. When should we use 'else' clause with a loop?
5. What is pass, break, and continue statements in Python?

CHAPTER 6
Functions and Modules in Python

In the last chapter, we learned about loop and control statements in Python, which helps if we want to execute the same code multiple times.

Now, in this chapter, we will learn an essential construct of Python that is *function*. The function helps to write readable and reusable code. Writing task-specific function code is easy to maintain and is reusable. For example, suppose we need to write the same functionality multiple times instead of writing the same code block numerous times. In that case, it is better to write a function for that and call it whenever needed.

As we move forward with this chapter, we will learn essential concepts and ways to use the function in Python.

Structure

In this chapter, we will discuss the following topics:

- Defining a function
- Using a function
- Passing the arguments in function
- Lambda function

- Map, filter, and reduce in Python
- Module in Python

Objectives

After studying this chapter, you should be able to:

- Understand and implement Python functions.
- Understand various types of arguments.
- Understand what lambda function is and its use.
- Understand the use of functions **map()**, **filter()**, and **reduce()**.
- Understand the module in Python and its use.

Defining a function

In general, a function is a block of code with statements written to perform a specific task. Functions make the code reusable and modular, making the code easy to read, manage, and maintain. The function will execute when they get a function call.

Syntax:

```
def yourFunctionName(input_parameter(s)):
    """"function doc string"""""
    statement(s)
    return returning_expression
```

The following is the coding snippet to demonstrate the defining and calling function.

```
1  def myPythonFunction():
2      '''This fucntion willpring a string '''
3      print("Welcome to Data Analysis with Python Course!!!")
4
5  # calling a function
6  print("Output :")
7  myPythonFunction()
```

```
Output :
Welcome to Data Analysis with Python Course!!!
```

Figure 6.1: *myPythonFunction()*

Here, in this example, we have defined a Python function `myPythonFunction()` with the help of keyword **def**, and line 2 and 3 is the function body (in this part, we are supposed to write our action or the logic we want to perform when this function is going to be called. In line 7, we have called this function using its name with open and closed parentheses, meaning `myPythonFunction()`. So, when program control comes at this line, it will invoke the function and immediately trigger the function action/task mentioned in the function body.

Parameter(s) and argument(s) in a function

In a function, parameter(s) is a variable mentioned inside the parentheses while defining a function but argument(s) is the value passed while making a function call to invoke the function.

Types of arguments

In Python, we have the following types of arguments:

1. **Positional arguments (required)**: Positional arguments or required arguments must follow the positional order; also, the number of arguments must be the same as per the definition of the function. The following is the coding snippet to demonstrate how to use positional argument:

```
1  # defining a function
2  def divisionOfTwoNumbers(a,b):
3      return a/b
4  #calling a function as passing the arguments
5  print("Output:") |
6  divisionOfTwoNumbers(10,30)
7
```

Output:

0.3333333333333333

Figure 6.2: Positional arguments

In this example, argument 10 and 30 are the positional arguments, meaning they will assign the parameters to position, i.e., in this example, 10 will be assigned to a, and 20 will be assigned to b. If we change the positions, meaning, if we call the function like `divisionOfTwoNumbers(30,10)`, then we will get different output so that it will be 30/10 =3.0. Another observation at line 3 is that we can see a **return** keyword, this is a keyword used to return the outcome of the function.

Note: It is necessary to pass all arguments for all positional parameters defined in the function. For example, if we call function divisionOfTwoNumbers(10) will cause an error.

2. **Keyword arguments**: The keyword argument is a way to pass the information into a function as *key=value pairs*; where the parameter name defined in the function's definition is a Key. Unlike the positional arguments with keyword arguments, it is not necessary to follow the orders to their definition. Given below is the coding snippet to demonstrate the same concept:

```
1  def divisionOfTwoNumbers(a,b):
2      return a/b
3
4  print("Output :")
5  divisionOfTwoNumbers(b=2,a=10)
```

Output :

5.0

Figure 6.3: Keyword arguments

Here in this example, we can see that we used keywords a and b with their values, while calling the function, so we don't need to bother about their positions.

3. **Default arguments**: Default arguments assume a predefined default value when the argument is not given while calling a function. We can overwrite the default argument by providing the value at the time of calling the function.

```
1  def divisionOfTwoNumbers(a,b=10):
2      return a/b
3
4  print("Output:")
5  divisionOfTwoNumbers(100)
```

Output:

10.0

Figure 6.4: Keyword arguments

In this example, we have used 10 as a default value for parameter b, so in this case, if we do not pass any argument for b, it will take 10 as a default value. But if we give any argument, it will overwrite the default value.

4. **Variable-length/Arbitrary arguments**: Sometimes, we don't know the number of arguments passed into the Python function. Python has a variable-length argument passing option to handle such a situation. In the positional variable-length argument, we define a function with asterisk (*) before the parameter name. We define a function with two asterisks (**) before the parameter name for the keyword variable-length argument.

Syntax:

```
# Positional variable- length function
def yourFunctionName(*args):
    """"function doc string"""
    statement(s)
    return returning_expression


# Key-Word variable- length
def yourFunctionName(**kwargs):
    """"function doc string"""
    statement(s)
    return returning_expression
```

- **Positional variable-length arguments**

    Given below is the coding snippet to demonstrate the positional variable-length argument:

```
1  # Non-keyword/Positional variabl-length parameter
2  def nNumberAddition(*args):
3      result=0
4      for num in args:
5          result=result+num
6      return result
7
8  print("Output:")
9  nNumberAddition(1,11,111,1111)
```
Output:

Figure 6.5: Positional variable length arguments

In this example, we have defined ***args** as a parameter in the function. We will pass 1,11,111,1111 as multiple arguments, we can even pass more, and at last it will calculate the sum of them as defined in the function's body.

- **Key-word variable-length arguments**

  Given below is the coding snippet to demonstrate the positional key-word variable-length argument:

  ```
  # Keyworld parameter
  def selfIntro(**kwargs):
      values = list(kwargs.values())
  
      print('''Hi! My name is {}.
  I am working in {} department.
  I am from {}.'''.format(values[0],values[1],values[2]))
  
  print("Output:")
  
  selfIntro(Name="Rohit",dept="IT",city="Delhi")
  ```

  Output:
  Hi! My name is Rohit.
  I am working in IT department.
  I am from Delhi.

  Figure 6.6: Key-word variable length arguments

  In this example, we have used ****kwargs** as a parameter for the function and passed the multiple key-value pairs as arguments at the function's call time.

Lambda function/anonyms function in Python

In Python, lambda functions or anonymous functions do not have a formal function definition. We can write a lambda function using the **lambda** keyword.

Syntax:

lambda input_parameters: function_expression

Let us see the following example for the lambda function:

```
# 2 number addition
twoNumberAddition = lambda a,b:a+b

print("Output:")
#calling the lambda function
twoNumberAddition(10,30)
```

Output:

40

Figure 6.7: Lambda function

In this example, we used a lambda function to add two numbers.

The map(), filter(), and reduce() functions in Python

In Python, mostly, we use the lambda function with **map()**, **reduce()**, and **filter()** functions to manipulate the elements of iterables (list, tuple, and so on) by using some specific function.

1. map()

   This **map()** function will execute the specific function using each iterable element.

   Syntax:

   map(some_function,iterables)

```
1  #map
2  number_list = [1,11,111,1111]
3
4  squared_number_list = list(map(lambda num:num**2,number_list))
5
6  print("Output:")
7  print("squared_number_list :",squared_number_list)

Output:
squared_number_list : [1, 121, 12321, 1234321]
```

Figure 6.8: map()

   We print the squad values for the list elements using the **map()** function in this example.

2. filter()

   This function applies some Python function on all elements of an iterable and gives a filtered list of values, for which specified function returns 'True'.

   Syntax:

   filter(some_function,iterables)

```
1  #filter()
2  number_list = [1,5,67,89,90,4,5,7,45]
3  even_number_list = list(filter(lambda num:num%2==0,number_list))
4
5  print("Output:")
6  print("even_number_list :",even_number_list)

Output:
even_number_list : [90, 4]
```

Figure 6.9: filter ()

We filter out the odd numbers from the list and print only even numbers in this example.

3. **reduce()**

   This function is a folding function; that means it takes a sequence or iterable and applies the specified position on a sequential pair of sequence values in a rolling fashion and gives a cumulative computed value as a result. For example, suppose we want the total sum from a list of numbers.

   To use the **reduce()** function, we need to import the **functools** module as this function is for the **functools** module. We will see the Python module and learn how to use them in detail, in the upcoming topic. To use any function from a Python module, first, we need to import that and only then can we use that.

   Syntax:

   `# to use reduce() function we need import functools module`

   `import functools`

   `reduce ( some_function, iterables[, initial])`

```
1  # reduce
2  import functools   # explain this part in later in this chapter
3  number_list = [1,34,56,78,91,11,23,44]
4  sum_of_number_list = functools.reduce(lambda num1,num2:num1+num2,number_list)
5
6  print("Output:")
7  print("sum_of_number_list :",sum_of_number_list)
```

```
Output:
sum_of_number_list : 338
```

Figure 6.10: reduce()

Here in this example, first, we import the **functools** module as **reduce()** function belong to this module. We get the total sum of the series using **reduce()** function.

Note:
1. We can do all the stuff done by these functions (map, reduce, and filter) using Python loops, which is not recommended to handle such cases.

2. We have used the lambda function with the map, reduce, and filter functions in the example above, but we can also pass a formally defined function name instead of the lambda function.

Python modules

Python modules are the Python code files with the **.py** extension, which contains Python code blocks and statements.

Modulus helps to logically organize Python code-specific modules, which also increases the code readability.

Python has various built-in modules like the system module, OS module, RE, and so on. In the previous topic, while we're doing an example of the **reduce()** function, we have used the **functools** module to access and use the **reduce()** function.

Not only can we use the built-in function, but we can also create and use our custom Python modules. In the next part of this chapter, we will see how to create and use custom Python modules.

How to create and use Python modules

In this section of the chapter, we will see how to create and use Python modules.

Creating a Python module

The simplest way to create a custom module in Python is to create a file with Python code and put it with **.py** extension; for example, to create a module with the name **mypythonmodule**, you need to create a **mypythonmodule.py** and write the required Python code inside this file.

Given below is the **mypythonmodule.py** custom Python module with **trafficLightAction()** and **vehicleSpeedCheck()** functions. We have created our first Python module. Next, we need to use this module in our current code.

mypythonmodule.py

```python
def trafficLightAction(color_of_light):
    color_of_light = color_of_light.lower()
    if color_of_light=='red':
        return "Stop!"
    if color_of_light=="yellow":
        return "Get Reday!"
    if color_of_light=="green":
        return "Keep Going!"

def vehicleSpeedCheck(speed_of_vehicle):
    max_speed_limit = 50
    if speed_of_vehicle <= max_speed_limit:
        return ("Pass: Vehicle speed ({} kmph) is less than or equal to allowed speed({} kmph)".format(speed_of_vehicle,max_speed_limit))
    else:
        return ("Violation: Vehicle speed({} kmph) is higher than allowed speed({} kmph)".format(speed_of_vehicle,max_speed_limit))
```

Figure 6.11: Custom python module python script

Using a Python module: Using the import statement, we can import the other modules in the current Python code, and then use functions from the imported module. There are various ways to write the import statements; the following are some of them:

Import statement: We need to use the import statement to import any other module in the current Python code. The following are the variations in writing import statements. We can choose any of them according to requirements.

1. `Import module_name`: This will import the complete Python module with all its functions.

```
1  # importing the python module
2  import mypythonmodule
3
4  traffic_light_color = "Green"
5  Speed=80
6
7
8  print("Output:")
9
10 print("Traffic_light_color :",traffic_light_color)
11
12 # calling the trafficLightAction function of mypythonmodule
13 print(mypythonmodule.trafficLightAction(traffic_light_color))
14
15 # calling the vehicleSpeedCheck function of mypythonmodule
16 print("\nVehicle Speed Check :",mypythonmodule.vehicleSpeedCheck(Speed))
17
```

```
Output:
Traffic_light_color : Green
Keep Going!

Vehicle Speed Check : Violation: Vehicle speed (80 kmph) is less than or equal to allowd speed (50 kmph)
```

Figure 6.12: import module

In this example, we used the keyword import to import the custom module **mypythonmodule**.

2. `import module1[, module2, module3...]`: This way, we can import more than one modulus in one statement.

```
1  import datetime,math
2
3  print("Log 1 value =",math.log(1))
4  print("Month=",datetime.datetime.now().strftime("%B"))
5
```

```
Log 1 value = 0.0
Month= December
```

Figure 6.13: Import multiple modules

We imported two Python built-in modules in this example and used their functions.

3. **`import module_name as some_alias`**: In the first example, everywhere we use the imported module function, we have to give the complete name of the module rather than the function name (**mypythonmodule.vehicleSpeedCheck()**). If we need to change some directory structure of the modules, then we need to go and change it everywhere in code, which is not a good practice, so to solve this problem, we can create an alias while importing a module and then we can use that alias as the module name.

```
1  # importing the python module with alias
2  import mypythonmodule as mypymod
3
4  traffic_light_color = "Green"
5  Speed=80
6
7  print("Output:")
8  print("traffic_light_color :",traffic_light_color)
9
10 # calling the trafficLightAction function of mypythonmodule
11 print(mypymod.trafficLightAction(traffic_light_color))
12
13 # calling the vehicleSpeedCheck function of mypythonmodule
14 print("\nVehicle Speed Check :",mypymod.vehicleSpeedCheck(Speed))
15
```

```
Output:
traffic_light_color : Green
Keep Going!

Vehicle Speed Check : Violation: Vehicle speed (80 kmph) is less than or equal to allowd speed (50 kmph)
```

Figure 6.14: Import module with alias

In this example, we have an import module with the alias **mypymod**. This is another way to import modules. Alias name makes it easy to read.

From… import and from… import * statements: Using the 'from….import' statement, we can import specific objects from the module, and 'from…import *' will import all objects from the imported module.

In the following example, we have imported **trafficLightAction** and **vehicleSpeedCheck** functions from our custom module.

```
1   # importing the python module
2   from mypythonmodule import trafficLightAction,vehicleSpeedCheck
3
4   traffic_light_color = "Green"
5   Speed=80
6
7   print("Output:")
8   print("traffic_light_color :",traffic_light_color)
9
10  # calling the trafficLightAction function of mypythonmodule
11  print(trafficLightAction(traffic_light_color))
12
13  # calling the vehicleSpeedCheck function of mypythonmodule
14  print("\nVehicle Speed Check :",vehicleSpeedCheck(Speed))
15
```

```
Output:
traffic_light_color : Green
Keep Going!

Vehicle Speed Check : Violation: Vehicle speed (80 kmph) is less than or equal to allowd speed (50 kmph)
```

Figure 6.15: An example of from...import ...

This is the most recommended way to import the modules and their functions; we are not supposed to import all functions from a module that causes unnecessary memory consumption.

Note: While importing the objects from other modules, importing only the required attributes is always recommended. Never use import all kinds of statements. This will cause more memory consumption.

Conclusion

In this chapter, we have seen how to write a function in Python and the various ways to call and pass the arguments to a function. Also, get familiar with a Python module and how to use them, a custom module, and built-in modules.

In the next chapter, we will demonstrate how to read and write a file in Python.

Questions

1. Why do we need functions in Python?
2. What is a lambda function? Write a lambda function for adding two numbers.
3. What is the difference between parameter and argument?
4. What is the use of map (), reduce (), and filter () functions? Explain with a suitable example.
5. What is the Python module?
6. How can we import and use the other module's function in another program? Explain with a suitable example using the Python code.

CHAPTER 7
Working with Files I/O in Python

In the last chapter, we learned about Python functions and modules that help write the Python code in a more reusable and modular way. In day-to-day work, it is a widespread need to read the information from text files and write the data into those files to store them for future purposes or further downstream processing. Python has provided various methods and functions to work with file handling. So, in this chapter we will cover how to read, write, and manipulate files in Python.

Structure

In this chapter, we will discuss the following topics:

- Opening a file and its various modes
- Reading the file's content using multiple functions
- Important I/O functions of a file in Python
- Writing the content into a file

Objectives

After studying this chapter, you should be able to:

- Understand how to open a file
- Understand the various file opening modes
- Know the important I/O functions of a file
- Write the content into a file

Opening a file in Python

To open a file with Python, we will have an **open()** function, which we will use to open a file.

Syntax:

fle_object = open(<file_path>,<file_mode>)

Here, **<file_path>** is the file name which we want to open (**python_wiki.txt**) if the file is present in the current directory of Python code, else, we need to give a full path starting from the root folder.

And **<file_mode>** is the mode in which the file has been opened, like **r** for reading, **w** for write, **a** for append, and so on. Given below is a list of various file modes:

File Mode	Description
R	Read-only mode opens a file for reading.
W	Write-only mode opens a file for writing the content. The existing file will be overwritten, but it will create a new file if it does not exist on a specified path.
X	EXCLUSIVE mode opens a file for exclusive creation. If the file already exists, the operation fails.
A	Append mode opens a file for appending at the end of the file. It also creates a new file if it does not exist.
T	Text mode opens in text mode.
B	Binary mode opens in a binary way.
+	Update mode opens a file for both reading and writing.

Table 7.1: Various file modes

The following is a coding snippet to demonstrate how to open a file using the Python method:

```python
1  # Opening a file in Python and checking status
2
3  # variable containg filepath
4  input_file_path = r"python_wiki.txt"
5
6  # dfining the file object
7  file_object = open(input_file_path,"r")
8
9
10 print("Output:")
11
12 #printing the file status
13 print("Is file closed ?:",file_object.closed)
14
15 #printing the file open mode
16 print("File is open with mode :",file_object.mode)
17
```

```
Output:
Is file closed ?: False
File is open with mode : r
```

Figure 7.1: Open file

Let's understand the given coding snippet. Here, in this piece of code at line 4, we have defined a variable named **input_file_path**, which contains the full path of the file. In this example, only the filename (**python_wiki.txt**) is given, so the programme will try to check in the current directory for this file. In case your file is not in the current directory, you can give an absolute path for this. In line 7, we used the **open()** function by passing the file path with the mode of working (**r** for reading mode only) and created an object assigned to the variable **file_object**. In line 13, we used the invoked closed method (**file_object.closed**), so if the file connection is open, it will return 'False' else 'True'. In our case, we can see that the output for this is False, which means that the file connection is active and ready to use. At line 16, we are printing in the mode of file operation using the model method, and we can see it returned **r**, which is correct as we have opened this connection with **r** mode.

Closing a file in Python

After completing the work with the file object, we are supposed to close the file-object connection to release the resources. You will not get any error if you don't close the file connection, but that is not recommended. To close the file connection, we have the **close()** method.

As it is always recommended to close the file connection after use, the following example demonstrates how to close active file connections:

```
1  # Closing the file
2
3  file_object.close()
4
5  print("Output :")
6  #prining the file status
7  print("Is file closed ?:",file_object.closed)
8
9
```

```
Output :
Is file closed ?: True
```

Figure 7.2: *Closing the file*

In this example, we can see that at line 3 we used the **close()** function to close the file connection. And now, if we check the connection status for the file, we should see that it is closed, as shown in line 7, which returned 'True', indicating that the file is closed.

There is another way to open a Python file using the "with" clause, where it will automatically close the file connection once after its use. So, you do need to explicitly close the file connection. The snippet given below shows how to open a file using the "with" clause.

```
1  # opening a Files using with clause
2
3  with open(input_file_path,"r") as f:
4      # printing tehe file status
5      print("Is file closed ?:",f.closed)
6
7  # printing tehe file status
8  print("Is file closed ?:",f.closed)
9
```

```
Is file closed ?: False
Is file closed ?: True
```

Figure 7.3: *Closing the file*

In this example, we used another approach to open a file, which has a 'with' clause, so in this approach, you don't need to bother about closing the file explicitly. If you are using this method to open a file, close the file connection automatically and destroy the file object once you are done with the file operation programme. We can confirm the same by seeing the output for this coding snippet. At line 8, you can see that, we have printed the file object connection status, and we are getting 'True' for closed, so it is confirmed that with this approach closing the connection is automatically taken care of.

So, we always recommend using this approach.

Reading the content of a file in Python

In Python, to read the file, we need to open a file that will give the file object and then use the appropriate method to **read()**, **readline()**, or **readlines()** according to our needs.

Given below is a text file that we will use to demonstrate other concepts:

```
1  Python is an interpreted high-level general-purpose programming language.
2  Its design philosophy emphasizes code readability with its use of significant
   indentation.
3  Its language constructs as well as its object-oriented approach aim to help
   programmers write clear, logical code for small and large-scale projects.
4  Python is dynamically-typed and garbage-collected. It supports multiple
   programming paradigms, including structured (particularly, procedural), object
   -oriented and functional programming.
5  It is often described as a "batteries included" language due to its
   comprehensive standard library.
6  Guido van Rossum began working on Python in the late 1980s, as a successor to
   the ABC programming language, and first released it in 1991 as Python 0.9.0.
7  Python 2.0 was released in 2000 and introduced new features, such as list
   comprehensions and a cycle-detecting garbage collection system (in addition t
   o reference counting).
8  Python 3.0 was released in 2008 and was a major revision of the language that
   is not completely backward-compatible.
9  Python 2 was discontinued with version 2.7.18 in 2020.
```

Figure 7.4: python_wiki.txt

Let's see the following functions that are used to read data from a text file:

- **read():** it reads the data character-wise. If we pass the argument (number of characters to read) to this function, it will read a specified number of characters from the file. But in default, it will read all the characters from the file. The following snippet is the code that demonstrates reading the file's data using the **read()** function.

```
1  #read()
2  with open(input_file_path,"r") as f:
3      data=f.read(50)
4
5
6  print("Display the data from file using readline() :")
7  print(data)
8
```

Display the data from file using readline() :
Python is an interpreted high-level general-purpos

Figure 7.5: read() function

In this example, we have used the **read()** function to read the data from an input file. We have given 50 as argument value in reading () function, which means it will read only 50 characters from the starting of the file pointer. We can see the same in the output which has printed the data.

- **readline()**: This method will read the current line from the file. The following is a snippet of a code that demonstrates reading the file's data using the **readline()** function:

```
1  #readline()
2  with open(input_file_path,"r") as f:
3      data=f.readline()
4
5  
6  print("Display the data from file using readline() :")
7  print(data)
8
```

Display the data from file using readline() :
Python is an interpreted high-level general-purpose programming language.

Figure 7.6: read() function

In this example, we have used the function **readline()** to read the data from the file. As we have discussed, the **readline()** function reads the first line from the file pointer, and we can see the output of the same with **print(data)**.

- **readlines()**: It gives a list of all the lines from a file. The following is a snippet of a code that demonstrates reading the data from the file using the **readlines()** function.

```
#readline()
with open(input_file_path,"r") as f:
    data=f.readlines()



print("Display the data from file using readlines() :")
print(data)

```

```
Display the data from file using readlines() :
['Python is an interpreted high-level general-purpose programming language.\n', 'Its design philosoph
y emphasizes code readability with its use of significant indentation. \n', 'Its language constructs
as well as its object-oriented approach aim to help programmers write clear, logical code for small a
nd large-scale projects.\n', 'Python is dynamically-typed and garbage-collected. It supports multiple
programming paradigms, including structured (particularly, procedural), object-oriented and functiona
l programming.\n', 'It is often described as a "batteries included" language due to its comprehensive
standard library.\n', 'Guido van Rossum began working on Python in the late 1980s, as a successor to
the ABC programming language, and first released it in 1991 as Python 0.9.0.\n', 'Python 2.0 was rele
ased in 2000 and introduced new features, such as list comprehensions and a cycle-detecting garbage c
ollection system (in addition to reference counting).\n', 'Python 3.0 was released in 2008 and was a
major revision of the language that is not completely backward-compatible.\n', 'Python 2 was disconti
nued with version 2.7.18 in 2020.']
```

Figure 7.7: readlines() function

This example shows that it used the **readlines()** function to read the data, which reads, streams, and returns the list of lines.

Writing the content into a file in Python

Python has a **write()** function; we can write the content into a file using this function. First, we need to create a file object using **open()** with the correct mode (**w**, **a**, and so on.); after that, we can pass the content string on the writing function to write the data into the file. In the following example, we will first write some content to a file and then read the same file to verify if the data has been correctly written into the file.

The following is the snippet of a code that demonstrates writing the data onto the file:

```
# writing a the conent into a file
with open("Outfile.txt","w") as f:
    data = ''' This is Line number 1 in output file.
    This is Line number 2 in output file.
    This is Line number 3 in output file.
    This is Line number 4 in output file.
    This is Line number 5 in output file.
    This is Line number 6 in output file.
    
    ...
    f.write(data)
```

Figure 7.8: write() function

We used the open function with mode **w** (write mode) and the **write()** to write the information onto the file.

Following is the file that the previous example has produced:

```
output_file.txt - Notepad
File  Edit  Format  View  Help
This is Line#1 in output file.
    This is Line#2 in output file.
    This is Line#3 in output file.
    This is Line#4 in output file.
    This is Line#5 in output file.
```

Figure 7.9: Output file with written data

Following is the coding snippet to read the previously written file:

```
1  #read()
2  with open("output_file.txt","r") as f:
3      print(f.read())
```

```
This is Line#1 in output file.
    This is Line#2 in output file.
    This is Line#3 in output file.
    This is Line#4 in output file.
    This is Line#5 in output file.
```

Figure 7.10: To read the output file

In this example, we read the file **output_file.txt** using the **read()** function.

Conclusion

In this chapter, we learned how to work with file I/O in Python, the various ways to read the file, like **open()** and with clauses, and we also learned how to write information onto an external file. We have also become familiar with the various modes of opening a file.

Now, we have enough Python programming knowledge to learn data analysis using Python tools.

In the next chapter, we will learn the various data analysis concepts and their tools.

Questions

1. Write the pseudo code to read the file (emp.txt) in Python.

2. Write the pseudo code to write the "Data Analysis using Python" string to file "DataFile.txt".

3. What are the different modes to open a file?

4. What is the benefit of using 'with' open clause when we need to open the file?

5. Explain the functionality of read(), readline(), and readlines() methods.

CHAPTER 8
Introducing Data Analysis

In the previous chapter, we learned how to work with file I/O with Python. We have gone through various hands-on examples of reading and writing files using Python. So far, we have learned most of the essential building blocks of core Python programming, which is the elementary prerequisite in learning data analysis using Python.

The current age is the age of data, and data is increasing rapidly day by day. For any data-driven business, it is essential to get good insights into its data to make improved decisions. So, it is necessary for anyone who wants to learn data analysis to understand fundamental concepts and methods.

This chapter will build up an understanding of the basic concepts of data analysis, which will help you understand what data analysis is and the basic steps that need to be followed to get it done correctly.

Structure

In this chapter, we will discuss the following topics:

- What is data analysis?
- Data analysis versus data analytics

- Why do we need data analysis?
- Types of data analysis
- Process flow of data analysis
- Types of data
- Tools for data analysis in Python

Objectives

After studying this chapter, you should be able to understand the following:

- Definition of data analysis and why it is essential in business
- What is the process flow of data analysis and its fundamental concepts?
- Different types of data and the various tools needed to perform data analysis work

What is data analysis

Different data scientists and data analysts have different views on data analysis definition. But, in general, we can say that *Data analysis is the process of discovering useful information from the raw data to empower data-driven business decisions.*

As per Wikipedia – *Data analysis is a process of inspecting, cleansing, transforming, and modeling data with the goal of discovering useful information, informing conclusions, and supporting decision-making.*

Link to Wikipedia: **https://en.wikipedia.org/wiki/Data_analysis**

If we look at the implementation or working view of data analysis, it is a process of some sequential steps; by applying those, we will discover the insights from the raw data.

Data analysis versus data analytics

Data analysis and analytics are often used interchangeably in the current world, so are they identical? The answer is no, and they have different meanings. The dictionary meaning of both terms are as follows:

Data analysis: It is a detailed examination of the elements or structure of something.

Data analytics: It is a systematic computational analysis of data or statistics.

Data analysis is a subpart of data analytics, and it is a process of collecting, transforming, and examining the data to uncover profound insights of the data. We analyze the past data to understand the contributing factors or reasons behind some activities that have already occurred. In contrast, data analytics uses the outcome of data analysis and goes to the next level of analysis. It uses compressive computational models to analyze data at the next level, predicting future possibilities.

In simple words, data analysis gives insight into what happened or the current trend; however, data analytics provides insight into what may happen in the future.

Why data analysis?

Now we clearly understand the definition of data analysis and how data analysis differs from data analytics. However, one question remains: Why do we need data analysis?

If we see in our lives, we often do data analysis knowingly or unknowingly to make day-to-day decisions. For example, to purchase any product from the e-commerce site, often, we see the previous customer's ratings and feedback on that product. Then, after analyzing product rating, feedback, and other factors, we buy a new product.

In the previous example, we review and analyze the available data related to our interest and then decide that this is nothing but a simple data analysis.

Similarly, data analysis helps organizations make better decisions and make their business more profitable.

So, we can say that data analysis is the backbone of any data-driven business decision.

Types of data analysis

In general, there are four types of data analysis. The following are the details and examples for those various types of data analysis:

Descriptive data analysis

Descriptive analysis is one of the most common and primary forms of data analysis. Descriptive data analysis is helpful to find the *"what is/has happening/happened?"* in business. Usually, we take the help of descriptive data analysis to track the **Key Performance Indicators (KPIs)**, sales profit/loss, and so on. Example: publishing weekly sales report.

Diagnostic data analysis – (Why something happened in the past?)

Diagnostic data analysis helps find out the *"Why did something happen?"* Once we get the report of what happened from descriptive analysis, diagnostic data analysis helps us understand which factors caused something to happen. It has more complexities than descriptive analysis.

Example: analyzing the reasons/factors for fewer sales in the previous year.

Predictive data analysis – (What can happen in the future?)

Predictive data analysis is used to forecast or predict what can likely happen by analyzing the historical data, which helps us understand *"what will probably happen in the future?"* For example, by analyzing the past years of sales reports, it is possible to predict the coming year's sales, but this task does not come easily. It is needed in advanced data analysis and **Machine Learning** (**ML**).

Example: predicting the unemployment ratio for upcoming years.

Prescriptive data analysis – (What actions should I take?)

Predictive analysis is not always sufficient to make improved business decisions; instead, we need corrective actions to improve decisions. For that, prescriptive data analysis comes into the picture. Prescriptive data analysis uses the outcomes of all the data analysis. It will help find the *"what action should be taken?"* to counter a problem or predicted problem. So, it prescribes the action(s) as a solution to counter the specific situation. It needs advanced machine learning and real-time artificial intelligence.

Example: Dynamic pricing of taxi fares depends on demand, weather, and social conditions.

Process flow of data analysis

Now, you are clear about data analysis and its types. Next, let's see the various steps we need to follow in data analysis. The following are the different steps in the data analysis process:

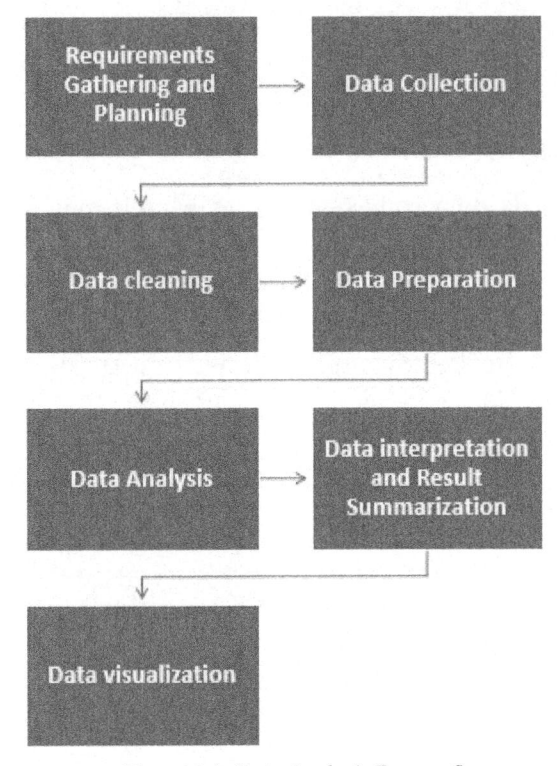

Figure 8.1: Data Analysis Process flow

Requirements: gathering and planning

In the requirement gathering step, we understand the problem statement and set the goals for the data analysis task. Here, we try to get answers to the following questions:

Why do we need data analysis? What is the business domain of the problem statement? What type of data analysis should we apply? What data do we need to deal with? What are the possible challenges/gaps with data? And how to overcome those?

So, this phase is for understanding/brainstorming the problem statement and its domain and then creating/planning the roadmap for the data analysis process.

Data collection

In this step, we will collect data from different sources (From the web, some transactional systems, data from users in flat files or data from sensors or machines, and so on). In data collection, only collecting the data is not enough, but the timing of data (at which time and how frequent) is also essential. So, always consider this point while going for the data collection step.

Data cleaning

The data collected at the data collection step is raw; it may have some corrupt, irrelevant, or dirty data. For example, it may have white spaces, quotes, inconsistencies, corrupted records, or some part/records of that collected data that are irrelevant to our problem.

So, here, we will detect and remove the corrupted, inaccurate, and irrelevant data from the collected raw data set and build a cleaner subset from that.

Data preparation

Here, at this data preparation step, we manipulate the data and add the required derived variable (columns/fields) to make it ready for accurate and consistent data analysis. For example, suppose we have a user's contact number with the country code (like +91-1234567890); now, if we split this into two columns, `contact_number` (124567890) and `country` (India), here, the country is a derived column.

Data analysis

We will analyze previously prepared data by following the finalized approach and plan, which we decided at the requirements gathering and planning step. Here, we do data analysis with the help of a data analysis framework, tools, and utilities like Excel, R, SAS, Python, Hadoop, Spark, and so on.

Data interpretation and result summarization

This is where we will interpret the results from the data analysis step and build the conclusion by summarizing the findings.

Data visualization

Data visualization is the final step. Here, we will represent our findings and conclusion graphically with the help of an appropriate visual plot, like Bar Charts, Histograms, Pie charts, and so on.

Also, we must communicate the data analysis insights in Reports/Dashboards with the higher management for their review and information.

Type of data

It is essential to understand the different data types for data analysis. Based on the organizing structure of data, we can categorize the data into three classes as follows:

Structured data

Structured data have a fixed, predefined, and consistent structure. This type of data is most effective for analysis. For example, relational data is organized in rows and columns.

Semi-structured data

Semi-structure has a partially defined structure. Though it does not have entire relational data, it is manageable to understand the data structure and process. For example, CSV data, JSON data, XML data, and so on.

Unstructured data

Unstructured data means there is no predefined structure of the data. This is a bit complex to process and store, and we need some advanced capacity, tools, and methods to analyze and process such data. For example, pdf, image, text log, audio/video data, and so on.

Tools for data analysis in Python

Python has many libraries for data analysis, data visualization, and data modeling like IPython, Pandas, NumPy, Matplotlib, Seaborn, Scikit-Learn, NLTK, Keras, TensorFlow, and so on. All are not in scope for this book, but some are common and used by the data science and data analytics community.

IPython

IPython is a web-based interactive shell notebook for several programming languages but is mainly used with Python to write, test, and execute the Python programme to analyze and visualize the data.

Pandas

Pandas is a trendy data analysis and data exploration library that provides a structured representation of data. It helps to do data manipulation, cleansing, aggregation, merging, and so on effortlessly.

NumPy

NumPy is a fundamental library for doing array and vector-based mathematical operations.

Matplotlib

Matplotlib library is a vastly used data visualization library. It helps us represent the data in various visual graphs, such as line plots, bar charts, histograms, etc.

Conclusion

In this chapter, we have developed our understanding of the data analysis concepts. We have learned what data analysis is and how essential it is to make data-driven decisions. We have seen different data analytics types and the different steps in the data analysis process.

Also, we learned about the three types of data and got some ideas on different data analysis tools.

The following chapters will explore the data analysis library Pandas with good hands-on examples. Pandas is a prosperous Library in terms of methods and features for doing data analysis, so it is essential to learn if we want to do data analysis using Python.

Questions

1. What is data analysis, and why is it important?
2. What are the different types of data analysis?
3. List some Python libraries that help in the data analysis task.
4. What are the different types of data based on their organizing structures?
5. What are the different steps in the data analysis process?

CHAPTER 9
Introducing Pandas

In the previous chapter, we have learned about the fundamentals of data analysis, like what is data analysis, its types, and the different steps to perform a data analysis task. Also, we got a brief introduction to the data analysis tools/utilities in Python. Having a good understanding of all these concepts is very important and helpful to perform any data analysis task.

This chapter will explore a wildly used data analysis library, pandas, in-depth. It makes data analysis in Python easy and has a rich collection of features and functions.

Structure

In this chapter, we will discuss the following topics:

- What is pandas?
- Why use pandas?
- Pandas data structure
- Creating pandas' data frame using Python collections
- Importing the data from external files into pandas' data frame
  - Importing the data from a CSV file

- Importing the data from an Excel file
- Importing the data from JSON file
- Exploring the data of a DataFrame
- Selecting and filtering the data from DataFrame
- Data cleaning in pandas DataFrame
  - Handling duplicate data
  - Handling missing values in data
- Grouping and aggregation
- Sorting and ranking
- Adding/appending row/column in DataFrame
- Deleting/dropping the row/column from DataFrame
- Concatenating the dataframes
- Merging/Joining the dataframes
- Writing the dataframes content to external files
  - Writing the CSV file
  - Writing the Excel file
  - Writing the JSON file

Objectives

After studying this chapter, you should be able to:

- Understand about pandas.
- Work with pandas' data structures.
- Create DataFrame from Python collections.
- Load data from different external files (CSV, EXCEL, and JSON).
- Explore, select, and filter the data using pandas' essential functions.
- Understand how to handle duplicate data and missing values in DataFrame.
- Group, aggregate, sort and rank the data.
- Append and drop the row or column into/from DataFrame.
- Concatenate, merge, and join the dataframes.
- Write the dataframes content to external files (CSV, EXCEL, and JSON).

Defining pandas library

Pandas is an open-source data analysis library for Python.

According to pandas' official document: pandas is an open-source, BSD-licensed library providing high-performance, easy-to-use data structures and data analysis tools for the Python programming language.

Why do we need pandas library?

Why do we need pandas, and how does data analysis make life easy? Let's solve a straightforward problem with and without pandas to understand this.

Suppose we have been given an input file with employee details like **emp_name**, **emp_salary**, **emp_department**, and so on. Now, we need to find the sum of employees' salaries for each department (or sum of salaries department wise).

Following are the solutions to solve this problem with two approaches:

1. The first approach uses core Python programming to solve it without using the pandas library.
2. In a second approach, we used the pandas library to solve the problem.

If we observe the following solutions, it is self-explanatory that approach one has approximately four times more lines of code than approach two, and approach two will take less time to compute the following solution.

So, now it is well observed that pandas is quite helpful, easy, and fast to perform the data analysis work, compared to core Python programming.

```
1  input_file_path = "data/emp.csv"
2  with open(input_file_path,'r') as f:
3      lines = f.readlines()
4  header = lines[0]
5  lines_wo_header = lines[1:]
6  dept_list = [row.split(",")[1] for row in lines_wo_header ]
7  dept_list_no_dups = list(set(dept_list))
8  sum_sal_dept_wise_dict={}
9  for dept in dept_list_no_dups:
10     sum_sal_dept_wise_dict[dept] = 0
11 for line in lines_wo_header:
12     line = line.split(",")[1:3]
13     sum_sal_dept_wise_dict[line[0]] = int(sum_sal_dept_wise_dict[line[0]])+ int(line[1])
14
15 print("Output :\n")
16 print("Department : sum_of_sal")
17 for k in sorted(list(sum_sal_dept_wise_dict.keys())):
18     print(k," : ",sum_sal_dept_wise_dict[k])
```

Figure 9.1: Solution - Without using the pandas library

Output :

```
Department : sum_of_sal
Accounting   :  22500
Advertising  :  45609
Asset Management  :  26885
Customer Relations  :  34939
Customer Service  :  15687
Finances  :  26259
Human Resources  :  7919
Legal Department  :  24534
Media Relations  :  22325
Payroll  :  22079
Public Relations  :  28010
Quality Assurance  :  12934
Research and Development  :  30320
Sales and Marketing  :  15919
Tech Support  :  23232
```

Figure 9.2: *Output of the Solution - Without using the pandas library*

Now, let's see the solution with the pandas library:

```
1  df = pd.read_csv("data/emp.csv")
2  sal_dept_by_df = df.groupby("Department").sum("Salary_in_dollor").reset_index()
3  sal_dept_by_df.columns = ['Department', 'sum_of_sal']
4  print("Output :\n")
5  sal_dept_by_df
```

Figure 9.3: *Solution using the pandas library*

Output :

	Department	sum_of_sal
0	Accounting	22500
1	Advertising	45609
2	Asset Management	26885
3	Customer Relations	34939
4	Customer Service	15687
5	Finances	26259
6	Human Resources	7919
7	Legal Department	24534
8	Media Relations	22325
9	Payroll	22079
10	Public Relations	28010
11	Quality Assurance	12934
12	Research and Development	30320
13	Sales and Marketing	15919
14	Tech Support	23232

Figure 9.4: *Output of the solution using pandas library*

Pandas data structure

We will start with a brief, non-comprehensive overview of the data structures in pandas. Given below are the important data structures in pandas:

1. **Series**

    Pandas series is a one-dimensional array with index labels, more in technical term, these labels are also referred to as axis index. So, in other words, the pandas series is the collection of objects in one dimension with an axis index.

    o **Creating the pandas series**

    We have the function **pandas.Series(data,index=index)** and it can create a pandas series. In the following example, we have created a pandas series from the Python list.

```
1  import pandas as pd # importing the pandas library
2  import numpy as np
3  #Pandas Series
4  num_list = [1,2,3,4,5]
5  num_series=  pd.Series(num_list)
6  print("data type of num_series :{}".format(type(num_series)))
7  num_series
```

```
data type of num_series :<class 'pandas.core.series.Series'>
0    1
1    2
2    3
3    4
4    5
dtype: int64
```

Figure 9.5: Pandas series

2. **DataFrame**

    Pandas DataFrame is the data structure with two-dimensional labels, one is axis index (row label), and the second is axis column (column label). We can think of it as a table in SQL where data is organized in rows and columns. DataFrame is the most commonly used data structure of pandas. In the next part of this chapter, we will explore various features and functions of pandas DataFrame.

    o **Creating pandas DataFrame**

    In pandas library, we have the function **Pandas.DataFrame(data,index=index,columns=[column(s)])**, which can be used to create a pandas DataFrame. We have created pandas

DataFrame from the Python list and Python dictionary in the following examples:

If you see in the first example, where we have created DataFrame using Python list, we have passed 'number' as a column name (**Pandas.DataFrame(num_list, columns = ['number']**)) but we have not given the indexes as an argument in the function. So pandas automatically assigned the index labels [0,1,2,3,4] to the DataFrame and now we know that if we haven't passed index labels or column labels, pandas will automatically create them.

Coding example(s)

Creating the pandas DataFrame from Python list:

```
import pandas as pd # importing the pandas library
import numpy as np
# Pandas DataFrame
num_list = [1,2,3,4,5]
num_df= pd.DataFrame(num_list,columns = ['number'])
print("data type of num_series :{}".format(type(num_df)))
num_df
```

data type of num_series :<class 'pandas.core.frame.DataFrame'>

	number
0	1
1	2
2	3
3	4
4	5

Figure 9.6: Creating the pandas DataFrame from the Python list

Creating the pandas DataFrame from Python dictionary :

```
1  import pandas as pd # importing the pandas library
2  import numpy as np
3  # creating Pandas data frame using Python list
4  num_list_df =  pd.DataFrame(num_list, columns=['number'])
5  print ("data type of num_list_df is {}".format(type(num_list_df)))
6  print("printing the data frame num_list_df:")
7  num_list_df
```

```
data type of num_list_df is <class 'pandas.core.frame.DataFrame'>
printing the data frame num_list_df:
```

	number
0	1
1	2
2	3
3	4
4	5

Figure 9.7: Creating the pandas DataFrame from python Dictionary

Loading data from external files into DataFrame

Pandas library has various functions to read and load the data from different files into the DataFrame. The following are examples of loading the data from commonly used file formats like CSV, EXCEL, and JSON:

- **Loading the data from CSV into DataFrame:**

    CSV is the abbreviation of **Comma Separated Values**, so typically, the CSV file contains the common separated values. Given below is the snapshot of a CSV file with a header:

    ```
     1  Name,Department,Salary_in_dollor,city
     2  Porter,Advertising,5383,Connah's Quay
     3  Abraham,Media Relations,8181,Beauwelz
     4  Victoria,Accounting,7921,Neerrepen
     5  Hiroko,Customer Relations,7443,Sanzeno
     6  Kathleen,Legal Department,9476,Minneapolis
     7  Amela,Public Relations,9900,Carterton
     8  Timon,Advertising,5222,Portland
     9  Barclay,Accounting,8224,Sanzeno
    10  Knox,Finances,6089,Alken
    11  Malachi,Quality Assurance,5858,Wazirabad
    12  Macy,Public Relations,9470,Richmond Hill
    13  Demetria,Advertising,8282,Wanneroo
    14  Lawrence,Payroll,7538,Sanzeno
    15  Lavinia,Tech Support,9775,Temuka
    ```

    Figure 9.8: CSV file

We have the **read_csv()** function in the pandas library to create the DataFrame by reading the data from a CSV file. There could be various scenarios working with CSV files; some of them are the following:

o   CSV file which contains header information

o   CSV file which doesn't have header information

o   Instead of a common separator, there will be some other character separator like the pipe (" | ")

We will see the hands-on examples for all the above cases.

- **Loading data from CSV file with a header into a DataFrame**

    The **read_csv()** function automatically picked up the first line as header and assigned the column names in DataFrame accordingly. Following is the snapshot of a CSV with a header. Now, we will load data from this file into a DataFrame.

    Input CSV file snap-shot:

```
1  Name,Department,Salary_in_dollor,city
2  Porter,Advertising,5383,Connah's Quay
3  Abraham,Media Relations,8181,Beauwelz
4  Victoria,Accounting,7921,Neerrepen
5  Hiroko,Customer Relations,7443,Sanzeno
```

Figure 9.9: Input CSV file

The code snippet is to import/load the CSV file and display the first five rows from DataFrame.

```
1  import pandas as pd # importing the pandas library
2  import numpy as np
3  # csv
4  csv_df = pd.read_csv("data/emp.csv") # Will take elemnt(s) of first line as column(s)
5  csv_df.head() # printing the first 5 records from DataFrame
```

	Name	Department	Salary_in_dollor	city
0	Porter	Advertising	5383	Connah's Quay
1	Abraham	Media Relations	8181	Beauwelz
2	Victoria	Accounting	7921	Neerrepen
3	Hiroko	Customer Relations	7443	Sanzeno
4	Kathleen	Legal Department	9476	Minneapolis

Figure 9.10: Importing CSV file and creating pandas the frame

- **Loading data from CSV file without header into a DataFrame:**

    If the CSV file doesn't have a header, we have to pass header or column details as an argument during calling the **read_csv()** function to load the data from CSV to a data frame. The function will be like – **Pandas.read_csv(<Input_CSV_file_Path>,names = [col1,col2…coln])**. If neither file has a header nor applies the values to the names keyword, then by default, pandas will assign the first row's value(s) as a column name(s) to the DataFrame.

    Given below is the snapshot of a CSV file without a header. Now, we will load data from this file into a DataFrame.

    Input CSV File without header snapshot

    ```
    1  Porter,Advertising,5383,Connah's Quay
    2  Abraham,Media Relations,8181,Beauwelz
    3  Victoria,Accounting,7921,Neerrepen
    4  Hiroko,Customer Relations,7443,Sanzeno
    5  Kathleen,Legal Department,9476,Minneapolis
    ```

    Figure 9.11: Input CSV file without header

Given below is the code snippet to import/load the CSV file above and display the first five rows from DataFrame:

```
1  import pandas as pd # importing the pandas library
2  import numpy as np
3  my_header= ['name','department','salary_in_dollor','city']
4  # passing the header information explicitly to names parameter
5  no_header_csv_df =  pd.read_csv("data/emp_no_header.csv",names=my_header)
6  no_header_csv_df.head() # printing the first 5 records from DataFrame
```

	name	department	salary_in_dollor	city
0	Porter	Advertising	5383	Connah's Quay
1	Abraham	Media Relations	8181	Beauwelz
2	Victoria	Accounting	7921	Neerrepen
3	Hiroko	Customer Relations	7443	Sanzeno
4	Kathleen	Legal Department	9476	Minneapolis

Figure 9.12: Import the CSV file (without header) and create a data frame with a custom head

- **Loading data from pipe ("|") separated file into a DataFrame**

  If a flat-file contains data, separated by some other character except comma (","), then to load that file into a DataFrame, need to explicitly specify the separator as an argument while calling the **read_csv()** function.

  Following is the snippet of a pipe-separated file, now we will load data from this file into a DataFrame:

  Input file snippet

  ```
  Name|Department|Salary_in_dollor|city
  Porter|Advertising|5383|Connah's Quay
  Abraham|Media Relations|8181|Beauwelz
  Victoria|Accounting|7921|Neerrepen
  Hiroko|Customer Relations|7443|Sanzeno
  ```

  Figure 9.13: Pipe delimited input file

  The code snippet is to import/load the data from the pipe separated file above into a DataFrame and display the first five records.

  ```
  import pandas as pd # importing the pandas library
  import numpy as np
  text_file_df = pd.read_csv("data/emp.txt",sep ="|")
  text_file_df.head()
  ```

  Figure 9.14: Importing pipe-delimited input file and creating pandas dataframe

  The following is the output of this code:

	Name	Department	Salary_in_dollor	city
0	Porter	Advertising	5383	Connah's Quay
1	Abraham	Media Relations	8181	Beauwelz
2	Victoria	Accounting	7921	Neerrepen
3	Hiroko	Customer Relations	7443	Sanzeno
4	Kathleen	Legal Department	9476	Minneapolis

  Figure 9.15: Output from example

- **Loading the data from excel file into DataFrame**

   To load data from a Microsoft Excel file into a DataFrame, we have the **read_excel()** function. It will be – **pd.read_excel(<excel_file_path>,sheet_name=<excel_sheet_name>)**

   Given below is the code snippet to load data from Excel into a DataFrame and display the first five rows:

```
1  # Loading the data from excel file
2  excel_df = pd.read_excel("data/emp.xlsx",sheet_name='emp')
3  excel_df.head()
```

	Name	Department	Salary_in_dollor	city
0	Porter	Advertising	5383	Connah's Quay
1	Abraham	Media Relations	8181	Beauwelz
2	Victoria	Accounting	7921	Neerrepen
3	Hiroko	Customer Relations	7443	Sanzeno
4	Kathleen	Legal Department	9476	Minneapolis

Figure 9.16: Importing excel data into the pandas dataframe

- **Loading the data from JSON file into DataFrame:**

   A JSON file format is the commonly used file format across the system and platforms. It organizes the data in key-value pairs and the order's list. The following is the snippet of a JSON file:

```
1  [{"Name":"Rosalyn","Department":"Customer Relations","Salary":"$8757","city":"Ibadan"},
2  {"Name":"Bell","Department":"Media Relations","Salary":"$8915","city":"Senneville"},
3  {"Name":"Salvador","Department":"Payroll","Salary":"$5134","city":"Adria"},
4  {"Name":"Reece","Department":"Asset Management","Salary":"$5451","city":"Balfour"},
5  {"Name":"Jermaine","Department":"Asset Management","Salary":"$5146","city":"Recoleta"},
6  {"Name":"Naomi","Department":"Tech Support","Salary":"$5173","city":"Neerrepen"}]
```

Figure 9.17: Input JSON file's example

We have the **read_json( )** function in the pandas library to load the JSON file data into a DataFrame.

Let's see the following code snippet in which we are loading the data from a data frame and displaying its first five rows:

```
# loading the JSON file data
json_df = pd.read_json('data/emp.json')
json_df.head()
```

	Name	Department	Salary	city
0	Rosalyn	Customer Relations	$8757	Ibadan
1	Bell	Media Relations	$8915	Senneville
2	Salvador	Payroll	$5134	Adria
3	Reece	Asset Management	$5451	Balfour
4	Jermaine	Asset Management	$5146	Recoleta

Figure 9.18: Importing the JSON file into the pandas dataframe

Exploring the data of a DataFrame

So far, we have a good idea of the pandas DataFrame and how we can create them. Now, we will learn some essential functions to explore the data of a DataFrame.

The following are some important functions/methods of the pandas library:

- **DataFrame.shape**

    The **shape** will return a tuple containing the number of rows and columns of the DataFrame. The following is the code snippet to demonstrate this:

    ```
    # createing the dataframe from a csv file
    emp_df = pd.read_csv("data/emp.csv")
    
    
    shape_of_df = emp_df.shape
    print("shape_of_df :",shape_of_df)
    ```

    ```
    shape_of_df : (50, 4)
    ```

    Figure 9.19: dataframes shape method

- **DataFrame.head(n)**

    The **head(n)** function returns a DataFrame containing the first n rows from the Input DataFrame. The following is the code snippet to demonstrate this function:

    ```
    print("Dispalying the first 6 Rows from DataFrame")
    emp_df.head(6)
    ```

    Dispalying the first 6 Rows from DataFrame

	Name	Department	Salary_in_dollor	city
0	Porter	Advertising	5383	Connah's Quay
1	Abraham	Media Relations	8181	Beauwelz
2	Victoria	Accounting	7921	Neerrepen
3	Hiroko	Customer Relations	7443	Sanzeno
4	Kathleen	Legal Department	9476	Minneapolis
5	Amela	Public Relations	9900	Carterton

    Figure 9.20: head() function

- **DataFrame.tail(n)**

    The **tail(n)** function returns a DataFrame containing the last **n** rows of the input DataFrame. The following is the code snippet to demonstrate this function:

    ```
    print("Dispalying the last 6 Rows from DataFrame")
    emp_df.tail(6)
    ```

    Dispalying the last 6 Rows from DataFrame

	Name	Department	Salary_in_dollor	city
44	Cecilia	Customer Relations	7480	Cumberland
45	Tobias	Media Relations	8619	Westlock
46	Palmer	Quality Assurance	7076	Ospedaletto d'Alpinolo
47	Hayes	Asset Management	6381	Malahide
48	Xyla	Asset Management	6531	Poole
49	Orlando	Customer Service	8524	Caramanico Terme

    Figure 9.21: tail() function

- **DataFrame.info()**

  The `info()` function prints the data frame information like index, columns, not null values, and so on. The following is the code snippet to demonstrate this function:

  ```
  1  emp_df.info()
  ```

  ```
  <class 'pandas.core.frame.DataFrame'>
  RangeIndex: 50 entries, 0 to 49
  Data columns (total 4 columns):
   #   Column           Non-Null Count  Dtype
  ---  ------           --------------  -----
   0   Name             50 non-null     object
   1   Department       50 non-null     object
   2   Salary_in_dollor 50 non-null     int64
   3   city             50 non-null     object
  dtypes: int64(1), object(3)
  memory usage: 1.7+ KB
  ```

  Figure 9.22: info() function

- **DataFrame.describe()**

  The `describe()` function generates the descriptive statistics. By default, it returns the statistics for the numeric column, but it explicitly applies this to some other type like string column; it will generate the respective statistics. Given below is the code snippet to demonstrate this function:

  ```
  1  # Generating the Statistics for numeric column
  2  emp_df.describe()
  ```

	Salary_in_dollor
count	50.000000
mean	7183.020000
std	1360.504866
min	5015.000000
25%	6099.250000
50%	7161.000000
75%	8213.250000
max	9900.000000

  Figure 9.23: Describe() function

The following is the code snippet to **describe()** the non-numeric column:

```
1  # Generating the Statistics for non numeric column
2  emp_df[['city']].describe()
```

	city
count	50
unique	31
top	Sanzeno
freq	9

Figure 9.24: describe() function -non numeric

- **DataFrame.dtypes:**

    The **dtypes()** function returns the data types in DataFrame. The following is the code snippet to demonstrate this function:

```
1  # Return the DataTypes in Dataframe
2  emp_df.dtypes
```

```
Name              object
Department        object
Salary_in_dollor   int64
city              object
dtype: object
```

Figure 9.25: The dtypes() function

- **DataFrame.columns**

    The **columns** method returns the column labels of the DataFrame. The following is the code snippet to demonstrate this function:

```
1  # print the all columns of the data frame
2  print ("Columns in the DataFrame :\n",emp_df.columns)
```

```
Columns in the DataFrame :
 Index(['Name', 'Department', 'Salary_in_dollor', 'city'], dtype='object')
```

Figure 9.26: The columns method

Selecting data from DataFrame

There are various ways to select and filter the data from the pandas DataFrame. Some of them (like **DataFrame.head(n)**, **DataFrame.tail(n)**, and so on) we have already discussed in the last part of this chapter. We can use the following methods to select and filter the data as per our needs:

- **Selecting the data for the subset of columns**

    To select the subset of columns out of all, we can use a function like - **<dataframe name>[[col1,col2…]]**. This will return a DataFrame with selected columns. The following is an example where we will select the name and city from **emp_df** and will display the first five rows from the returned DataFrame.

    Coding example(s)

    ```
    1  print("Columns present in DataFrame:",emp_df.columns)
    2  print("Selecting the data for Name and city column from DataFrame")
    3  new_df = emp_df[['Name','city']]
    4  new_df.head() # Displaying the first 5 rows from new dataframe with column Name and city
    ```

    ```
    Columns present in DataFrame: Index(['Name', 'Department', 'Salary_in_dollor', 'city'], dtype='object')
    Selecting the data for Name and city column from DataFrame
    ```

	Name	city
0	Porter	Connah's Quay
1	Abraham	Beauwelz
2	Victoria	Neerrepen
3	Hiroko	Sanzeno
4	Kathleen	Minneapolis

    Figure 9.27: Selecting the specific column's values from dataframe

- **Selecting the data using simple conditions**

    It is like selecting some data from a table in SQL with the 'where' clause. Similarly, in pandas' also, we can select the data from the pandas DataFrame with some condition. For example, from an employee data frame (**emp_df**), we want to get all the records of the city Sanzeno (meaning, city = Sanzeno). The following is an example for selecting the data with the condition:

    Coding example(s)

```
1  #filter the data
2  # display all records which have city='Sanzeno'.
3  new_df= emp_df[emp_df.city == 'Sanzeno']
4  new_df
```

	Name	Department	Salary_in_dollor	city
3	Hiroko	Customer Relations	7443	Sanzeno
7	Barclay	Accounting	8224	Sanzeno
12	Lawrence	Payroll	7538	Sanzeno
23	Tashya	Legal Department	8826	Sanzeno
26	Hakeem	Legal Department	6232	Sanzeno
27	Ezekiel	Advertising	6848	Sanzeno
29	Charity	Research and Development	5135	Sanzeno
34	Doris	Asset Management	8242	Sanzeno
39	Kieran	Tech Support	8061	Sanzeno

Figure 9.28: Selecting data from the data frame using simple condition -example#1

Let's take another example to explore it more. For example, let's assume that now we need to select all the employee names from the data frame **emp_df** with a salary of less than $6000. The following is a code snippet where we're doing the same:

Coding example(s)

```
1  # display employe name  which have salary less that $6000 .
2  emp_names_sal_lt_6k = emp_df[emp_df.Salary_in_dollor < 6000][['Name']]
3  # print(emp_names_sal_lt_6k)
4  emp_names_sal_lt_6k
```

	Name
0	Porter
6	Timon
9	Malachi
18	Christopher
20	Carla
28	Jaden
29	Charity
30	Quin
33	Rogan
35	Cassidy
42	Walker

Figure 9.29: Selecting data from the data frame using simple condition – example#2

- **Selecting the data with multiple conditions**

    Sometimes, just selecting the data on simple conditions is not enough to fill our requirements. In real-world problems, we have to select data by applying multiple conditions. We will see such cases in the following:

    CASE 1 : Condition 1 AND Condition 2 :

    We often have to select data by applying two or more conditions simultaneously. For example, suppose we need to select all such records from **emp_df** where:

    Condition 1: Salary is less than or equal to $10000.

    Condition 2: City is Sanzeno.

    So, in case of AND condition, we can select only those records that qualify for both the conditions. The following is an example to demonstrate this case:

    Coding example(s)

    ```
    1  out_df = emp_df[(emp_df.Salary_in_dollor <= 10000) & (emp_df.city == 'Sanzeno')]
    2  out_df
    ```

	Name	Department	Salary_in_dollor	city
3	Hiroko	Customer Relations	7443	Sanzeno
7	Barclay	Accounting	8224	Sanzeno
12	Lawrence	Payroll	7538	Sanzeno
23	Tashya	Legal Department	8826	Sanzeno
26	Hakeem	Legal Department	6232	Sanzeno
27	Ezekiel	Advertising	6848	Sanzeno
29	Charity	Research and Development	5135	Sanzeno
34	Doris	Asset Management	8242	Sanzeno
39	Kieran	Tech Support	8061	Sanzeno

    Figure 9.30: CASE #1 : Condition1 AND Condition2

    CASE 2: Condition 1 OR Condition 2

    Let's assume that we need to fetch out such records from the **emp_df**, where:

    Condition 1: Salary is less than or equal to $5000.

    Condition 2: City is Sanzeno.

    So, in this case, we can select records that either qualify condition 1 or condition 2. Such arrangement of the condition is OR, meaning if any one of the conditions is True or gets passed, we will pick up that record. The following is an example to demonstrate the case #2 (OR)

```
1  out_df = emp_df[(emp_df.Salary_in_dollor < 5000) | (emp_df.city == 'Sanzeno')]
2  out_df
```

	Name	Department	Salary_in_dollor	city
3	Hiroko	Customer Relations	7443	Sanzeno
7	Barclay	Accounting	8224	Sanzeno
12	Lawrence	Payroll	7538	Sanzeno
23	Tashya	Legal Department	8826	Sanzeno
26	Hakeem	Legal Department	6232	Sanzeno
27	Ezekiel	Advertising	6848	Sanzeno
29	Charity	Research and Development	5135	Sanzeno
34	Doris	Asset Management	8242	Sanzeno
39	Kieran	Tech Support	8061	Sanzeno

Figure 9.31: CASE# 2: Condition1 OR Condition2

Data cleaning in pandas DataFrame

It is essential for unbiased, accurate, and consistent results to have data free from the impurities like duplicate values/records, missing values, irrelevant data points, and so on. So, to solve the data problem, either we can manipulate and fix these impurities or remove such bad data records. In pandas, we have various functions/methods for the data cleaning task. Some of their essential methods/functions are the following:

- **Handling duplicate data**

    Duplicates in the data is a prevalent problem; it takes more space to save the identical records and can lead to inaccuracy in resultant insights. So, it is better if we should remove such duplicate records from our data. But before removing them, it is essential to identify the duplicate records first, and to understand the different ways to consider any record duplicate.

- **If the complete record is duplicate**

  Duplicate record means if more than one record has the same values for all columns. In the following snippet, `employee_id = 149` has duplicate records:

employee_id	employee_name	employee_salary_in_dollor	employee_city	employee_department	employe_joining_date
149	Leroy	8001	Meeswijk	Advertising	29/03/2021
149	Leroy	8001	Meeswijk	Advertising	29/03/2021
150	Kiona	9248	Saguenay	Customer Service	22/07/2015
151	Miranda	5962		Payroll	5/4/2017
152	Tyrone	5757		Human Resources	11/9/2017
153	Raymond	5870		Payroll	14/04/2021
154	Colby	6414	Saravena	Sales and Marketing	3/4/2019
155	Bethany	8677	Dover	Tech Support	4/7/2016
156	Allegra	5377	Saint-Marc	Media Relations	17/05/2015

  Figure 9.32: If the complete record is duplicate

- **A subset of columns has duplicate values**: Here, we will consider a record as duplicate if one or a subset of DataFrame columns (we can say those columns as key columns) instead of all columns have duplicate values. In the following example, `employee_id =111` has more than one column with the same values, but all columns don't.

	employee_id	employee_name	employee_salary_in_dollor	employee_city	employee_department	employe_joining_date
12	111	Cruz	6740	Lavacherie	Legal Department	24/06/2014
13	111	Cruz	6740		Legal Department	24/06/2014

  Figure 9.33: One or more columns have duplicate values

  The following are examples of identifying and dropping duplicate records from a DataFrame.

  Getting the number of duplicate records present in data.

  In *Example 1*, we will apply the `duplicated()` function on a complete data frame, which means it is considered a record duplicate if two or more than two records have the same values for all columns, while in *Example 2*, we are using `duplicated()` by passing the subset of dataframes columns, so it will consider any record duplicate if they have identical values for the subset of the key column(s).

```
#Example#1
# get the count of Duplicate Records [if complete row is duplicate then it will consider it duplicate ]
no_of_dups = emp_df_raw.duplicated().sum()
print("number of rows having complete row duplicate :",no_of_dups)

#Example#2
#Finding the duplicate recodrs on the basis of key column(s) instead of complete record.
no_of_dups = emp_df_raw.duplicated(['employee_id']).sum()
print("number of rows having duplicate employee ids:",no_of_dups)
```

```
number of rows having complete row duplicate : 4
number of rows having duplicate employee ids: 8
```

Figure 9.34: Duplicate rows count

Displaying the duplicate records

The following example shows the records from DataFrame that have duplicate values for column **employee_id**.

```
1  # displaying the duplicate records
2  emp_df_raw[emp_df_raw.duplicated('employee_id')] # Show Only Duplicate Rows
```

	employee_id	employee_name	employee_salary_in_dollor	employee_city	employee_department	employe_joining_date
11	111	Cruz	6740	NaN	Legal Department	24/06/2014
29	128	Colorado	9075	Gosselies	Media Relations	2/11/2019
35	132	Gisela	7879	Castellina in Chianti	Accounting	4/2/2016
45	NaN	Amir	9819	Püttlingen	Legal Department	18/10/2020
52	149	Leroy	8001	Meeswijk	Advertising	29/03/2021
68	NaN	Reese	5121	Orizaba	Public Relations	14/01/2021
73	168	Neil	6644	Drachten	Public Relations	22/06/2019
74	169	Rahim	9749	Neiva	Customer Service	12/9/2015

Figure 9.35: *Printing the duplicate records from dataframe*

Dropping/deleting the duplicate records

To get rid of the duplicate records, we can drop them from our DataFrame. We can do it with the help of the **drop_duplicates()** function. If we did not pass any list of subset columns to this, it would drop only these records from the data frame, which have duplicity in the value s for all columns, but if we pass the essential columns list, it will drop records that show duplicity in values for specified columns only. In the following example, we will drop all duplicate row(s) from the data frame; duplicate values for **employee_id** columns:

```
1  # Droping or deleting the duplicate recods from DataFrame
2  #Drop All Duplicate Rows Keep only single record
3  emp_df_raw_no_dups = emp_df_raw.drop_duplicates('employee_id')
4  dups_reord_count = emp_df_raw_no_dups.duplicated(['employee_id']).sum()
5  print("Duplicate recods count =",dups_reord_count)
6
7
8  # Now no dups df have only single record for employee_id=111
9  emp_df_raw_no_dups[emp_df_raw_no_dups.employee_id=='111']
```
Duplicate recods count = 0

	employee_id	employee_name	employee_salary_in_dollor	employee_city	employee_department	employe_joining_date
10	111	Cruz	6740	Lavacherie	Legal Department	24/06/2014

Figure 9.36: *Dropping the duplicate rows*

- **Handling missing values in data**

    Handling the missing values is a very crucial and essential task. The most straightforward approach is removing the records from the DataFrame that have missing values. But it will not help since in all cases we can lose some important facts from our data. So, another way is to impute the values for the missing data, and there is no single or fixed method to find such values. It depends on several factors like what type of problem it is, its domain, and the business need, or how it will impact our outcomes. In pandas, we have a good list of functions/methods to handle missing data in DataFrame.

- **Dropping the rows which have missing data**

    In pandas, we have the **dropna()** function to drop the rows with the missing values. We can use this function with various options like:

    o   If all columns have missing values (**dropna(how='all')**)…

    o   If any column has missing values (dropna(how='any')…

    o   If subset of columns or specified columns have missing value (**drop_na(subset=[col1,col2…])**)…

    The following are the examples for the same:

    Example: Use of **dropna(how='all')**

```
1  df_drop_na_all = df.dropna(how='all')
2  custom_display(df,df_drop_na_all,titles=["|Input : Raw DataFrame|","|Output : df with dropna(how='all') "])
```

	Name	Department	Salary_in_dollor	city		Name	Department	Salary_in_dollor	city
			|Input : Raw DataFrame|					|Output : df with dropna(how='all')|	
0	Jim	Advertising	7921.0	Connah's Quay	0	Jim	Advertising	7921.0	Connah's Quay
1	Abraham	NaN	7787.0	Sanzeno	1	Abraham	NaN	7787.0	Sanzeno
2	Porter	Accounting	7921.0	NaN	2	Porter	Accounting	7921.0	NaN
3	Victoria	HR	NaN	Neerrepen	3	Victoria	HR	NaN	Neerrepen
4	Hiroko	Accounting	7443.0	Sanzeno	4	Hiroko	Accounting	7443.0	Sanzeno
5	NaN	NaN	NaN	NaN	6	NA		0.0	
6	NA		0.0						

Figure 9.37: Dropping the rows using dropna(how='all')

Example: Use of **dropna(how='any')**

```
1  df_drop_na_any = df.dropna(how='any')
2  custom_display(df,df_drop_na_any,titles=["|Input : Raw DataFrame|","|Output : df with dropna(how='any') "])
```

	Input : Raw DataFrame						Output : df with dropna(how='any')			
	Name	Department	Salary_in_dollor	city		Name	Department	Salary_in_dollor	city
0	Jim	Advertising	7921.0	Connah's Quay	0	Jim	Advertising	7921.0	Connah's Quay
1	Abraham	NaN	7787.0	Sanzeno	4	Hiroko	Accounting	7443.0	Sanzeno
2	Porter	Accounting	7921.0	NaN	6	NA		0.0	
3	Victoria	HR	NaN	Neerrepen
4	Hiroko	Accounting	7443.0	Sanzeno
5	NaN	NaN	NaN	NaN
6	NA		0.0	

Figure 9.38: *Dropping the rows using dropna(how='any')*

Example: Use of **dropna(subset)**

```
1  df_drop_na_subset = df.dropna(subset=['Name','city'])
2  custom_display(df,df_drop_na_subset,
3                 titles=["|Input : Raw DataFrame|","|Output : df with dropna(how='any',subset=[col]) "])
```

	Input : Raw DataFrame						Output : df with dropna(how='any',subset=[col])			
	Name	Department	Salary_in_dollor	city		Name	Department	Salary_in_dollor	city
0	Jim	Advertising	7921.0	Connah's Quay	0	Jim	Advertising	7921.0	Connah's Quay
1	Abraham	NaN	7787.0	Sanzeno	1	Abraham	NaN	7787.0	Sanzeno
2	Porter	Accounting	7921.0	NaN	3	Victoria	HR	NaN	Neerrepen
3	Victoria	HR	NaN	Neerrepen	4	Hiroko	Accounting	7443.0	Sanzeno
4	Hiroko	Accounting	7443.0	Sanzeno	6	NA		0.0	
5	NaN	NaN	NaN	NaN
6	NA		0.0	

Figure 9.39: *Dropping the rows using dropna(subset)*

- **Filling the missing values**

  As discussed already, it is not always helpful to delete the records from DataFrame with the missing values. In many cases, we need to infer some values which we can fill or impute in place of missing data. So, to fill the missing values, we can use the **fillna()** or **replace()** function. These can be used with various options depending on our needs. The following is the code snippet to create a DataFrame **df** from a Python dictionary with missing values.

```
1  # creating a sample df
2  # np.nan means inserting the NaN values
3  emp_dict = {'Name':['Porter','Abraham','NA','Victoria','Hiroko'],
4  'Department':['Advertising',np.nan,'Accounting',"",'Accounting'],
5  'Salary_in_dollor':[7921,0,7921,np.nan,7443],
6  'city':["Connah's Quay","Sanzeno",np.nan,"Neerrepen","Sanzeno"]}
7
8  df = pd.DataFrame(emp_dict)
9  df
```

	Name	Department	Salary_in_dollor	city
0	Porter	Advertising	7921.0	Connah's Quay
1	Abraham		0.0	Sanzeno
2	NA	Accounting	7921.0	NaN
3	Victoria		NaN	Neerrepen
4	Hiroko	Accounting	7443.0	Sanzeno

Figure 9.40: Creating sample dataframe using dict

In the above DataFrame, all **Not a Number** (**NaN**) means missing values. In pandas, NaN is the missing value (means zero, blank, or space, and NA will not be considered as missing values by pandas).

Let's see how we can use **fillna()** and **replace()** functions to fill/replace the values in DataFrame.

DataFrame.fillna():

We can use this function as follows:

- **DataFrame.fillna(<value_to_be filled>)**

    Whatever we pass in the **fillna()** function will replace all NaN by default. See the following example where all NaN values were filled with the **MissingValue**.

```
1  # using fillna() , will fill all NaN values with new value
2  # print(" NaN filled with Missingvalue string :")
3  df_fillna = df.fillna("MissingValue")
4  #displaying the df side by side using custom function
5  custom_display(df,titles=["|Input : Raw DataFrame|"])
6  custom_display(df_fillna,titles=["|Output : Applyng fillna() function|"])
```

Figure 9.41: Using fillna() to fill missing values

Here, we can see the coding snippet, where we're using the **fillna()** function to fill the NaN values in DataFrame. Line 5 is a custom display function, which will display the Input data frame, and line 6 will show the dataframe **df_fillna** after applying the **fillna()** function. The following is the output screenshot:

|Input : Raw DataFrame|

	Name	Department	Salary_in_dollor	city
0	Jim	Advertising	7921.0	Connah's Quay
1	Abraham	NaN	7787.0	Sanzeno
2	Porter	Accounting	7921.0	NaN
3	Victoria	HR	NaN	Neerrepen
4	Hiroko	Accounting	7443.0	Sanzeno
5	NaN	NaN	NaN	NaN
6	NA		0.0	

|Output : Applyng fillna() function|

	Name	Department	Salary_in_dollor	city
0	Jim	Advertising	7921	Connah's Quay
1	Abraham	MissingValue	7787	Sanzeno
2	Porter	Accounting	7921	MissingValue
3	Victoria	HR	MissingValue	Neerrepen
4	Hiroko	Accounting	7443	Sanzeno
5	MissingValue	MissingValue	MissingValue	MissingValue
6	NA		0	

Figure 9.42: Output for fillna() functions demo

- **DataFrame.fillna(method = 'ffill')**

    If we use the forward fill method option with **fillna()**, all NaN values will be filled with the previous value of that column. The following example demonstrates this:

    ```
    #fillna(method = 'ffill'):
    df_fillna_w_ffill = df.fillna(method='ffill')


    sal_fillna_w_ffill = df[['Salary_in_dollor']].fillna(method='ffill')
    custom_display(df[['Salary_in_dollor']],sal_fillna_w_ffill,
                   titles=["|Input : Raw DataFrame|","|Output : Applyng fillna(method='ffill') function|"])
    ```

|Input : Raw DataFrame| Salary_in_dollor	|Output : Applyng fillna(method='ffill') function| Salary_in_dollor
0	7921.0	0	7921.0
1	7787.0	1	7787.0
2	7921.0	2	7921.0
3	NaN	3	7921.0
4	7443.0	4	7443.0
5	NaN	5	7443.0
6	0.0	6	0.0

    Figure 9.43: Output for fillna(method='ffill')

- **DataFrame.fillna(method = 'bfill')**

    If we use the 'backward fill' option with **fillna()**, all NaN values will be filled from the next value of its column. The following example demonstrates this:

    ```
    salry_w_bfill = df[['Salary_in_dollor']].fillna(method='bfill')
    custom_display(df[['Salary_in_dollor']],
                   salry_w_bfill,titles=["|Input : Raw DataFrame|",
                                         "|Output : Applyng method='bfill' function|"])
    ```

|Input : Raw DataFrame| Salary_in_dollor	|Output : Applyng method='bfill' function| Salary_in_dollor
0	7921.0	0	7921.0
1	7787.0	1	7787.0
2	7921.0	2	7921.0
3	NaN	3	7443.0
4	7443.0	4	7443.0
5	NaN	5	0.0
6	0.0	6	0.0

    Figure 9.44: Output for fillna(method='bfill')

- **fillna()** with **mean()**, **median()**, **mode()**

    We can fill the missing values with more appropriate ones using the **fillna()** function's statistical function. For example, suppose we found some missing values in the salary column. In that case, filling with some constant value is not good; rather, filing that with average of all salaries or median of all salaries will be more appropriate. See the following examples where we will handle the missing values with **mean()**, **median()** and **mode()** functions:

    The following example demonstrates how to use the **fillna()** function with **mean()** of specific columns value.

```
1  #fillna() with mean()
2  df_fillna_w_mean = df[['Salary_in_dollor']].fillna(df['Salary_in_dollor'].mean())
3
4  custom_display(df[['Salary_in_dollor']],df_fillna_w_mean,
5                 titles=["|Input : Raw DataFrame|",
6                         "|Output : df_fillna_w_mean "])
7
```

	Input : Raw DataFrame	 Salary_in_dollor		Output : df_fillna_w_mean Salary_in_dollor
0	7921.0	0	7921.0
1	7787.0	1	7787.0
2	7921.0	2	7921.0
3	NaN	3	6214.4
4	7443.0	4	7443.0
5	NaN	5	6214.4
6	0.0	6	0.0

Figure 9.45: Output for fillna() with means()

The following example demonstrates how to use the **fillna()** function with **median()** of specific columns value:

```
1  #fillna() median()
2  df_fillna_w_median = df[['Salary_in_dollor']].fillna(df['Salary_in_dollor'].median())
3
4  custom_display(df[['Salary_in_dollor']],df_fillna_w_median,
5                 titles=["|Input : Raw DataFrame|","|Output : df_fillna_w_median "])
6
```

	Input : Raw DataFrame	 Salary_in_dollor		Output : df_fillna_w_median Salary_in_dollor
0	7921.0	0	7921.0
1	7787.0	1	7787.0
2	7921.0	2	7921.0
3	NaN	3	7787.0
4	7443.0	4	7443.0
5	NaN	5	7787.0
6	0.0	6	0.0

Figure 9.46: Output for fillna() with median()

The following example demonstrates how to use the **fillna()** function with **mode()** of specific columns value.

```
1  #fillna() with mean(),median() or mode
2  df_fillna_w_mode = df[['city']].fillna(df['city'].mode()[0])
3  custom_display(df[['city']],df_fillna_w_mode,
4              titles=["|Input : Raw DataFrame|","|Output : df_fillna_w_mode "])
```

|Input : Raw DataFrame| city	|Output : df_fillna_w_mode| city
0	Connah's Quay	0	Connah's Quay
1	Sanzeno	1	Sanzeno
2	NaN	2	Sanzeno
3	Neerrepen	3	Neerrepen
4	Sanzeno	4	Sanzeno
5	NaN	5	Sanzeno
6		6	

Figure 9.47: Output for fillna() with mode()

DataFrame.replace()

If you observed the previous examples for **fillna()** function, it deals with only the NaN values (as pandas consider NaN as missing value); it does not replace values like 'NA,' 0, blank/space, but these values can also be considered as missing in real-time problem cases. For example, we have a city column, but it has blank/space for some cell or 0 in the salary column, which is also supposed to be considered missing values. So, if we can replace these values with some other values using **replace()** function, we need to pass **old_value** and **new_value** in this function to get **new_value** by replacing the **old_value**. Following are the examples which demonstrates how to implement this **replace()** function with various options.

The following example demonstrates the uses of **replace()** function with all columns:

```
1  # Replacing All data frames values
2  df_replace = df.replace({'NA':'Not applicable',0:5000,"":'Blank',np.nan:'Not a Number'})
3  custom_display(df,df_replace,titles=["|Input : Raw DataFrame|","|Output : df with replace() "])
```

		Input : Raw DataFrame						Output : df with replace()		
	Name	Department	Salary_in_dollor	city		Name	Department	Salary_in_dollor	city
0	Porter	Advertising	7921.0	Connah's Quay	0	Porter	Advertising	7921	Connah's Quay
1	Abraham	NaN	0.0	Sanzeno	1	Abraham	Not a Number	5000	Sanzeno
2	NA	Accounting	7921.0	NaN	2	Not applicable	Accounting	7921	Not a Number
3	Victoria		NaN	Neerrepen	3	Victoria	Blank	Not a Number	Neerrepen
4	Hiroko	Accounting	7443.0	Sanzeno	4	Hiroko	Accounting	7443	Sanzeno

Figure 9.48: replace() function – for all columns

The following example demonstrates uses of **replace()** function with specific columns:

```
1  # Replacing All selected columns values
2  salary_replaced = df[['Salary_in_dollor']].replace({0:5000,np.nan:5000})
3  custom_display(df[['Salary_in_dollor']],salary_replaced,titles=
4                 ["|Input : Raw DataFrame|","|Output : df with replace() "])
```

	Input : Raw DataFrame	 Salary_in_dollor		Output : df with replace() Salary_in_dollor
0	7921.0	0	7921.0
1	0.0	1	5000.0
2	7921.0	2	7921.0
3	NaN	3	5000.0
4	7443.0	4	7443.0

Figure 9.49: The replace() function -with specific column at a time

Grouping and aggregation

Whenever we need to get the summary out from data, grouping and aggregation functions can be used. For grouping, pandas has **groupby()** function and for aggregation, it has various functions like **min()**, **max()**, **count()**, **sun()**, and so on. According to our requirements, we can choose the most appropriate function and use them.

Grouping

Let's understand how to use the **groupby()** function. In the following example, at:

Step#1: At this step, we need to import the **emp_agg.csv** file into **emp_df** dataframe

Step#2: At this step, **groupby()** function gets called with the 'Department' as argument and prints the grouped object, which will create a grouped object for the column Department where all distinct values of this column will represent the group keys.

Step#3: At this step, we will print all group keys from the grouped object.

```
#Step#1
#importing the emp_agg.csv file into emp_df dataframe
emp_df = pd.read_csv("data/emp_agg.csv")

#Step#2
#creating the grouped object on Department column
emp_dept_grouped_df = emp_df.groupby('Department')
print("Grouped Object:",emp_dept_grouped_df)

#Step#3
# get the all groups key from groupped object
groups = emp_dept_grouped_df.groups.keys()
print("\nGroup_Keys : ",groups)
```
Grouped Object: <pandas.core.groupby.generic.DataFrameGroupBy object at 0x000002639B9FA4F0>

Group_Keys : dict_keys(['Accounting', 'Advertising', 'Customer Relations', 'Legal Department', 'Media Relations', 'Public Relations'])

Figure 9.50: Use of groupby() function and display groups

So, if you want to do grouping on one or more than one column(s), you can use the function **groupby()** as – **DataFrame.groupby([col1,col2…con])**

Aggregation

Let us discuss how to use the aggregate function with the **group ()** function. The syntax will look like **DataFrame.groupby([col1,col2…]).<aggregate_function>()**. We can apply the aggregate function to the grouped data to get the aggregation result. For example, suppose we need to display the salaries for each department. In that case, we first need to do grouping of the data on the column department, then apply aggregate function **sum()** on **Salary** column. The following is an example of this:

```
emp_df.groupby(['Department'])[['Salary_in_dollor']].sum()
```

Department	Salary_in_dollor
Accounting	97504
Advertising	85610
Customer Relations	43819
Legal Department	41351
Media Relations	43013
Public Relations	47854

Figure 9.51: Use of groupby() with aggregate function sum()

There is another way to write the aggregation statements; we can use **agg({agg_function1(),agg_function2()...})** instead of directly calling the aggregation function on top of grouped data. As you see in the following example, we have solved the same query using **agg()** function. We can call aggregate functions by passing the dictionary inside the **agg()** function.

```
1  out_df = emp_df.groupby(['Department'])['Salary_in_dollor'].agg({'sum','mean','max','min','count'})
2  out_df
```

Department	min	count	sum	mean	max
Accounting	5396	13	97504	7500.307692	9470
Advertising	5222	13	85610	6585.384615	9864
Customer Relations	5196	6	43819	7303.166667	8640
Legal Department	5015	6	41351	6891.833333	9476
Media Relations	5740	6	43013	7168.833333	8224
Public Relations	5135	6	47854	7975.666667	9900

Figure 9.52: The use of groupby() with multiple aggregate functions using agg()

Sorting and ranking

We often have such requirements that we have to arrange the data in some order or rank in our data. For example, get the salaries in ascending order or give the rank to the students based on their obtained marks. So, to do such activities, pandas have provided sorting and ranking functions. We will discuss them with examples.

- **Sorting**

    Pandas has provided **sort_index()** and **sort_value()** functions to sort the data. Function **sort_index()** will sort the data based on the dataframes index values, while **sort_values()** will sort the data based on the column values. The function will sort the data. By default, these functions will sort the data in ascending order.

    In the following example, we have sorted the data using the **sort_index()** function. If we see in the input dataframe, the index has values 1,4,2,3, but after using the **sort_index()**, it sorts the dataframe, and in the output dataframe, we have 1,2,3,4.

sort_index()

```
1  # Sample Data frame
2  emp_dict = {'emp_id':[101,105,108,100],
3              'city':['Sanzeno','Beauwelz','Minneapolis','Carterton'],
4              'sal':[5000,8989,5634,9634]}
5
6  df = pd.DataFrame(emp_dict,index=[1,4,2,3])
7
8  # sorting the data usinf sort_index()
9  df_sorted_on_index = df.sort_index()
10 custom_display(df,df_sorted_on_index,
11             titles=["|Input DataFrame|","|O/P: df.sort_index()|"])
12
```

	|Input DataFrame|			|O/P: df.sort_index()|	
	emp_id	city	sal		emp_id	city	sal
1	101	Sanzeno	5000	1	101	Sanzeno	5000
4	105	Beauwelz	8989	2	108	Minneapolis	5634
2	108	Minneapolis	5634	3	100	Carterton	9634
3	100	Carterton	9634	4	105	Beauwelz	8989

Figure 9.53: Use of sort_index()

The functions **sort_values()** will sort the data in the column values; in the following example, we have sorted the input data frame's data based on **emp_id** column's values in the ascending order.

sort_values()

```
1  df_sorted_on_values = df.sort_values(['emp_id'])
2  print("Using sort_values() with default ")
3  custom_display(df,df_sorted_on_values,
4             titles=["|Input DataFrame|","|O/P :sort_values(['emp_id'])|"])
5
```

Using sort_values() with default

	|Input DataFrame|			|O/P :sort_values(['emp_id'])|	
	emp_id	city	sal		emp_id	city	sal
1	101	Sanzeno	5000	3	100	Carterton	9634
4	105	Beauwelz	8989	1	101	Sanzeno	5000
2	108	Minneapolis	5634	4	105	Beauwelz	8989
3	100	Carterton	9634	2	108	Minneapolis	5634

Figure 9.54: Use of sort_values()

If you see in the preceding examples, all sorting is done in ascending order by default. But to get the sorted data in descending order, we must pass the **ascending=False** as an argument with the ascending order sorting functions. In the following example, we have sorted the data based on **emp_id** in the descending order, meaning higher to lower order.

```
1  print("Using sort_values() with option ascending=False ")
2  df_sorted_on_values_desc = df.sort_values(['emp_id'],ascending=False)
3  custom_display(df,df_sorted_on_values_desc,
4                 titles=["|Input DataFrame|","|O/P:df.sort_values(['emp_id'],ascending=False)|"])
```

Using sort_values() with option ascending=False

	|Input DataFrame|			|O/P:df.sort_values(['emp_id'],ascending=False)|	
	emp_id	city	sal		emp_id	city	sal
1	101	Sanzeno	5000	2	108	Minneapolis	5634
4	105	Beauwelz	8989	4	105	Beauwelz	8989
2	108	Minneapolis	5634	1	101	Sanzeno	5000
3	100	Carterton	9634	3	100	Carterton	9634

Figure 9.55: Use of sort_values() with descending order

- **Ranking**

    For ranking, we have the **rank()** function. This function assigns the ranks to the values of a column starting from 1. The **rank()** function also has options to order the data in ascending and descending order. The following are the examples for this:

    ```
    1  df['sal_rank_asc']= df['sal'].rank()
    2  df
    ```

	emp_id	city	sal	sal_rank_asc
1	101	Sanzeno	5000	1.0
4	105	Beauwelz	8989	3.0
2	108	Minneapolis	5634	2.0
3	100	Carterton	9634	4.0

    Figure 9.56: Use of rank() function

    In this example, if you see it, it assigns the rank based on the ascending order of the values, which means lower to higher.

Let's see how we can assign the rank from higher to lower; the following is the example for this, where we pass **ascending =False** in rank function, assigning the ranks from higher to lower.

```
1  df['sal_rank_desc']= df['sal'].rank(ascending=False)
2  df
```

	emp_id	city	sal	sal_rank_asc	sal_rank_desc
1	101	Sanzeno	5000	1.0	4.0
4	105	Beauwelz	8989	3.0	2.0
2	108	Minneapolis	5634	2.0	3.0
3	100	Carterton	9634	4.0	1.0

```
1
```

Figure 9.57: Use of rank() function in descending order

Adding row into DataFrame

Using the **append()** function, we can add a new row in the existing data frame.

We can pass a new row as dictionary, panda in this function: series and **Pandas. DataFrame**. Let's consider that the following DataFrame is the existing data frame, and we are supposed to add a new row in this data frame.

Input DataFrame :

```
1  # Adding Row
2  emp_dict = {'emp_id':[101,105,108,100],
3              'city':['Sanzeno','Beauwelz','Minneapolis','Carterton'],
4              'sal':[5000,8989,5634,9634]}
5
6  df = pd.DataFrame(emp_dict)
7  df
```

	emp_id	city	sal
0	101	Sanzeno	5000
1	105	Beauwelz	8989
2	108	Minneapolis	5634
3	100	Carterton	9634

Figure 9.58: Creating a sample dataframe using dict

The following is an example of adding a new row of type Dict into the above DataFrame df.

```python
# Adding a new row, When new row type is Dict
row = {'emp_id':999,'city':'Minneapolis','sal':6789}
print(type(row))

df = df.append(row,ignore_index=True)
df
```

<class 'dict'>

	emp_id	city	sal
0	101	Sanzeno	5000
1	105	Beauwelz	8989
2	108	Minneapolis	5634
3	100	Carterton	9634
4	888	Minneapolis	6789
5	777	Minneapolis	6789
6	999	Minneapolis	6789

Figure 9.59: Adding new row in existing dataframe

The following is an example. We will add a new row of type pandas series into the above DataFrame **df**.

```python
# Adding a new row, When new row type is Pandas series
row = pd.Series(data = {'emp_id':888,'city':'Minneapolis','sal':6789},name=6)
print(type(row))

df = df.append(row,ignore_index=False)
df
```

<class 'pandas.core.series.Series'>

	emp_id	city	sal
0	101	Sanzeno	5000
1	105	Beauwelz	8989
2	108	Minneapolis	5634
3	100	Carterton	9634
4	999	Minneapolis	6789
6	888	Minneapolis	6789

Figure 9.60: Adding new row in existing dataframe with type pandas series

The following is the example of adding a new row of type pandas DataFrame into the existing DataFrame **df**.

```
1  # adding a column with constant singel value for each row in dataframe
2  df['constant_value_col'] = 'New_value'
3  df
```

	emp_id	city	sal	constant_value_col
0	101	Sanzeno	5000	New_value
1	105	Beauwelz	8989	New_value
2	108	Minneapolis	5634	New_value
3	100	Carterton	9634	New_value
4	999	Minneapolis	6789	New_value
6	888	Minneapolis	6789	New_value
0	777	Minneapolis	6789	New_value

Figure 9.61: Adding a new row in the existing dataframe with type pandas dataframe

Adding column into DataFrame

We can add a new column in the existing data frame using the following ways:

- **Adding New Column with one constant value**

    We can follow the following method if we need to add a new column into the pandas DataFrame by assigning the fixed constant value for all records.

```
1  # adding a column with constant singel value for each row in dataframe
2  df['constant_value_col'] = 'New_value'
3  df
```

	emp_id	city	sal	constant_value_col
0	101	Sanzeno	5000	New_value
1	105	Beauwelz	8989	New_value
2	108	Minneapolis	5634	New_value
3	100	Carterton	9634	New_value
4	999	Minneapolis	6789	New_value
6	888	Minneapolis	6789	New_value
0	777	Minneapolis	6789	New_value

Figure 9.62: Adding a new column in the existing dataframe with a default value

In the preceding example, we added a new column named **constant_value_col** by assigning the constant string value (**New_value**) to that column.

- **Adding a column with a list of values**

    Sometimes, we need to add a new column into the dataframe with predefined different values (list of values). So, in such cases, we can follow the following method.

    ```
    # adding a column with list of values
    df['new_col'] = [1,2,3,4]
    df
    ```

	emp_id	city	sal	constant_value_col	new_col
0	101	Sanzeno	5000	New_value	1
1	105	Beauwelz	8989	New_value	2
2	108	Minneapolis	5634	New_value	3
3	100	Carterton	9634	New_value	4

    Figure 9.63: adding new column in existing dataframe with a list of values

    In the preceding example, we added a new column named **new_col** by assigning the list values [1,2,3,4].

- **Adding column by applying the transformation logic**

    This is a prevalent scenario in data analysis when we need to add a new column into the exiting data frame by applying some transformation function to populate its values. For example, suppose we have a dataframe with employee salary detail. Now, we need to add a new column **updated_salary** by increasing the salary of all employees by ten percentage. We can perform this using the **apply()** function.

    The **apply()** function allows us to write our custom Python function and use that on the dataframe or any one of its columns.

    The following is the coding example for this. In this example, first, we have created the dataframe **df** and written a Python function **sal_with_10_percent_hike()**, which will return the new salary by increasing the 10 % in the old one. After that, we used **apply()** function by passing the Python custom function and assigned the values to a new column named **updated_salary**.

```python
# creating dataframe df
emp_dict = {'emp_id':[101,105,108,100],
            'city':['Sanzeno','Beauwelz','Minneapolis','Carterton'],
            'sal':[5000,8989,5634,9634]}

df = pd.DataFrame(emp_dict)
# print("data frame df =>\n",df)
custom_display(df,titles=["Input Data Frame"])

# adding a column in df with applying somefucntion to calculate value
def sal_with_10_percent_hike(old_sal):
    """ Function will new salary by adding 10%with current salry"""
    return int(old_sal)+int(old_sal)*.1



#  Adding new column updated_salary by apply the fucntion sal_with_10_percent_hike
df['updated_salary'] = df['sal'].apply(sal_with_10_percent_hike)
df
custom_display(df,titles=["Output DataFrame with New Added column"])
```

Figure 9.64: Adding new column and using transformation function to assign its values.

The following screenshot shows the output from this coding example:

Input Data Frame

	emp_id	city	sal
0	101	Sanzeno	5000
1	105	Beauwelz	8989
2	108	Minneapolis	5634
3	100	Carterton	9634

Output DataFrame with New Added column

	emp_id	city	sal	updated_salary
0	101	Sanzeno	5000	5500.0
1	105	Beauwelz	8989	9887.9
2	108	Minneapolis	5634	6197.4
3	100	Carterton	9634	10597.4

Figure 9.65: Output of the executed code

We can use the lambda function here also, instead of the regular Python function. See the following example to achieve the same using the lambda function.

```
# creating dataframe df
emp_dict = {'emp_id':[101,105,108,100],
            'city':['Sanzeno','Beauwelz','Minneapolis','Carterton'],
            'sal':[5000,8989,5634,9634]}

df = pd.DataFrame(emp_dict)
# print("data frame df =>\n",df)
custom_display(df,titles=["Input Data Frame"])


 
# Adding new column updated_salary using lambda fucntion
df['updated_salary'] = df['sal'].apply(lambda sal:int(sal)+int(sal)*.1)
custom_display(df,titles=["Output DataFrame with New Added column"])

```

Figure 9.66: :Output of the executed code.

The following is the output from this example:

Input Data Frame

	emp_id	city	sal
0	101	Sanzeno	5000
1	105	Beauwelz	8989
2	108	Minneapolis	5634
3	100	Carterton	9634

Output DataFrame with New Added column

	emp_id	city	sal	updated_salary
0	101	Sanzeno	5000	5500.0
1	105	Beauwelz	8989	9887.9
2	108	Minneapolis	5634	6197.4
3	100	Carterton	9634	10597.4

Figure 9.67: Output from the example

Here, it is recommended to use the lambda function as much as possible whenever you need to apply the custom function on the data frame to fulfill your requirement.

Dropping the row/column from DataFrame

Pandas have provided the **drop()** function to drop the row or column from the DataFrame. We need to pass index label and axis information (axis= 0 for row and axis=1 for the column) in this **drop()** function to drop a row or column. Let's understand this from the coding examples given below.

In the following example, we are dropping the row with index=2.

```
# creating dataframe df
emp_dict = {'emp_id':[101,105,108,100],
            'city':['Sanzeno','Beauwelz','Minneapolis','Carterton'],
            'sal':[5000,8989,5634,9634]}

custom_display(df,titles=["Input Data Frame"])


# deleting the row from DataFrame
# Here only row will be delete but existing ddataframe willnot update
new_df = df.drop([2],axis=0)
new_df
custom_display(new_df,titles=["Output Data Frame"])
```

Figure 9.68: Use of drop() function – to drop row from the data frame

The following is the output from this example:

Input Data Frame

	emp_id	city
0	101	Sanzeno
1	105	Beauwelz
2	108	Minneapolis
3	100	Carterton

Output Data Frame

	emp_id	city
0	101	Sanzeno
1	105	Beauwelz
3	100	Carterton

Figure 9.69: Output from the example.

Now, let's see how to drop a column from DataFrame. In the following coding snippet, we drop the column **sal** from the DataFrame. So, we need to pass **column_name** and **axis=1** in **drop()** function. But here, you can see another option. We have used that is in **place=True**, which means it will first drop the column and update the existing data frame with a new result (see the previous example of dropping the row from DataFrame where we haven't used this function). So, we capture the output in a new DataFrame named **new_df**.

```
# creating dataframe df
emp_dict = {'emp_id':[101,105,108,100],
            'city':['Sanzeno','Beauwelz','Minneapolis','Carterton'],
            'sal':[5000,8989,5634,9634]}

df = pd.DataFrame(emp_dict)

custom_display(df,titles=["Input Data Frame"])


# deleting the column from DataFrame

df.drop('sal',axis=1,inplace=True)
# new_df
custom_display(df,titles=["Output Data Frame"])
```

Figure 9.70: drop() function – to drop a column from dataframe.

Following is the output from this example:

Input Data Frame

	emp_id	city	sal
0	101	Sanzeno	5000
1	105	Beauwelz	8989
2	108	Minneapolis	5634
3	100	Carterton	9634

Output Data Frame

	emp_id	city
0	101	Sanzeno
1	105	Beauwelz
2	108	Minneapolis
3	100	Carterton

Figure 9.71: Output from the example.

Concatenating the dataframes

We have **concat()** and **append()** functions to concat the pandas DataFrame of series objects.

To use `concat()`, we must pass the list of dataframe objects and the axis information. By default, it considered axis=0. If we haven't given any axis, it will try to append the next DataFrame at the bottom of the previous. We will explore these functions by doing some hands-on examples.

The following is the code snippet where we create the three dataframes **df1**, **df2**, and **df3**, which we will use to understand the concatenation examples:

```
# Creating the dataframes
emp_dict1 = {'emp_id':[101,105,108,100],
             'city':['Sanzeno','Beauwelz','Minneapolis','Carterton']}

emp_dict2 = {'emp_id':[111,112,113,114],
             'city':['Delhi','Banglore','Panjab','Chennai']}

emp_dict3 = {'id':[101,105,108,100] ,#111,112,113,114],
             'sal':[5555,6666,7777,8888]}#,9999,6543,7654,8765]}

df1 = pd.DataFrame(emp_dict1)
df2 = pd.DataFrame(emp_dict2)
df3 = pd.DataFrame(emp_dict3)
custom_display(df1,df2,df3,titles=['df1','df2','df3'])
```

	df1		df2		df3	
	emp_id	city	emp_id	city	id	sal
0	101	Sanzeno	111	Delhi	101	5555
1	105	Beauwelz	112	Banglore	105	6666
2	108	Minneapolis	113	Panjab	108	7777
3	100	Carterton	114	Chennai	100	8888

Figure 9.72: sample data frames

Now, see the following examples where we concatenate the **df1** and **df2** using the default options of function **concate()**.

```
1  # When 2 dfs has same column name and number
2  df_concat_axis_0 = pd.concat([df1,df2])
3  df_concat_axis_0
4  custom_display(df1,df2, df_concat_axis_0,titles=['Input : df1', 'Input : df2',
5                                                   'O/P : pd.concat([df1,df2])',])
```

	Input : df1			Input : df2			O/P : pd.concat([df1,df2])	
	emp_id	city		emp_id	city		emp_id	city
0	101	Sanzeno	0	111	Delhi	0	101	Sanzeno
1	105	Beauwelz	1	112	Banglore	1	105	Beauwelz
2	108	Minneapolis	2	113	Panjab	2	108	Minneapolis
3	100	Carterton	3	114	Chennai	3	100	Carterton
						0	111	Delhi
						1	112	Banglore
						2	113	Panjab
						3	114	Chennai

Figure 9.73: Use of concat() function with default options

In this example, we have concatenated **df1** and **df2** and get a new dataframe, but if you observe the result, we can see that the index values have been preserved from both dataframes. Suppose we want the indexes in the result as [0,1,2,….N-1], then, in that case, we can use the **ignore_index=True** option with this function. The following is an example to demonstrate the same:

```
1  out_df = pd.concat([df1,df2],keys=['df1','df2'],ignore_index=True)
2  out_df
3  custom_display(df1,df2, out_df,titles=['Input : df1', 'Input : df2',
4                                         'O/P : pd.concat([df1,df2],ignore_index=True)'])
```

	Input : df1			Input : df2			O/P : pd.concat([df1,df2],ignore_index=True)	
	emp_id	city		emp_id	city		emp_id	city
0	101	Sanzeno	0	111	Delhi	0	101	Sanzeno
1	105	Beauwelz	1	112	Banglore	1	105	Beauwelz
2	108	Minneapolis	2	113	Panjab	2	108	Minneapolis
3	100	Carterton	3	114	Chennai	3	100	Carterton
						4	111	Delhi
						5	112	Banglore
						6	113	Panjab
						7	114	Chennai

Figure 9.74: use of concat() function with ignore_index=True

Now, let's see one more example of how to use the option **axis=1**. In the following example, we concatenate **df1** and **df3** with option **axis=1**.

```
1  df_concat_axis_1 = pd.concat([df1,df3],axis=1)
2  df_concat_axis_1
3  custom_display(df1,df3,df_concat_axis_1,titles=['Input : df1', 'Input : df3',
4                                                  'O/P : pd.concat([df1,df3],axis=1)'])
```

	Input : df1		Input : df3		O/P : pd.concat([df1,df3],axis=1)			
	emp_id	city	id	sal	emp_id	city	id	sal
0	101	Sanzeno	101	5555	101	Sanzeno	101	5555
1	105	Beauwelz	105	6666	105	Beauwelz	105	6666
2	108	Minneapolis	108	7777	108	Minneapolis	108	7777
3	100	Carterton	100	8888	100	Carterton	100	8888

Figure 9.75: Use of concat() function with axis=1

We can also concatenate two dataframes using the **append()** function. Let's see how we can do it.

```
1  out_df =df1.append(df2)
2  out_df
3  custom_display(df1,df2,out_df,titles=['Input : df1', 'Input : df2',
4                                        'O/P :df1.append(df2)'])
```

	Input : df1		Input : df2		O/P :df1.append(df2)	
	emp_id	city	emp_id	city	emp_id	city
0	101	Sanzeno	111	Delhi	101	Sanzeno
1	105	Beauwelz	112	Banglore	105	Beauwelz
2	108	Minneapolis	113	Panjab	108	Minneapolis
3	100	Carterton	114	Chennai	100	Carterton
0					111	Delhi
1					112	Banglore
2					113	Panjab
3					114	Chennai

Figure 9.76: Use of append() function

Here, in this example, we concatenate **df1** and **df2** with the **append()** function, which gives the same result as the **concat()** function in the previous example.

Merging/joining the dataframes

Pandas provided a fully featured facility to merge and join the different data frames, which have features almost like an SQL join.

We will discuss both **merge ()** and **join ()** functions with their primary and essential options going forward.

The following are the dataframes **emp_df** and **dept_df** that we will use to demonstrate our examples:

```
1   # Creating the data frame to explain the function
2
3   emp_dict = {'emp_id':[101,105,108,111,],
4               'city':['Sanzeno','Beauwelz','Minneapolis','Carterton']}
5
6   dept_dict = {'emp_id':[101,105,108,100],
7                'dept':['Customer Relations','Legal Department','Public Relations','Advertising']}
8
9
10
11  emp_df = pd.DataFrame(emp_dict)
12  dept_df = pd.DataFrame(dept_dict)
13
14  custom_display(emp_df,dept_df,titles=['emp_df','dept_df'])
```

	emp_df			dept_df	
	emp_id	city		emp_id	dept
0	101	Sanzeno	0	101	Customer Relations
1	105	Beauwelz	1	105	Legal Department
2	108	Minneapolis	2	108	Public Relations
3	111	Carterton	3	100	Advertising

Figure 9.77: Sample dataframes

The merge() function

Pandas merge function takes two dataframes as input and returned merged DataFrame as output. Let's understand the syntax of the **merge()** function and some of its essential parameters.

Syntax: **pandas.merge(left, right, how='inner', on=None, left_on=None, right_on=None)**

The following are the details about its parameters:

left: Left DataFrame object

right: Right DataFrame object

how : How we want to merge dataframes ['inner', 'left', 'right', 'outer']; default is inner

on : Column or index lable to join in must be present in both the dataframes

left_on : Column or index lable to join in from left DataFrame

right_on : Column or index lable to join in from right DataFrame

The following are the examples of using the **merge()** function with various options:

- **If both dataframes have the same column name key to merge on**:

    Let's take the first case when both dataframes have a key column with the same name. For example, suppose we want to join the dataframes mentioned above **emp_df** and **dept_df**, where **emp_df** have columns **emp_id** and **city** other side **dept_df** have columns **emp_id** and **dept**. Now, we can see that our joining key column is present in both the dataframes with the same name. In this case, we can pass the column name as value to parameter 'on' (**on='emp_id'**).

    The following are the examples with different types of joins with the same name key column:

    Example #1 (how =' inner '):

    Performing the merge with **how=inner** option can think like inner join operation in SQL. This will return the DataFrame with the records from both dataframes, with the matching key. See the following examples where we get records for **emp_id** 101,105, and 108 as these employee ids are present in both dataframes.

```
1  #Example#1
2  merged_df_inner = pd.merge(emp_df,dept_df,on='emp_id',how='inner')
3  merged_df_inner
4
5
6  custom_display(emp_df,dept_df,merged_df_inner,titles=['emp_df','dept_df',
7                                           "pd.merge(emp_df,dept_df,on='emp_id',how='inner')"])
```

	emp_df			dept_df		pd.merge(emp_df,dept_df,on='emp_id',how='inner')			
	emp_id	city		emp_id	dept		emp_id	city	dept
0	101	Sanzeno	0	101	Customer Relations	0	101	Sanzeno	Customer Relations
1	105	Beauwelz	1	105	Legal Department	1	105	Beauwelz	Legal Department
2	108	Minneapolis	2	108	Public Relations	2	108	Minneapolis	Public Relations
3	111	Carterton	3	100	Advertising				

Figure 9.78: Use of merge() function

Example #2 (how='left'):

Performing the merge with the **how=left** option, we can think of it as a left join operation in SQL. This will return a DataFrame with all records from the left (**emp_df**) DataFrame and matching key records from the right (**dept_df**) dataframe. In the following example, we can observe that:

- Output dataframe (**merged_df_left**) have all records from left (**emp_df**) DataFrame and only matching records for key from right (**dept_df**) DataFrame. Record for **emp_id=100** has been discorded in output as there is no matching **emp_id** present in left (**emp_df**) dataframe.

- If there is no matching key record present in right(**dept_df**) dataframe, then all columns for right (**dept_df**) dataframe will be assigned with value NaN in returned and merged dataframe. Record for **emp_id=111** has **dept=NaN** in output as it does not have matching **emp_id** in right(**dept_df**) dataframe.

```
1  #Example#2
2  merged_df_left = pd.merge(emp_df,dept_df,on='emp_id',how='left')
3  merged_df_left
4
5  custom_display(emp_df,dept_df,merged_df_left,titles=['emp_df','dept_df',
6                                          "pd.merge(emp_df,dept_df,on='emp_id',how='left')"])
```

	emp_df			dept_df			pd.merge(emp_df,dept_df,on='emp_id',how='left')		
	emp_id	city		emp_id	dept		emp_id	city	dept
0	101	Sanzeno	0	101	Customer Relations	0	101	Sanzeno	Customer Relations
1	105	Beauwelz	1	105	Legal Department	1	105	Beauwelz	Legal Department
2	108	Minneapolis	2	108	Public Relations	2	108	Minneapolis	Public Relations
3	111	Carterton	3	100	Advertising	3	111	Carterton	NaN

Figure 9.79: Use of merge() function with how=left

Example #3 (how=right) :

Performing the merge with the **how=right** option, we can think of it as the correct join operation in SQL. This will return the dataframe with all records from the right dataframe(**dept_df**) and matching key records from the left dataframe(**emp_df_df**). In the following example, we can observe that:

- Output dataframe (**merged_df_right**) has all records from the right (**dept_df**) DataFrame and only matching records for the key from the left (**emp_df**) DataFrame. The record for **emp_id=111** has been discorded in output as there is no matching **emp_id** present in the right (**dept_df**) DataFrame.

- If there is no matching key record present in the left(**emp_df**) dataframe, then all columns for left(**emp_df**) dataframe will be assigned with the value NaN in the returned and merged DataFrame. Record for **emp_id=100** has **dept=NaN** in output as it does not have matching **emp_id** in **left(emp_df)** DataFrame.

```
1  #Example#3
2  merged_df_right = pd.merge(emp_df,dept_df,on='emp_id',how='right')
3  merged_df_right
4
5
6  custom_display(emp_df,dept_df,merged_df_right,titles=['emp_df','dept_df',
7                          "pd.merge(emp_df,dept_df,on='emp_id',how='right')"])
```

	emp_df			dept_df		pd.merge(emp_df,dept_df,on='emp_id',how='right')		
	emp_id	city		emp_id	dept		emp_id	city	dept
0	101	Sanzeno	0	101	Customer Relations	0	101	Sanzeno	Customer Relations
1	105	Beauwelz	1	105	Legal Department	1	105	Beauwelz	Legal Department
2	108	Minneapolis	2	108	Public Relations	2	108	Minneapolis	Public Relations
3	111	Carterton	3	100	Advertising	3	100	NaN	Advertising

Figure 9.80: *The use of merge() function with how=right*

Example #4 (how='outer') :

Performing the merge with the **how='outer'** option, we can think of it as an outer join operation in SQL. This will return a DataFrame with all the records from both dataframes. In the following example, we can observe that:

- Output DataFrame (**merged_df_right**) has all the records from both DataFrame.

- If there is no matching key record present in the **left(emp_df)** DataFrame, all columns for the **left(emp_df)** dataframe will be assigned with the value NaN, which is the returned and merged dataframe. We can see this case for **emp_id=100**.

- If there is no matching key record present in the **right(dept_df)** DataFrame, all the columns for the right (**dept_df**) DataFrame will be assigned with the value NaN, which is the returned and merged DataFrame. We can see this case for **emp_id=111**.

Introducing Pandas   161

```
1  #Example#4
2  merged_df_outer = pd.merge(emp_df,dept_df,on='emp_id',how='outer')
3  merged_df_outer
4
5  custom_display(emp_df,dept_df,merged_df_outer,titles=['emp_df','dept_df',
6                                                       "pd.merge(emp_df,dept_df,on='emp_id',how='outer')"])
```

	emp_df			dept_df		pd.merge(emp_df,dept_df,on='emp_id',how='outer')		
	emp_id	city		emp_id	dept		emp_id	city	dept
0	101	Sanzeno	0	101	Customer Relations	0	101	Sanzeno	Customer Relations
1	105	Beauwelz	1	105	Legal Department	1	105	Beauwelz	Legal Department
2	108	Minneapolis	2	108	Public Relations	2	108	Minneapolis	Public Relations
3	111	Carterton	3	100	Advertising	3	111	Carterton	NaN
						4	100	NaN	Advertising

Figure 9.81: Use of merge() function with how=outer

- **If both the dataframes have different column names as key to merge on :**

    So, for the examples we have seen above, for the **merge()** function has the same key column name present in both the dataframes, what if we have different name's key columns? We can pass key columns information using **left_on** and **right_on** parameters in such a case.

    For example, we have two dataframes, **emp_df** and **dept_df**; both dataframes have employee ides, but the key column name in **emp_df** is **emp_id**, and **dept_df** is **id**. As we keep **emp_df** as left DataFrame and **dept_df** as the right DataFrame, the values for parameter **lef_on** and **eight_on** will be **left_on='emp_id' right_on='id'**.

    In the following example, we have explained the merging of **emp_df** and **dep_df** using **left_on** and **right_on** with parameter **how ='inner'**.

```
1   #Example#5
2   # Creating the data frame to explain the function
3
4   emp_dict = {'emp_id':[101,105,108,111,],
5               'city':['Sanzeno','Beauwelz','Minneapolis','Carterton']}
6
7   dept_dict = {'id':[101,105,108,100],
8               'dept':['Customer Relations','Legal Department','Public Relations','Advertising']}
9
10  emp_df = pd.DataFrame(emp_dict)
11  dept_df = pd.DataFrame(dept_dict)
12
13
14  merged_df = pd.merge(emp_df,dept_df,left_on='emp_id',right_on='id',how='inner')
15  merged_df
16
17  custom_display(emp_df,dept_df,merged_df,
18              titles=['emp_df','dept_df',
19              "pd.merge(emp_df,dept_df,left_on='emp_id',right_on='id',how='inner')"])
```

Figure 9.82: Use of merge() function with how=inner

Now, the output is:

	emp_df			dept_df		pd.merge(emp_df,dept_df,left_on='emp_id',right_on='id',how='inner')			
	emp_id	city		id	dept		emp_id	city	id	dept
0	101	Sanzeno	0	101	Customer Relations	0	101	Sanzeno	101	Customer Relations
1	105	Beauwelz	1	105	Legal Department	1	105	Beauwelz	105	Legal Department
2	108	Minneapolis	2	108	Public Relations	2	108	Minneapolis	108	Public Relations
3	111	Carterton	3	100	Advertising					

***Figure 9.83**: Output from merge() function with how=inner*

Similarly, we can go for left, right, and outer merge also.

The join() function

The `join()` function is used to join the columns from another DataFrame. It is somehow like the `merge()` function, but the `join()` function joined the data on the dataframes indexes.

Let's understand the important parameters for this function.

Syntax: `DataFrame.join(other, on=None, how='left', lsuffix='', rsuffix='')`

The following are the details about its parameters:

other: Left DataFrame object

how: How to join data frames? ['inner', 'left', 'right', 'outer',] Default is left.

on: Column or index lable to join on, must be present in both DataFrame.

lsuffix: Add a suffix to the left DataFrames overlapping columns.

rsufficx: Add a suffix to the right data frame's overlapping columns.

Let's understand the `join()` function more by doing some examples.

The following code snippet is for creating the two dataframes **emp_df** with index: [1,2,3,4] and **dept_df** with indexes :[0,1,5,4].

```
1  # Creating the dataframe to explain the join() function
2
3  emp_dict  = {'emp_id':[101,105,108,111,],
4              'city':['Sanzeno','Beauwelz','Minneapolis','Carterton']}
5
6  dept_dict = {'emp_id':[101,105,108,100],
7              'dept':['Customer Relations','Legal Department','Public Relations','Advertising']}
8
9
10
11 emp_df = pd.DataFrame(emp_dict,index=[1,2,3,4])
12 dept_df = pd.DataFrame(dept_dict,index=[0,1,5,4])
13 # print(emp_df)
14 # print(dept_df)
15
16 custom_display(emp_df,dept_df,titles=['emp_df','dept_df'])
```

	emp_df emp_id	city		emp_id	dept_df dept
1	101	Sanzeno	0	101	Customer Relations
2	105	Beauwelz	1	105	Legal Department
3	108	Minneapolis	5	108	Public Relations
4	111	Carterton	4	100	Advertising

Figure 9.84: Sample dataframes

We can use a **join()** function in two ways, the first is joined on indexes values, and the second is by making a key column as the index.

- **Use the join() on the index**

    In the following example, we join the **emp_df** with **dep_df** using **how=inner**, **lsuffix='_left'** and **rsuffi='_right'**.

    Also, we can observe that in the result DataFrame (**joined_df**).

    o   As we are using **how='inner'** so, in output, we have only records that have common indexes (key index values present in both).

o You can see in the output that the overlapping columns from both DataFrame have **suffi =x** values which we have passed, which means **emp_id** has **emp_id_left** and **emp_id_right**.

```
1  #joining on index
2  joined_df = emp_df.join(dept_df,lsuffix='_left',rsuffix='_right',how='inner')
3  joined_df
4
5  custom_display(emp_df,dept_df,joined_df,titles=['emp_df',
6                                                  'dept_df',
7                     "emp_df.join(dept_df,lsuffix='_left',rsuffix='_right',how='inner')"])
```

	emp_df			dept_df			emp_df.join(dept_df,lsuffix='_left',rsuffix='_right',how='inner')		
	emp_id	city		emp_id	dept		emp_id_left	city	emp_id_right	dept
1	101	Sanzeno	0	101	Customer Relations	1	101	Sanzeno	105	Legal Department
2	105	Beauwelz	1	105	Legal Department	4	111	Carterton	100	Advertising
3	108	Minneapolis	5	108	Public Relations					
4	111	Carterton	4	100	Advertising					

Figure 9.85: Inner join() function

With **join()** function also we can pass all other values like the **merge()** function for parameter "how" as per our need. As we have seen in the **merge()** function examples, this will have the same behavior.

- **Use the join() function on the key column by making that as index**

    Now, let us assume that instead of indexes, we have a common column in both dataframes, and we want to join the DataFrame on that column. In this case, we first have to make the column index in both dataframes then apply the **join()** function. For example, in our sample dataframes **emp-df** and **dept_df**, both have the **emp_id** column; now, we want to join both the DataFrame using **how=inner**.

    So, first, we have to make those columns the index in both dataframes; we can use function **DataFrame.set_index(<col_name>)** for this. After that, we will use the **join()** function.

Setting the column emp_id as index:

```
1  # setting up emp_id column as index in Data frames
2  emp_df = emp_df.set_index('emp_id')
3  dept_df = dept_df.set_index('emp_id')
4  custom_display(emp_df,dept_df,titles=['emp_df','dept_df'])
```

emp_df		dept_df	
	city		dept
emp_id		emp_id	
101	Sanzeno	101	Customer Relations
105	Beauwelz	105	Legal Department
108	Minneapolis	108	Public Relations
111	Carterton	100	Advertising

Figure 9.86: Setting column emp_id as index

Joining the dataframes:

```
1  # Joining the datframe
2  joined_df = emp_df.join(dept_df,how='inner')
3  joined_df
4
5  custom_display(emp_df,dept_df,joined_df,titles=['emp_df','dept_df',"emp_df.join(dept_df,how='inner')"])
```

emp_df		dept_df		emp_df.join(dept_df,how='inner')		
	city		dept		city	dept
emp_id		emp_id		emp_id		
101	Sanzeno	101	Customer Relations	101	Sanzeno	Customer Relations
105	Beauwelz	105	Legal Department	105	Beauwelz	Legal Department
108	Minneapolis	108	Public Relations	108	Minneapolis	Public Relations
111	Carterton	100	Advertising			

Figure 9.87: join() when the key column is an index

In the example above, we can see no overlapping column present in dataframes, so we haven't used lsuffix and rsuffix parameters this time.

Writing the DataFrame to external files

So far, we have learned various functions/methods in pandas which we use in data analysis by going through many examples. Let's see how to export/write the output dataframes results to the external file like CSV, Excel, and so on.

Pandas support various file formats to write the data frames onto CSV, Excel, JSON, Parquet, ORC, and so on. The following are the examples to show how to work with some of them file formats.

We will use the following DataFrame as input for the next set of examples, writing the dataframes to external files:

```
1  emp_dict = {'emp_id':[101,105,108,111,],
2              'city':['Sanzeno','Beauwelz',
3                      'Minneapolis','Carterton']}
4
5  df=pd.DataFrame(emp_dict)
6  df
```

	emp_id	city
0	101	Sanzeno
1	105	Beauwelz
2	108	Minneapolis
3	111	Carterton

Figure 9.88: Sample dataframe

The following are the examples to demonstrate how to use pandas' different functions to write the dataframes on various file formats:

- **Writing the CSV file**

    To write the DataFrame to the CSV file, pandas has provided the **to_csv()** function. Let's see some examples to understand this function better.

    Example#1: DataFrame.to_csv(<file_path>)

    In the following examples, we pass the output file path into the **to_csv()** function. By default, it will write the comma-separated file with indexes on the specified file path (complete path with filename).

```
1  # writing the output on csv file with default to_csv() funtion
2  df.to_csv("data/out.csv")
```

Figure 9.89: writing the dataframe content into a CSV file.

The following is the CSV file content that we have written on this:

```
out.csv
1  ,emp_id,city
2  0,101,Sanzeno
3  1,105,Beauwelz
4  2,108,Minneapolis
5  3,111,Carterton
6
```

Figure 9.90: CSV file's snippet

Example#1: `DataFrame.to_csv(<file_path>,index=False)`

In the last example, if you see, you will find that in the first column, the index column is generated by the pandas automatically. If you don't want the index column's data on the output file, you can use the parameter **index =False** in the **to_csv()** function. The following is an example of this:

```
1  # writing Df to file excluding indexes
2  df.to_csv("data/out_wo_index.csv",index=False)
3
```

Figure 9.91: Write the dataframe content into a CSV file without an index

The following is the snippet of the CSV file without having an index column:

```
out_wo_index.csv
1  emp_id,city
2  101,Sanzeno
3  105,Beauwelz
4  108,Minneapolis
5  111,Carterton
6
```

Figure 9.92: Written CSV without index column

Example#1: `DataFrame.to_csv(<file_path>,index=False,sep=<char>)`

Instead of the comma, we can write the file's output on a flat-file with some other characters. For example, pipe (" | "). In the following example, we used parameter sep and given that value as " | " to write the dataframes output on file with pipe separator.

```
1  # Writing the delimited file with other delimeter like pipe (|)
2  df.to_csv("data/out_pipe.txt",index=False,sep="|")
```

Figure 9.93: Writing the dataframe content into a text file with the pipe as a delimiter

The following is the snippet of the flat(`.txt`) file with the pipe separator:

```
out_pipe.txt
1  emp_id|city
2  101|Sanzeno
3  105|Beauwelz
4  108|Minneapolis
5  111|Carterton
```

Figure 9.94: Written data into a file with pipe delimiter

- **Writing the Excel file**

    Pandas is provided **to_excel()** function to write the content of DataFrame on excel file. See the following example:

    ```
    # wrtiitng  the df to excel
    df.to_excel("data/out.xlsx",index=False)
    ```

    Figure 9.95: Writing the dataframes content into an excel file

    The following is the snippet of the output excel file that we have generated from the code above by writing the content of the DataFrame.

emp_id	city
101	Sanzeno
105	Beauwelz
108	Minneapolis
111	Carterton

    Figure 9.96: Excel file with data frame's content which we have written in the example

- **Writing the JSON file**

    Pandas is provided **to_json()** function to write the content of dataframe on the JSON file. See the following example:

    ```
    # writing the dtafrma content to json file
    df.to_json("data/out.json")
    ```

    Figure 9.97: writing the dataframes content into a JSON file

    The following is the snippet of the output JSON file that we have generated from the code above by writing the content of the dataframe:

    ```
    {"emp_id":{"0":101,"1":105,"2":108,"3":111},
     "city":{"0":"Sanzeno","1":"Beauwelz","2":"Minneapolis","3":"Carterton"}}
    ```

    Figure 9.98: JSON has written the dataframes content.

Conclusion

In this chapter, we have learned about the various features and functions of the pandas library. We have got the understanding and a good hands-on practice on what pandas is. We also understand how helpful it is in data analysis activities like creating the DataFrame, importing the data into DataFrame, cleaning and preprocessing, analyzing, summarizing the results, and exporting those onto the external files for reporting.

In the next chapter, we will learn another important Python library, Numpy. Numpy is quite helpful in the case of numerical data analysis.

Questions

1. What is pandas, and why is it so popular?
2. What is the difference between the pandas series and pandas dataframe?
3. How will you create a pandas dataframe using python list and dictionary?
4. What are the different ways to sort the data for pandas dataframe?
5. What are the important aggregate function pandas? Explain with examples.

CHAPTER 10
Introduction to NumPy

In the last chapter, we learned about pandas, the famous data analysis library. We have learned the various functions and features of this library.

Pandas is quite good at handling and analyzing labeled and relational data, but it is not optimized enough in the case of numeric or scientific data analysis. So, when we need to deal with numeric data analysis, the NumPy library comes into the picture.

NumPy library is specially used for numerical data analysis and scientific computation. It is pretty famous among the data scientists community. It is much more memory efficient than pandas. Also, it has a rich collection of functions to analyze numeric data like numeric series data, multidimensional numeric arrays like matrix, and so on. So, in this chapter, we are going to learn how to use NumPy for numeric data analysis.

Structure

In this chapter, we will discuss the following topics:

- What is NumPy?
- NumPy array object
- Creating the NumPy array

- Creating NumPy arrays using the Python list and tuple
- Creating the array using numeric range series
- Indexing and slicing in NumPy array
- Data types in NumPy
  - Getting the datatype and memory storage information of the NumPy Array
  - Creating the NumPy array with defined datatype
  - Structured datatype or record type
- NumPy array shape manipulation
- Inserting and deleting array element(s)
- Joining and splitting NumPy arrays
- Statistical functions in NumPy
- Numeric operations in NumPy
- Sorting in NumPy
- Writing data into files
- Reading data from files

Objectives

After studying this chapter, you should be able to:

- Know what NumPy is, and why we need it for numeric data analysis.
- Create the 1-D and n-D arrays.
- Do array manipulation and data analysis using various in-built functions and methods.
- Understand various functions to import that data from file to an array.
- Write or export the n-D array's data into an external file.

What is NumPy?

NumPy (Numerical Python) is a vastly used Python library for scientific computation; it is memory efficient and fast. It has N-dimensional array objects and a rich collection of routines to process and analyze them. NumPy is suitable for numeric and scientific data analysis. The following are some important areas where we can use NumPy:

- Mathematical/logical functions on numeric series and multidimensional numeric arrays
- Statical operations on numeric series
- Performing the function of linear algebra

NumPy array object

In NumPy, a multidimensional homogeneous array is a fundamental object. NumPy array can contain only the same types of elements (like an array of integers), unlike the Python list. In the NumPy array, the dimension of array is referred to as axes. For example, a 1-D array ([1,2,3]) would behave like one axis with three elements. More precisely, we can say that it has a length of 3. For 2-D arrays [[1.0,2.0,3.0],[4.0,6.0,7.0]], it would be two axes: the first axis (axis=0) has a length of 2, and the second axis (axis=1) has a length of 3.

Creating the NumPy array

In NumPy, we can create the N-D array using the **array()** function; We can create a NumPy array by passing any regular Python list or tuple in the array () function. The following is an example of the same:

```python
import numpy as np

#1D array in Numpy
array1_1D = np.array([1,2,3,4,5])
array2_1D = np.array((2,3,4,5))

print("Output:")
print("array1_1D:", array1_1D)
print("array2_1D:", array2_1D)

Output:
array1_1D: [1 2 3 4 5]
array2_1D: [2 3 4 5]
```

Figure 10.1: Creating the 1-D NumPy array

In this example, we have used a regular Python list to create the one dimensional array (**array1_1D**), and second, we have used a standard Python tuple and made a 1-D NumPy array (**array2_1D**).

We can also explicitly pass the datatypes of the array using the **dtype** option of the **array ()** function. Let's see the following example:

```
import numpy as np

#1D array with dtype
array1_1D = np.array([1,3,5],dtype='complex')

print("Output:")
print("array1_1D:", array1_1D)

Output:
array1_1D: [1.+0.j 3.+0.j 5.+0.j]
```

Figure 10.2: Creating the 1-D NumPy array

So, if we want to datatype **int** or **float**, and so on, that can be passed instead of complex datatype. Later in the chapter, we will see the various types of data types in NumPy.

From this example, we can make another observation that the array() function transforms the sequences ([1,2,3,4,5] and (2,3,4,5)) into 1-D Array. So, if we need to create a 2-D Array, then we have to pass sequences of sequences, and if we need a 3-D Array, then sequences of sequences, and so on. Let's see the following example of 2-D array creation using the **array()** function:

```
import numpy as np

# 2D Array
import numpy as np
num_arry_2d = np.array([(1,3,5),(2,4,6)])

print("Output:")
num_arry_2d

Output:

array([[1, 3, 5],
       [2, 4, 6]])
```

Figure 10.3: Creating the 2-D NumPy array

We passed the two tuples list in this coding snippet, and the array function transformed it into a 2-D array. Here, the length of the first axis is two and the second, three.

In NumPy, we can create special arrays, such as an array of zeros, ones, and an empty array, and so on.

The following are the examples for some special arrays:

- **Array with zeros**

    NumPy has the **zeros()** function to create an n-D array. See the following example:

    ```
    import numpy as np

    # Array with zeros
    array_zeros = np.zeros((2,3))

    print("Output:")
    array_zeros
    ```

    Output:

    ```
    array([[0., 0., 0.],
           [0., 0., 0.]])
    ```

    Figure 10.4: Creating the array with zeros

    In this example, we have created an array of zeroes by passing the shape (2,3) in the **np.** The **Zeros ()** function, as we can see, created a two-dimensional array with three elements.

- **Array with ones**

    Numpy has the **ones()** function to create an n-D array. See the following example:

    ```
    import numpy as np

    #Array with ones
    array_ones = np.ones((2,3))

    print("Output:")
    array_ones
    ```

    Output:

    ```
    array([[1., 1., 1.],
           [1., 1., 1.]])
    ```

    Figure 10.5: Creating the array with ones

In this example, we have created an array of zeroes by passing the shape (2,3) in the **np.ones()** function. As we can see in this example's output, it created a two-dimensional array with three elements.

- **Empty array**

    Numpy has the **empty()** function to create an n-D array, this **empty() function()** is not like the **zeros()** function. The **Zeros()** function always returns the array with zeros of the chosen datatype, while **empty()** may or may not.

```
1  import numpy as np
2  # creating an empty array
3  array_empty = np.empty((3,3))
4
5  print("Output:")
6  array_empty
```

Output:

```
array([[0.00000000e+000, 0.00000000e+000, 0.00000000e+000],
       [0.00000000e+000, 0.00000000e+000, 5.88926250e-321],
       [9.34608431e-307, 1.42410974e-306, 2.56761491e-312]])
```

Figure 10.6: Creating the empty array

This example shows that it returns a 3,3 array with random values.

Creating NumPy arrays using the Python list and tuple

We can create the NumPy array using the existing Python list or tuple, using the function as **array()**. The following are the example for the same:

```
1  import numpy as np
2  # creating array with python list
3  t1=[1,2,3]
4  print("\n1-D Array from Python list:\n",np.asarray(t1,dtype='int16'))
5
6
7  t2=[[1,2,3],[2,3,4]]
8  print("\n2-D Array from Python list:\n",np.asarray(t2,dtype='int16'))
```

```
1-D Array from Python list:
 [1 2 3]

2-D Array from Python list:
 [[1 2 3]
 [2 3 4]]
```

Figure 10.7: Creating the NumPy array from python List

In this example, we have passed list **t1** to **assarry()** function with **dtype='int16'** and it has returned the respective 1-D array, and in others we passed the 2-D list to create a 2-D array.

We can create the NumPy array using the Python tuple as well, and we can pass any tuple to the **assarry()** function like we passed the list in the last example. Let's see the following example to understand this:

```
1  import numpy as np
2  # Creating array with Python tuple
3  t1=((1,2,3))
4  print("\n1-D Array from Python Tuble:\n",np.asarray(t1,dtype='int16'))
5
6  t12=((1,2,3),(2,3,4))
7  print("\n2-D Array from Python Tuble:\n",np.asarray(t1,dtype='int16'))
```

```
1-D Array from Python Tuble:
 [1 2 3]

2-D Array from Python Tuble:
 [1 2 3]
```

Figure 10.8: Creating the NumPy array from Python tuple

In this example, the first part creates the 1-D array using a tuple, and the second creates the 2-D array.

Creating the array using numeric range series

We have the option to create an array from a numeric range; NumPy has the function **arange(star, stop, step)**. With the help of this function, we can create an array as well.

Let's see the following example:

```
1  import numpy as np
2  #creating array using arange() fucntion
3  #np.arange(start, stop, step, dtype)
4  np.arange(1,10,2)
```

```
array([1, 3, 5, 7, 9])
```

Figure 10.9: Creating the NumPy array using arange()

In this example, we have used the **arange()** function, where we have passed 1,10 and 2 as arguments. The first argument is the starting point (1) of the number series, and second (10) is the ending point of this series, but it is not included in returned numeric series, and third is Step (2), which jumps the given number of steps from the previous to next pint, in our example. So, as we have passed 1,10 and 2, it returned an array starting from 1 till 9 with a 2-step gap from the previous to the next, meaning 1,3,5,7,9.

Indexing and slicing in NumPy array

To access the content of an **ndarray** object, we have a mechanism of indexing and slicing.

For **ndarray** object, indexing and slicing work similar to the Python list, which we have already seen in the previous chapters.

NumPy **ndarray** object is also a zero-based index, which means the first element of the **ndarray** object assigned 0 indexes. It also supports the negative index like -1, which means the last element of the array.

Syntax: array[start: end]; the start indexed value is included in a returned slice of the array, but the end is excluded.

The following is an example to explain this concept better:

```
1  import numpy as np
2
3  a = np.arange(10, 20, 2)
4  print("Input Array:\na =", a)
5
6  print("\nSlicing Examples:")
7
8  print("\nExample#1 : a[:] =", a[:])
9  print("\nExample#2 : a[0:2] =", a[0:2])
10 print("\nExample#3 : a[:3] =", a[:3])
11 print("\nExample#4 : a[3:] =", a[3:])
12 print("\nExample#4 : a[-3:-1] =", a[-3:-1])
```

```
Input Array:
a = [10 12 14 16 18]

Slicing Examples:

Example#1 : a[:] = [10 12 14 16 18]

Example#2 : a[0:2] = [10 12]

Example#3 : a[:3] = [10 12 14]

Example#4 : a[3:] = [16 18]

Example#4 : a[-3:-1] = [14 16]
```

Figure 10.10: 1-D Array Slicing

In this example at line#3, we have created a 1-D array- [10 12 14 16 18] using the **arange()** function. Let us see the following cases that we have used in the example:

For the [:], the full array will be returned in this case.

For the [0:2], the slice of the array starting from index 0 and till index 1, means [10 12], will be returned.

For the [:3], the elements from array staring from index 0 till 2 will be returned, slice is [10 12 14].

For the [3:], in this case, we have mentioned stop here so that it will take max value of this, which means the sliced array starting from 0 till the end [16 18] will be returned.

For the [-3:-1], here, we have given negative index so it will start -3 index, means, the third element from last to -1 first element, but it will be excluded so index -3,-2 values as sliced array [14 16] will be returned.

Multi-dimensional slicing

For a multidimensional array, the syntax will be like a 1-D array, but we have separately defined the slices for each dimension. For example, in 2-D array, we have two dimensions (rows and columns), so we have to define the slices for the row and column both, the syntax will be like array [**dim1_slice,cdim2_slice**], or it can also represent it as array [**row_slice,column_slice**], similar in the case of n dimensions.

It would be like array [**dim_1_slice : dim_1_slice: dim1_slice…dim_n_slie**], where the start index value is included in the returned slice of the slice array, but the end is excluded.

The following is the example of slicing on 2 dimensional array; though the basic concept will be like the last example, the dimension scope will increase:

```
1  import numpy as np
2  # indexing and sclicing in Multidiemtioni arra
3  b = np.arange(20)
4  b.resize(4, 6)
5  print("Input multi-diemnstional Array:\n b=", b)
6
7  print("\n Slicing Examples:")
8  print("\nExample#1 : b[0] =", b[0])
9  print("\nExample#2 : b[0:2] =", b[0:2])
10 print("\nExample#3 : b[0:2, 0:2] =", b[0:2, 0:2])
11 print("\nExample#4 : b[2:, 4:] = ", b[2:, 4:])
```

```
Input multi-diemnstional Array:
b= [[ 0  1  2  3  4  5]
 [ 6  7  8  9 10 11]
 [12 13 14 15 16 17]
 [18 19  0  0  0  0]]

 Slicing Examples:

Example#1 : b[0] = [0 1 2 3 4 5]

Example#2 : b[0:2] = [[ 0  1  2  3  4  5]
 [ 6  7  8  9 10 11]]

Example#3 : b[0:2, 0:2] = [[0 1]
 [6 7]]

Example#4 : b[2:, 4:] =  [[16 17]
 [ 0  0]]
```

Figure 10.11: 2-D array slicing

In this example, we have a 2-dimensional array b; let's see the various examples referred to in the given coding snippet.

Example# 1: b[0], this means we have just defined the slice for rows only, so the 0th index for row 1, thus we have array [0 1 2 3 4 5] as output.

Example# 2: b[0:2], here also, it defines the row slice 0:2, meaning starting from row index 0 till 1 (excluding the index 2) so the returned array will be [[0 1 2 3 4 5] [6 7 8 9 10 11]].

Example# 3: b[0:2, 0:2], for this example, we have to define slices for both the dimensions, meaning row and column, so in this case, it will be the returned element from row starting from index 0 till 1 (as index 2nd is excluding). It will pick row 1 and row 2 from the 2D array and from the column class, it will return the sliced array starting from index 0 to till 1 (excluding index 2) meaning column 1 and column 2 values from a 2-D array. So, the output will be [[0 1] [6 7]].

Example # 4: b[2:,4:] in this example, we can see for both dimensions we have not defined the end index, so it means it will return all the elements from start till end for both rows and columns. The input array b has 4 rows (index 0,1,2,3) and 6 columns (index 0,1,2,3,4,5), so the returned sliced 2D array will be like [[index 2,3] [index 4,5]] so the final output will be [[16 17][0 0]].

Data types in NumPy

NumPy supports a bigger number of numeric types than Python does. *Table 10.1* is the list of basic data types in NumPy.

Data type	Character code	Description
int	i	signed integer : int8,int16,int32,int64 or int1,int2,int4,int8 (here int8 means 8-bit integer, int16 means 16bit integer and so on)
uint	u	unsigned integer : unit8,uint16,uint32 and unit64
float	f	floating-point : float16, float32 ,float64
bool	?	boolean: True or False, stored as byte
complex	c	complex number : complex64, complex128(real and imaginary components)
string	S	
Unicode string	U	
datetime	m	
timedelta	M	

Table 10.1: Basic data types in NumPy

In NumPy array, all the elements have the same data type, which means, if there is any n-D array, 'a' is a type of int8 (8-bit integer), then each element of this array will be able to store an 8-bit integer value.

- **Getting the datatype and memory storage information of NumPy array**

    In NumPy, we have **numpy.dtype** class with the help for this, we can get the information about the data type of the array, and by using the **itemsize** attribute of this class, we can get the info about one element of the array.

The following is the coding snippet demonstrating the same:

```
# get the datatype and storage info of any array

import numpy as np
a=np.array([1,2,3,45])

print("Array datatype is {}.".format(a.dtype))

print("Memory size of one array element is {} byte(s).".format(a.itemsize))

print("Total memory size of array is {} byte(s).".format(a.size * a.itemsize))

# we can use nbytes also to get the information about toaal memory size
print("Total memory size of array is {} byte(s).".format(a.nbytes))
```

```
Array datatype is int32.
Memory size of one array element is 4 byte(s).
Total memory size of array is 16 byte(s).
Total memory size of array is 16 byte(s).
```

Figure 10.12: Example of dtype and itemsize

In this example, first, we have created an array **a**, and then used the **a.dtype** to get the information about the data type of array **a**, which is **int32,** means the array type is a 32-bit integer. After line #8, in this line, we printed the memory size in bytes for one element of this array, which we got as 16 bytes. In line #10, we calculated the total memory size consumed by this array a. Last, we used the direct option **ndarray.nbytes** to get the total memory size consumed by the array **a**.

- **Creating the NumPy array with defined datatype**

    If we want to create an array with a defined datatype, we must pass the datatype argument with a valid NumPy type value in the **np**. Array () function while creating the NumPy array.

    The following coding snippet are examples to create the NumPy array with **int** type.

```
1  #Example #1
2  import numpy as np
3  a=np.array([1,2,3,45,],dtype='int')
4  print("Array :",a,"\nDataType:",a.dtype)
```

```
Array : [ 1  2  3 45]
DataType: int32
```

```
1  #Example #2
2  import numpy as np
3  a=np.array([1,2,3,45,],dtype='int16')
4  print("Array :",a,"\nDataType:",a.dtype)
5
```

```
Array : [ 1  2  3 45]
DataType: int16
```

```
1  #Example #3
2  import numpy as np
3  a=np.array([1,2,3,45,],dtype='i2')
4  print("Array :",a,"\nDataType:",a.dtype)
5
```

```
Array : [ 1  2  3 45]
DataType: int16
```

Figure 10.13: Datatype -int examples(s)

Let's understand the examples mentioned in this coding snippet.

Example#1: We created an array with an integer type by passing the **dtype=int**; this will create the array with an integer type with default storage; in this case, it is a 32-bit integer.

Example#2: If we want some defined storage size of array elements, we can pass the valid datatype with storage values like int8, int 16, and so on. So, in this example, we create an array with a 16-bit integer.

Example#3: In this example, we used the character code with storage value (bytes) means **dtype=i2**, which is the same as int16, so this is another way to achieve the same.

In a similar way, we can create arrays as per need. The following are the examples to create an array with float datatype:

```
#Example#1
import numpy as np
a=np.array([1,2,3,45,],dtype='float')
print("Array :",a,"\nDataType:",a.dtype)
```

```
Array : [ 1.  2.  3. 45.]
DataType: float64
```

```
#Example#2
import numpy as np
a=np.array([[1,2,],[3,45,]],dtype='float16')
print("Array :",a,"\nDataType:",a.dtype)
```

```
Array : [[ 1.  2.]
 [ 3. 45.]]
DataType: float16
```

```
#Example#3
import numpy as np
a=np.array([[1,2,],[3,45,]],dtype='f2')
print("Array :",a,"\nDataType:",a.dtype)
```

```
Array : [[ 1.  2.]
 [ 3. 45.]]
DataType: float16
```

Figure 10.14: Datatype -float examples(s)

The following is the coding snippet to demonstrate the array creation with boolean type:

```
#Example1

b=np.array([True,False,True],dtype='bool')
print("Array :",b,"\nDataType:",b.dtype)

#Example2
b=np.array([True,False,True],dtype='?')
print("Array :",b,"\nDataType:",b.dtype)
```

```
Array : [ True False  True]
DataType: bool
Array : [ True False  True]
DataType: bool
```

Figure 10.15: Datatype -boolean examples(s)

The following is the coding snippet to demonstrate the array creation with String and Unicode string types.

```
1  #Example#1
2  b=np.array(["Python","Numpy","Pandas"],dtype='S')
3  print("Array :",b,"\nDataType:",b.dtype)
```

```
Array : [b'Python' b'Numpy' b'Pandas']
DataType: |S6
```

```
1  #Example#2
2  b=np.array(["Python","Numpy","Pandas"],dtype='U')
3  print("Array :",b,"\nDataType:",b.dtype)
```

```
Array : ['Python' 'Numpy' 'Pandas']
DataType: <U6
```

Figure 10.16: Datatype -String(s)

In this coding snippet, we can observe that we have just passed the type only. Still, in output, we can see some numbers also along with S and U. This is the length of string which will be assigned automatically according to the longest element of the array, which means if we put some string size with S and U while creating an array, it will truncate the data which have more characters that defined.

- **Structured DataType or record type**

    The structure data type is like Struct in C, or we can think of it like a row in SQL. This means it has a collection for fields that may or may not have the same data type, unlike the typically NumPy Array. We can create structured datatype using the function **NumPy.dtype()**. There are several ways to define the structured data type. One of them is passing the list of tuples with (**field_name**, `data_type`).

    Syntax: `struct_type = numpy.dtype([(filed1,filed1_type),(filed2,-filed2_type)...(filedn,filedn_type)])`

    Here, the field type will be the valid Numpy data types like int8,int16, float, and so on.

The following is an example where we have created a structured data type of employee:

```
1  import numpy as np
2  employee = np.dtype([('name','S10'), ('dept', 'S10'), ('sal', 'i4')])
3  print("Structured Data Type :",employee)
4
5  emp_array = np.array([('Jim','HR',7000),('Mark','IT',8000),('Allen','Admin',10000)], dtype=employee)
6  print("\nArray :",emp_array,"\nDataType:",emp_array.dtype)
7
```

```
Structured Data Type : [('name', 'S10'), ('dept', 'S10'), ('sal', '<i4')]
Array : [(b'Jim', b'HR', 7000) (b'Mark', b'IT', 8000)
 (b'Allen', b'Admin', 10000)]
DataType: [('name', 'S10'), ('dept', 'S10'), ('sal', '<i4')]
```

Figure 10.17: Datatype -Structure example

In this example, we have first created the structured data type employed, which has three fields **names**, **dept**, and **sal** associated with datatypes S10 (String with size ten chars), S10, i4 (32-bit integer), respectively. Line #5 has a statement to create an array with **datatype=employee**. We can see line #6 print the **dtype**, which we have defined already.

Similarly, if we can do the same in the case of a multidimensional array, we have to pass the third argument shape along with the field name and type.

NumPy array shape manipulation

We often have to deal with resizing or reshaping the shape of the NumPy array. The following is a list of essential functions we need for daily data analysis work:

Function/method	Description
`reshape()`	a returned new array with a specified shape without modifying data
`flat()`	flattens the array then returns the element of a specified index
`flatten()`	returns the one-dimensional copy of input array
`ravel()`	returns the one-dimensional view of input array
`transpose()`	transposes the axes
`resize()`	same as `reshape()`, but resize modifies the input array on which this has been applied, or modifies the referred array

Table 10.2: Essential functions for data analysis

See the following coding examples to understand these functions better:

```python
#NumPy Array Shape Manupulatio

# creating a array
import numpy as np
num_arry = np.arange(2, 10, 2)
# print("Input Array is :\n", num_arry)

#Example#1 - use of reshape()
araay_shape = num_arry.reshape(2, 2)
print("\nExample#1: Input before applying reshape() :\n", num_arry)
print("Output after applying reshape(2,2) :\n", araay_shape)

#Example#2 - use of flat
array_flat = araay_shape.flat[3]
print("\nExample#2: Input before applying flat[3] :\n", araay_shape)
print("Output after applying flat[3] :\n", array_flat)

#Example#3 - use of flatten()
array_flatten = araay_shape.flatten()
print("\nExample#3: Input Array before applying flatten() :\n", araay_shape)
print("Output after applying flatten() :\n", array_flatten)

#Exmple#4 -use of ravel()
array_ravel = araay_shape.ravel()
print("\nExample#4: Input Array before applying ravel() :\n", araay_shape)
print("Output after applying ravel() :\n", array_ravel )

#Example#5 -use of transpose()
array_transpose = araay_shape.transpose()
print("\nExample#5: Input Array before applying transpose() :\n", araay_shape)
print("Output after transpose() :\n", array_transpose)

#Example#6 -use of resize()
a = np.arange(2, 20, 2)
print("\nExample#6: Input Array before applying resize((5,4)) :\n", a)
a.resize((5,4))
print("Output after applying resize((5,4)) :\n", a)
```

Figure 10.18: Array manipulation functions

We have shown all the examples for the previously discussed functions; the following is the output after executing these examples:

```
Example#1: Input before applying reshape() :
[2 4 6 8]
Output after applying reshape(2,2) :
[[2 4]
 [6 8]]

Example#2: Input before applying flat[3] :
[[2 4]
 [6 8]]
Output after applying flat[3] :
8

Example#3: Input Array before applying flatten() :
[[2 4]
 [6 8]]
Output after applying flatten() :
[2 4 6 8]

Example#4: Input Array before applying ravel() :
[[2 4]
 [6 8]]
Output after applying ravel() :
[2 4 6 8]

Example#5: Input Array before applying transpose() :
[[2 4]
 [6 8]]
Output after transpose() :
[[2 6]
 [4 8]]

Example#6: Input Array before applying resize((5,4)) :
[ 2  4  6  8 10 12 14 16 18]
Output after applying resize((5,4)) :
[[ 2  4  6  8]
 [10 12 14 16]
 [18  0  0  0]
 [ 0  0  0  0]
 [ 0  0  0  0]]
```

Figure 10.19: Array manipulation functions -output

This snippet has the output for all the examples which we have executed.

Inserting and deleting array element(s)

This is a common need when adding an element(s) into the array or deleting the element(s) from the existing array; the following are the functions to achieve the same:

- **numpy.append()**

    This function returns a new array by appending the values at the last of the input array. Dimensions of the values we want to append must match the input array; otherwise, it will give an error.

Syntax: `numpy.append(existing_array,values,axis)`

```
1  # appending the element in existing array
2  num_array  = np.array([1,2,3,45,6,])
3
4  print("\nExisting Array:\n",num_array)
5
6  new_num_array = np.append(num_array,[10])
7  print("\nNew array with appended element:\n",new_num_array)
```

```
Existing Array:
 [ 1  2  3 45  6]

New array with appended element:
 [ 1  2  3 45  6 10]
```

Figure 10.20: *numpy.append()*

In this coding snippet, we have a 1-D array **num_array**, and we append the value 10 at the end of input array **num_array,** and create a new array **num_num_array**. In the following example, let's see how we work with 2-D arrays or array with multidimensions:

```
1   # appending the element in existing array
2   a = np.array([[1,2,3],[4,5,6]])
3   print("\nExisting Array:\n",num_array
4
5   a1 = np.append(a,[7,8,9])
6   print("\nNew array with appended element (without axis):\n",a1)
7
8   a2 = np.append(a,[[7,8,9]],axis=0)
9   print("\nNew array with appended element (without axis):\n",a2)
10
11  a3 = np.append(a,[[0],[1]],axis=1)
12  print("\nNew array with appended element (without axis):\n",a3)
```

```
Existing Array:
 [[1 2 3]
 [4 5 6]]

New array with appended element (without axis):
 [1 2 3 4 5 6 7 8 9]

New array with appended element (without axis):
 [[1 2 3]
 [4 5 6]
 [7 8 9]]

New array with appended element (without axis):
 [[1 2 3 0]
 [4 5 6 1]]
```

Figure 10.21: *Example of numpy.append() with axis argument*

In this example, we have an existing array, a 2-D array. Now, at line#5, we have created an array a1 by appending the values [7,8,9], but at this time, no argument value has been passed in the **append()** function, so, in this case, it will return a flattened input array with appended value(s), The same we can see in output as well.

Now, let's see at line#8 and 9, array a2 and a3 is created with axis=0 and axis=1 with append the function respectively. For axis=0, we can see that array 'a' has append values at row level or axis =0 (we can see that there is one more row [7 8 9] added) and in array a3, we can see values [[0],[1]] appended in the last of axis =1 or columns of the array.

- **numpy.insert()**

    This function is used to insert the values in the existing array at the specified index.

    See the following coding snippet where value [10] has been inserted at index 1 of the existing array nym-array.

    Syntax: `numpy.insert(existing_array,index,value(s))`

```
1  # inserting a new element in existing array
2  #np.insert(existing_arry,index,value)
3  num_array  = np.array([1,2,3,45,6])
4  print("\nExisting Array:\n",num_array)
5
6  new_num_array = np.insert(num_array,1,[10])
7  print("\nNew arry with inserted element:\n",new_num_array)
```

```
Existing Array:
 [ 1  2  3 45  6]

New arry with inserted element:
 [ 1 10  2  3 45  6]
```

Figure 10.22: numpy.insert()

- **numpy.delete()**

    This function will return an array by deleting the value(s) from the specified index of the existing **g** array.

    Syntax: `numpy.delete(existing_array,index)`

    Let us see the following example where the value of index 1 has been deleted from the existing array **num_array** and created a new array **new_num_array**.

```
1  # deleting an element in existing array
2  # np.delete(ndarray,index)
3
4  num_array   = np.array([1,2,3,45,6])
5  print("\nExisting Array:\n",num_array)
6
7  new_num_array = np.delete(num_array,1)
8  print("\nNew arry with inserted element:\n",new_num_array)
9
```

```
Existing Array:
 [ 1  2  3 45  6]

New arry with inserted element:
 [ 1  3 45  6]
```

Figure 10.23: *numpy.delete()*

Joining and splitting NumPy arrays

To join two arrays or split the array, we have various functions like **concate()**, **hstack()**, **vstack()**, **vslpit()**, and many more; we will understand them with the help of the following examples:

- **numpy.concatenate()**

    This function is used to concate two or more arrays into one array along an axis. If we haven't passed any argument in **NumPy.concatenate()**, it considers axis=0 by default and does concatenation along **axis=0**. But if we want to concatenate two or more arrays other than **axis=0**, we need to pass the specified axis value an argument of this function. For example, in the following coding snipped in example#2, we have concatenated **array_1** and **array_2** along **axis=1** or column level concatenation in case of a 2-D array. But we can see that we haven't passed any axis argument in example#1, in that case, it concatenated the input arrays **array_1** and **array_2** along with **axis =0,** which is default value for parameter axis. Please note that we want to concatenate input arrays in simple shape; otherwise, it will make an error.

Syntax: **numpy.concatenate((array1, array1, ... arrayn), axis)**

```
1  # Input arrays
2  array_1 = np.array([[1,2],[3,4]])
3  array_2 = np.array([[5,6],[7,8]])
4  print("\nFirst array :\n",array_1)
5  print("\nSecond array :\n",array_2)
6
7  #Example#1 - Row wise
8  array_concat = np.concatenate((array_1,array_2))
9  print("\nExample#1 :Concated Array with default axis :\n",array_concat)
10
11 #Example#2 -Column wise
12 array_concat = np.concatenate((array_1,array_2),axis=1)
13 print("\nExample#2 :Concated Array with axis=1 :\n",array_concat)
```

```
First array :
 [[1 2]
 [3 4]]

Second array :
 [[5 6]
 [7 8]]

Example#1 :Concated Array with default axis :
 [[1 2]
 [3 4]
 [5 6]
 [7 8]]

Example#2 :Concated Array with axis=1 :
 [[1 2 5 6]
 [3 4 7 8]]
```

Figure 10.24: *numpy.concatenate()*

- **numpy.hstack()**

    This function is similar to the **numpy.concate()** with **axis=1**. In the following example, we have used function **hstack()** to concatenate two arrays horizontally.

```python
1  #np.hstack() : stack the arrays horizontly like concat with axis=1
2
3  array_1 = np.array([[1,2],[3,4]])
4  print("\nFirst array :\n",array_1)
5
6  array_2 = np.array([[5,6],[7,8]])
7  print("\nSecond array :\n",array_2)
8
9  array_hstacked = np.hstack((array_1,array_2))
10 print("\nConcated Array with hstack() :\n",array_hstacked)
```

```
First array :
 [[1 2]
 [3 4]]

Second array :
 [[5 6]
 [7 8]]

Concated Array with hstack() :
 [[1 2 5 6]
 [3 4 7 8]]
```

Figure 10.25: numpy.hstack()

- **numpy.vstack()**

    This function is similar to the **numpy.concate()** with **axis=0**. In the following example, we have used function **vstacke()** to concatenate two arrays vertically or column-wise:

```python
1  #np.vstack() : stack the arrays vertically like concat with axis=0
2
3  # Row wise
4  array_1 = np.array([[1,2],[3,4]])
5  print("\nFirst array :\n",array_1)
6
7  array_2 = np.array([[5,6],[7,8]])
8  print("\nSecond array :\n",array_2)
9
10 array_vstacked = np.vstack((array_1,array_2))
11 print("\nConcated Array with vstack() :\n",array_vstacked)
```

```
First array :
 [[1 2]
 [3 4]]
Second array :
 [[5 6]
 [7 8]]
Concated Array with vstack() :
 [[1 2]
 [3 4]
 [5 6]
 [7 8]]
```

Figure 10.26: numpy.vstack()

- **numpy.split()**

    As per the name, this function splits the array into multiple sub-arrays along the defined axes. The following is a coding snipped to understand the implementation of this function. In the case of a multidimensional array, we can also opt to pass the axis along which we want to split. Also, please note that when we request the split, the number for splits must be a divisor of the total number of elements in the array; otherwise, it will throw an error.

    ```
    1  import numpy as np
    2
    3  a= np.array([1,2,3,4,5,6,7,8])
    4  print("\nInput array Before split()\n",a)
    5
    6  print("\nOutput array Aefore split()\n",np.split(a,4))
    7
    ```

    ```
    Input array Before split()
    [1 2 3 4 5 6 7 8]

    Output array Aefore split()
    [array([1, 2]), array([3, 4]), array([5, 6]), array([7, 8])]
    ```

    Figure 10.27: Example of a numpy.split()

    We split the array into 4 sub-arrays using this example's **split()** function.

- **numpy.hsplit()**

    This function is used to split the input array horizontally. For example, in the case of a 2-D array, it will split the array column-wise. This function is equivalent to **split()** with **axis=1**.

    ```
    1  array_input = np.array([(1,2,3,4),(6,7,8,9)])
    2
    3  array_1, array_2 = np.hsplit(array_input, 2)
    4
    5  print("\nArray Before hsplit()\n",array_input)
    6  print("\nHorizontal split array 1\n:",array_1)
    7  print("\nHorizontal split array 2\n:",array_2)
    ```

    ```
    Array Before hsplit()
    [[1 2 3 4]
     [6 7 8 9]]

    Horizontal split array 1
    : [[1 2]
     [6 7]]

    Horizontal split array 2
    : [[3 4]
     [8 9]]
    ```

    Figure 10.28: numpy.hsplit()

In this example, we used the function **hsplit()**: it splits the input array **array_input** in two arrays horizontally into **array_1** and **arry_2**.

- **numpy.vsplit()**

    This function is used to split the input array vertically. For example, in the case of a 2-D array, it will split the array column-wise. This functions is equivalent to **split()** with **axis=0**.

```
1  array_input = np.array([(1,2,3,4,10,11),(6,7,8,9,10,11)])
2
3  array_1, array_2 = np.vsplit(array_input, 2)
4
5  print("\nArray Before vsplit()\n",array_input)
6  print("\nvertically splited array 1:",array_1)
7  print("\nvertically splited  array 2:",array_2)
```

```
Array Before vsplit()
[[ 1  2  3  4 10 11]
 [ 6  7  8  9 10 11]]

vertically splited array 1: [[ 1  2  3  4 10 11]]

vertically splited  array 2: [[ 6  7  8  9 10 11]]
```

Figure 10.29: numpy.vsplit()

Here in this example, **vsplit()** function split **array_input** in two arrays (**array_1** and **array_2**).

Statistical functions in NumPy

To understand the data and its nature, we often take the help of some statistical information methods like mean, median, and so on. So, here in Numpy also we have such functions to get the statistical information of the data. The following are some important functions and their uses.

- **NumPy.amin()** and **NumPy.amax()**

    These functions **NumPy.amin()** and **NumPy.amaz()** give the minimum and maximum from the elements of the given array along the axis. If we haven't passed any axis information to this function, it will flatten the array and give a minimum or maximum value from the filter array, respectively.

    Syntax:

    o **numy.amin(input_array) / numpy.amax(input_array)**

    o **numy.amin(input_array,axis) / numpy.amax(input_array, axis)**

The following are the examples of **amin()** and **amax()** functions:

```python
import numpy as np
a = np.array([[23,45,11],[20,98,43],[20,65,33]])
print("Input Array a:\n",a)

# numpy.amin() - returns the minimum element from array
a_min = np.amin(a)
print("\nMinimum value from input array a is : {}".format(a_min))
# numpy.amax()- returns the minimum element from array
a_max = np.amax(a)
print("Maximum value from input array a is : {}".format(a_max))

# numpy.amin() - returns the minimum element from array
a_min_0 = np.amin(a,axis=0)
print("\nMinimum value along axis=0 from input array a is : {}".format(a_min_0))
# numpy.amax()- returns the minimum element from array
a_max_0 = np.amax(a,axis=0)
print("Maximum value along axis=0  from input array a is : {}".format(a_max_0))

# numpy.amin() - returns the minimum element from array
a_min_1 = np.amin(a,axis=1)
print("\nMinimum value along axis=1 from input array a is : {}".format(a_min_1))
# numpy.amax()- returns the minimum element from array
a_max_1 = np.amax(a,axis=1)
print("Maximum value along axis=1 from input array a is : {}".format(a_max_1))
```

```
Input Array a:
[[23 45 11]
 [20 98 43]
 [20 65 33]]

Minimum value from input array a is : 11
Maximum value from input array a is : 98

Minimum value along axis=0 from input array a is : [20 45 11]
Maximum value along axis=0  from input array a is : [23 98 43]
```

Figure 10.30: Examples of amin() and amax() functions

- **numpy.mean()**

    This function gives the mean value of the given array. The following is the coding snippet in which we have passed the array an into the **mean()** function and got the mean value 26.33:

```python
# numpy.mean()
import numpy as np
import numpy as np
a = np.array([23,45,11])
print("Input Array a:\n",a)
print("Mean value of the input array:",np.mean(a))

```

```
Input Array a:
[23 45 11]
Mean value of the input array: 26.333333333333332
```

Figure 10.31: Example of mean() function

- **numpy.average()**

    This function returns the weighted average, if we pass the weights array along with the input array. But if we do not give the weights as arguments, this will be like a **mean()** function.

    ```
    1  # numpy.average()
    2  import numpy as np
    3  input_arr = np.array([23,45,11])
    4  print("Input Array a:\n",input_arr)
    5  # average() fucntion without weights
    6  print("\nAverage() without weights :",np.average(input_arr))
    7
    8  # average() fucntion with weights
    9  wt_arr = np.array([0.5,2,3])
    10 print("\nAverage() with weights :",np.average(input_arr, weights=wt_arr))
    11
    12
    ```

    ```
    Input Array a:
    [23 45 11]

    Average() without weights : 26.333333333333332

    Average() with weights : 24.454545454545453
    ```

    Figure 10.32: Example of a mean() function

    In this example, we have an array **input_arr** as input array and we pass this array as an argument in the **average()** function without giving the weights. It returns 26.33 as the average value of the array, the same as the **mean()** in the last example. At line#9, we have defined another array, **wt_arry** array with weights, and at line #10, we calculate the weighted average by passing the weights (**np. average(input_arr,weights=wt_arr)**), and this time we got a value of 24.45 which is a weighted average.

- **NumPy.median()**

    This function returns the median value of the given array. The following is a coding snippet to demonstrate the use of the function **numpy.median()**:

    ```
    1  # numpy.median()
    2
    3  import numpy as np
    4  input_arr = np.array([23,45,11,3,1])
    5  print("Input Array a:\n",input_arr)
    6  print("\nMedian value of the input array:",np.median(a))
    7
    8
    ```

    ```
    Input Array a:
    [23 45 11  3  1]

    Median value of the input array: 23.0
    ```

    Figure 10.33: Example of median() function

- **numpy.std()**

    This function returns the standard deviation of the given array. The following is a coding snippet to demonstrate the use of the function **numpy.std()**:

    ```
    # numpy.std()
    import numpy as np
    input_arr = np.array([23,45,11,3,1])
    print("Input Array a:\n",input_arr)
    print("\nStandard Deviation of the give data:",np.std(input_arr))
    ```

    ```
    Input Array a:
     [23 45 11  3  1]

    Standard Deviation of the give data: 16.169106345126192
    ```

    Figure 10.34: std() function

- **numpy.var()**

    This function returns the variance of the given array. The following is a coding snippet to demonstrate the use of the function **numpy.var()**:

    ```
    # numpy.var()
    import numpy as np
    input_arr = np.array([23,45,11,3,1])
    print("Input Array a:\n",input_arr)
    print("\nVariance of the give data:",np.var(input_arr))
    ```

    ```
    Input Array a:
     [23 45 11  3  1]

    Variance of the give data: 261.44000000000005
    ```

    Figure 10.35: Example of var() function

- **numpy.percentile()**

    This function returns the nth percentile of the given array along the specified axis. In case no axis is given, it will provide the scalar value, else it will return the array of nth percentile values along the axis.

    Syntax: numpy.percentile(input_array,q,axis):

    Here, **input_arry** is the array for which we need the nth percentile value, q is the percentile value, and axis is the axis along which we want to calculate the percentile value.

The following coding snippet demonstrates the function **numpy.percentile()**:

```
# numpy.percentile()
import numpy as np
input_arr = [[1,2,3,4],
       [5,6,7,8],
       [3,4,5,6]]
print("Input Array a:\n",input_arr)

# Percentile when axis=None
print("\n25th Percentile of input_arr, axis = None : ",np.percentile(input_arr, 25))

# Percentile with  axis = 0
print("\n25th Percentile of input_arr, axis = 0 : ",np.percentile(input_arr, 25, axis =0))

# Percentile with  axis = 1
print("\n25th Percentile of input_arr, axis = 1 : ",np.percentile(input_arr, 25, axis =1))
```

```
Input Array a:
 [[1, 2, 3, 4], [5, 6, 7, 8], [3, 4, 5, 6]]

25th Percentile of input_arr, axis = None :  3.0

25th Percentile of input_arr, axis = 0 :  [2. 3. 4. 5.]

25th Percentile of input_arr, axis = 1 :  [1.75 5.75 3.75]
```

Figure 10.36: Example of percentile() function

Numeric operations in NumPy

NumPy also has various numeric functions to process the mentioned operations like addition, subtraction, division, and so on. The following are some essential numeric options in NumPy:

- **Add, subtract, multiply, and divide:**

    We have functions in NumPy to add, subtract, multiply, and divide. All these functions perform element-wise operations on input NumPy arrays. Let's see the following examples:

```
import numpy as np
arr1 = np.arange(12, dtype = np.float_).reshape(3,4)
arr2 = np.array([[1,2,3,4]],dtype = np.float_)

print("First array - arr1:\n",arr1)
print("Second array - arr2:\n",arr2)

result_add = np.add(arr1,arr2) # arr1+arr2#
result_subtract = np.subtract(arr1,arr2) # arr1-arr2#
result_multiply = np.multiply(arr1,arr2) # arr1*arr2#
result_divide =np.divide(arr1,arr2) # arr1/arr2#

print("\nResult after adding arr1 with arr2 (arr1+arr2) :\n",result_add)
print("\nResult after subtracting arr2 from arr1 (arr1-arr2) :\n",result_subtract)
print("\nResult after multiplying arr1 with arr2 (arr1*arr2):\n",result_multiply)
print("\nResult after dividing arr1 by arr2 (arr1/arr2) :\n",result_divide)
```

Figure 10.37: Example of addition, subtraction, multiplication, and division with NumPy arrays

For these coding examples, the following is the output snippet:

```
First array - arr1:
[[ 0.  1.  2.  3.]
 [ 4.  5.  6.  7.]
 [ 8.  9. 10. 11.]]
Second array - arr2:
[[1. 2. 3. 4.]]

Result after adding arr1 with arr2 (arr1+arr2) :
[[ 1.  3.  5.  7.]
 [ 5.  7.  9. 11.]
 [ 9. 11. 13. 15.]]

Result after subtracting arr2 from arr1 (arr1-arr2) :
[[-1. -1. -1. -1.]
 [ 3.  3.  3.  3.]
 [ 7.  7.  7.  7.]]

Result after multiplying arr1 with arr2 (arr1*arr2):
[[ 0.  2.  6. 12.]
 [ 4. 10. 18. 28.]
 [ 8. 18. 30. 44.]]

Result after dividing arr1 by arr2 (arr1/arr2) :
[[0.         0.5        0.66666667 0.75      ]
 [4.         2.5        2.         1.75      ]
 [8.         4.5        3.33333333 2.75      ]]
```

Figure 10.38: The output

- **numpy.power()**

    This function returns the first array elements raised to powers from the second array or scalar value, element-wise.

```
1  import numpy as np
2  arr1 = np.arange(12, dtype = np.float_).reshape(3,4)
3  print("Input array -> arr1:\n",arr1)
4
5  power_2_array = np.power(arr1,2)
6  print("Onput array :\n",power_2_array)
```

```
Input array -> arr1:
[[ 0.  1.  2.  3.]
 [ 4.  5.  6.  7.]
 [ 8.  9. 10. 11.]]
Onput array :
[[  0.   1.   4.   9.]
 [ 16.  25.  36.  49.]
 [ 64.  81. 100. 121.]]
```

Figure 10.39: power() function

In this example, we can see each element of the input array rise to the power of two.

- `numpy.mod()`

    This function returns the remainder of the division between two arrays corresponding to the elements of both the arrays. In the following example, we can see that if we pass **arr1** and **arr2** as the arguments of the function **NumPy.mod()**, it returns element-wise the reminders:

```
1  import numpy as np
2  arr1 = np.array([10,23,21,11])
3  arr2 = np.array([1,2,3,4])
4
5  print("First array - arr1:\n",arr1)
6  print("Second array - arr2:\n",arr2)
7
8  out_arr= np.mod(arr1,arr2)
9  print("Output array after mod(arr1,arr2):\n",out_arr)
```

```
First array - arr1:
 [10 23 21 11]
Second array - arr2:
 [1 2 3 4]
Output array after mod(arr1,arr2):
 [0 1 0 3]
```

Figure 10.40: mod() function

- `numpy.reciprocal()`

    This function returns the mathematical reciprocal of the input array. In the case of an integer type array, it will return 0 if the array element is greater than 1; the following coding snippet demonstrates examples to understand this function:

```
1  import numpy as np
2  input_arr1 = np.array([[0.5,3,0.8],[4,1,7]])
3  input_arr2 = np.array([[2,3,4],[4,1,7]])
4
5  #Example1 when array tyepe is float
6  print("Input array - arr1:\n",input_arr1)
7  print("Reciprocal of arr1:\n",np.reciprocal(input_arr1))
8
9  #Example2 when array type is int
10 print("\nInput array - arr2:\n",input_arr2)
11 print("Reciprocal of arr2:\n",np.reciprocal(input_arr2))
```

```
Input array - arr1:
[[0.5 3.  0.8]
 [4.  1.  7. ]]
Reciprocal of arr1:
[[2.         0.33333333 1.25      ]
 [0.25       1.         0.14285714]]
Input array - arr2:
[[2 3 4]
 [4 1 7]]
Reciprocal of arr2:
[[0 0 0]
 [0 1 0]]
```

Figure 10.41: *reciprocal() function*

In Example#2, we can see the type of input array is **int**, so it returns 0 for the array elements greater than 1.

Sorting in NumPy

Sorting means keeping the data in some order, and it is a common need while you are doing data analysis. NumPy has **numpy.sort()** function to sort the data. This function takes the input array and returns the sorted array.

Syntax: **numpy.sort(input_array, axis=- 1, kind=None, order=None)**, where

input_array : is input array that needs to be sorted .

axis : this parameter specified the axis along with input array that needs to be sorted. If axis= None, the array is flattened before sorting. The default is -1, which sorts along the last axis.

kind: this parameter is optional sorting algorithm ('quicksort,' 'mergesort', 'heapsort', 'stable') .The default is 'quicksort'.

order: this parameter used to sort the input array in order to the specified field name

The following is a coding snippet where various examples have been demonstrated:

```
1   a = np.array([[11,14],[13,11]])
2
3   print("Input Array is :\n",a)
4
5   # sort along the last axis
6   out1 = np.sort(a)
7   print("\nExample#1 :Output sorted array when no axis defined means defalut axis:\n",out1)
8
9   # sort the flattened array
10  out2 = np.sort(a, axis=None)
11  print("\nExample#2 :Output sorted array when axis=None:\n",out2)
12
13  # sort along the first axis
14  out3 = np.sort(a, axis=0)
15  print("\nExample#3 :Output sorted array when axis=0 :\n",out3)
```

```
Input Array is :
 [[11 14]
 [13 11]]

Example#1 :Output sorted array when no axis defined means defalut axis:
 [[11 14]
 [11 13]]

Example#2 :Output sorted array when axis=None:
 [11 11 13 14]

Example#3 :Output sorted array when axis=0 :
 [[11 11]
 [13 14]]
```

Figure 10.42: Examples of sort()

Let's understand these examples one by one:

Example#1: In example#1, we have sorted the array using function **sort()** without mentioning any information about an axis. In this case, it took default value for axis, i.e., row wise.

Example#2: In example 2, we have mentioned **axis=None**, which means no axis, so in this case, it will return the flat sorted array. The same we can see in the output.

Example#3: Example#3 has the **sort()** function with argument **axis=0,** which means it is the first axis to sort the array along the **axis=0**, i.e., column-wise. We can see in the output that the sorted array has values in columns.

Now, let's discuss the parameter order. This is optional, but if you have an array with field names to sort array to some field, this option can be useful. Let's see the following example to understand it better:

```
1  # Sort() function with order parameter
2
3  import numpy as np
4
5  emp_dt = np.dtype([('emp_name', 'S10'),('dept_no', int)])
6
7  arr_input = np.array([("Garima",101),("Sudesh",101),("Indra", 102),
8                       ("Chitra",103),("Aparna",101)], dtype = emp_dt)
9
10 print ("Input array is :\n",arr_input)
11
12 out_arr = np.sort(arr_input, order = 'emp_name')
13
14 print("\nOutptut sorted array order by emp_name field\n:",out_arr)
15
```

```
Input array is :
 [(b'Garima', 101) (b'Sudesh', 101) (b'Indra', 102) (b'Chitra', 103)
 (b'Aparna', 101)]

Outptut sorted array order by emp_name field
: [(b'Aparna', 101) (b'Chitra', 103) (b'Garima', 101) (b'Indra', 102)
 (b'Sudesh', 101)]
```

Figure 10.43: Example of sort() with order field name

In this example, we must first create a struct type(**emp_dt**), which has fields **emp_name** and **dept_no**. create an array **arr_input** at Line #7 with **dtype=emp_dt**. After that, at line#12, we created another array **out_arr**, which is the copy of the input array in sorted order by field name **emp_name**. So, we sort the input array **arr_input** order by the **emp_name**field. Similarly, we can sort this array into other fields also.

Writing data into files

NumPy has **numpy.save()** and **numpy.svetxt()** functions to store the data into the files. The following are more details and coding examples for the same functions:

- **numpy.save()**

    This function stores the **ndarry** object to file with **npy** (NumPy internal file format) extension. This function stores the data and stores the metadata related to that array, for example, shape and all.

    The following example shows how to use **numpy.save()** function to store the **ndarray** on a file:

```
 1  import numpy as np
 2
 3  emp_dt = np.dtype([('emp_name', 'U10'),('dept_no', 'int')])
 4  arr_input = np.array([("Ankit",101),("Ravi",101),("John", 102),
 5                        ("Sam",103)], dtype = emp_dt)
 6
 7  print ("Input array is :\n",arr_input)
 8
 9  #Example#1 save()
10
11  np.save("data/emp_dt.npy",arr_input)
12  print("\nfile {} been written using fucntion np.save()!!".format('data/emp_dt.npy'))
13
```

```
Input array is :
 [('Ankit', 101) ('Ravi', 101) ('John', 102) ('Sam', 103)]

file data/emp_dt.npy been written using fucntion np.save()!!
```

Figure 10.44: The save() function

- **numpy.savetxt()**

    This function stores the **ndarry** data to a plain text file (e.g., CSV, txt, etc.) with a user-specified delimiter and header.

    The following examples show how to use **numpy.savetxt()** function to store the ndarray on a file:

```
 1  import numpy as np
 2  emp_dt = np.dtype([('emp_name', 'U10'),('dept_no', 'int')])
 3  arr_input = np.array([("Ankit",101),("Ravi",101),("John", 102),
 4                        ("Sam",103)], dtype = emp_dt)
 5
 6  print ("Input array is :\n",arr_input)
 7  #Example#1 savetxt()
 8  np.savetxt("data/emp_dt.csv",arr_input,fmt = '%s',delimiter=',',header='emp_name,dept_no')
 9  print("\nfile {} been written using fucntion np.savetxt()!!".format('data/emp_dt.csv'))
10
11  #Example#2 savetxt()
12  num_array = np.array([[1,2,3,4], [5,6,7,8],[3,4,5,6]])
13
14  print ("\nInput array is :\n",num_array)
15  np.savetxt("data/num_array.csv",num_array,fmt = '%d',delimiter=',')
16  print("\nfile {} been written using fucntion np.savetxt()!!".format('data/num_array.csv'))
```

```
Input array is :
 [('Ankit', 101) ('Ravi', 101) ('John', 102) ('Sam', 103)]

file data/emp_dt.csv been written using fucntion np.savetxt()!!

Input array is :
 [[1 2 3 4]
 [5 6 7 8]
 [3 4 5 6]]

file data/num_array.csv been written using fucntion np.savetxt()!!
```

Figure 10.45: The savetxt() function

In this example, we first created an array **arr_input** with struct datatype **emp_dt**. After that, we have used **np.savetxt("data/emp_dt.csv", arr_input, fmt = '%s', delimiter=',', header='emp_name, dept_no')** where "**data/emp_dt.csv**" is output file name with the folder path

fmt: is the format in which we want the same file for string %S, and for int, it would be %d.

arr_input: is the NumPy Array array which we want to save on file.

delimiter = ',' : means want to save the file with comma delimiter also we can give other character as delimiter according to need .

header='emp_name, dept_no': want to header in the file, if not, we will not pass any value for this parameter it will save array data on file without any header. So this way, we can save the file using **savetxt()** function.

Example #2 first created an array names ad **num_array**, then stored the **num_array** data on file using the **savetxt()** function. Similar to example #1.

Reading data from files

We can read the file data into an ndarray using **numpy.load()** or **numpy.loadtxt()** function. The following are more about these functions and their uses:

- **numpy.load()**

    This function loads the ndarry object with the npy (numpy file format) extension.

```
1  import numpy as np
2
3  #Example#1
4  array_read1 = np.load("data/emp_dt.npy")
5
6  print("Array read from file (data/emp_dt.npy) using np.load() :\n",array_read1)
7
```

```
Array read from file (data/emp_dt.npy) using np.load() :
 [('Ankit', 101) ('Ravi', 101) ('John', 102) ('Sam', 103)]
```

Figure 10.46: load() function

In this example, we have loaded file **emp_dt.npy** into the array **array_read1**.

- **numpy.loadtxt()**

    This function loads the data into an ndarray object from delimited plain text files like CSV, txt, and so on.

The following examples demonstrate how to use function `loadtxt()`:

```
1  #Example#1
2  emp_dt = np.dtype([('emp_name', 'U10'),('dept_no', 'int')])
3
4  array_read2 = np.loadtxt("data/emp_dt.csv",delimiter=',',skiprows=1,dtype= emp_dt)
5  print("\nArray read from file (data/emp_dt.csv) using np.loadtxt() :\n",array_read2)
6
7  #Example #2
8  array_read3 = np.loadtxt("data/num_array.csv",delimiter=',',dtype= int)
9  print("\nArray read from file (data/num_array.csv) using np.loadtxt() :\n",array_read3)
```

```
Array read from file (data/emp_dt.csv) using np.loadtxt() :
 [('Ankit', 101) ('Ravi', 101) ('John', 102) ('Sam', 103)]

Array read from file (data/num_array.csv) using np.loadtxt() :
 [[1 2 3 4]
 [5 6 7 8]
 [3 4 5 6]]
```

Figure 10.47: loadtxt() function

In this coding snippet, we have two examples. Let us understand them one by one.

Example# 1: In this example, we are trying to load struct type data from a comma-delimited CSV file. So, first at line #2 we defined the struct datatype **emp_dt** and at line #4 we loaded data into array **array_read2** using **np.loadtxt("data/emp_dt.csv", delimiter=',', skiprows=1, dtype= emp_dt)**; where –

"**data/emp_dt.csv**": is the file path with directory location, which we need to load into an n array.

delimiter=',': is the field delimiter.

skiprows=1: will skip the first row while loading the data from the file into an array.

dtype= emp_dt : data type ,as in this example it is struct data type so giving **emp_dt**.

In the output for this example, we can see that now **array_read2** has loaded the correct data from the file and displayed it in output.

Example# 2, here as the data file has built in types, in this case, it is int, so we don't need to define any struct type unlike example#1. Also, if you observe, we haven't passed skiprows parameter while loading the data using the **savetxt()** function as there is no herder in the input file. In this way, we can load data from files.

Conclusion

In this chapter, we have learned about the various features and functions of the NumPy library. We understand and have a good hands-on practice of NumPy, how to use that, and various other useful functions and methods that we need to do numerical analysis.

In the next chapter, we will teach another important Python library, matplotlib. Matplotlib is also a popular library for data visualization.

Questions

1. What is NumPy, and why is it so popular?
2. What is array slicing?
3. What are the different ways to create the NumPy array?
4. How can we sort the ndarray data?
5. What are the essential statistical and arithmetic functions in NumPy? Explain with examples.

CHAPTER 11
Introduction to Matplotlib

In the last chapter, we learned about the NumPy library, a famous numerical data analysis library. We learned various functions and features of this library.

The data analysis process is not enough to conclude the results or summarize the data's insights. Since we have to present the data analysis results effectively and we need some graphs or charts to represent the analyzed results, hence, data visualization came into the picture.

Data visualization is an essential part of data analysis; in this chapter, we will learn the basics of data visualization with the help of Matplotlib library, a widely used Python library for data visualization.

Structure

In this chapter, we will discuss the following topics:

- What is data visualization?
- What is Matplotlib?
- Getting started with Matplotlib
- Simple line plot using Matplotlib

- Object-oriented API in Matplotlib
- The subplot() function in Matplotlib
- Customizing the plot
    - Adding a title
    - Adding axis labels
    - Adding text in plot
    - Adding markers
    - Adding the line style, line color, and line width
    - Adding gridlines
    - Setting the axis limits
    - Adding the ticks and ticklables
- Some basic types of plots in Matplotlib
    - Bar graph
    - Histograms
    - Scatter plots
    - Pie charts
- Exporting the plot into a file
    - Export the plot into a pdf file
    - Export the plot into a jpeg file

Objectives

After studying this chapter, you should be able to answer:
- What is Matplotlib, and why do we need data visualization?
- How to plot data using matplotlib's various methods and options?
- How to customize the plots as per need?
- How to export the plot into a pdf and jpeg file?

What is data visualization

Data visualization is the representation of data graphically, using visual charts, visual graphics, and so on. Data visualization aims to represent data in visuals to understand the story behind the data in an interactive manner. In other words, we can say data visualization is a way of telling the story of facts that we gathered or concluded from the data analysis process.

Various tools are available specifically for data visualization, like Tableau and Power BI. Python also has effective and useful libraries like Matplotlib, Seaborn, Ploty, Bokeh, and so on.

What is Matplotlib?

Matplotlib is a vastly used and powerful Python library which is used to represent information visually with the help of visual charts and graphs. It has various graphs to represent the data according to the need and specification.

We will cover the basics of Matplotlib in the upcoming part of this chapter.

Getting started with Matplotlib

If you use the Anaconda platform for Python, then Matplotlib is preinstalled. Otherwise, you need to install this using a repository manager like pip using the following command:

```
C:\>pip install matplotlib
```

Figure 11.1: pip install matplotlib

- Once you install the matplotlib, we have to import this. Then, we can use the underlying functions and methods for the plots. Let's see how we can import the matplotlib and print that version.

```
1  import matplotlib
2
3  print("Running Version of Matplotlib is :",matplotlib.__version__)
```

```
Running Version of Matplotlib is : 3.3.4
```

Figure 11.2: Checking the version

Simple line plot using Matplotlib

In Matplotlib, we have a submodule plot. So, with the help of this module we can plot our graph/chart. Let's see the following example to create a simple line graph:

```
1  import matplotlib.pyplot as plt
2
3  x= [1,2,3,4,5,6]
4  y=[1,2,3,4,5,6]
5
6  plt.plot(x,y)
7  # plt.show()
```

[<matplotlib.lines.Line2D at 0x1b49d7ee0a0>]

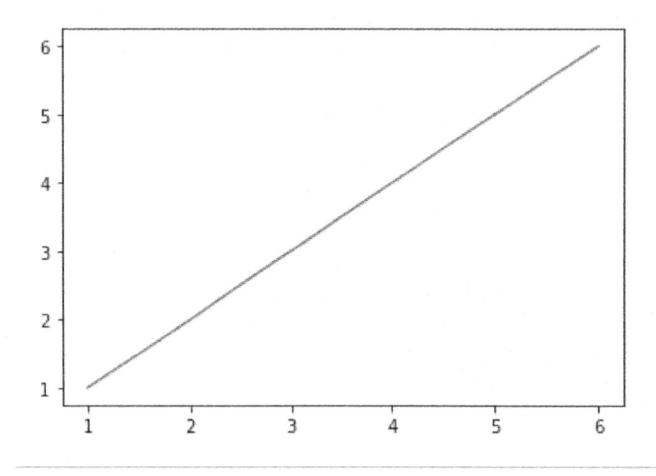

Figure 11.3: *Simple line plot*

Let's understand this example; here, first, we have imported the **pyplot** module of Matplotlib from.

In line#1, we have imported the **pyplot** submodule of Matpotlib with alias name **plt**.

In line#3 and #4, we have created two lists x and y with numbers that can be considered coordinates of the x-axis and y-axis on a two-dimensional graph.

In line#5, now we invoked the **plot()** function, which will take x and y coordinate values and plot the values on the graph. As we are using the Jupyter Notebook, we don't need to call the **show()** function here. But if there are more than one plot in one cell, we need to call **show()** after each plot to display all; otherwise in a notebook, it will display the very last plot. Now in the graph, we can see it draw a line graph.

Object-oriented API in matplotlib

We have seen the example of plotting a simple plot using the Matplotlib. **pyplot** module, which is a functional method and uses a state-based interface. But Matplotlib has another interface, which is the object-oriented interface. In this case, we use the instance or object of **matplotlib.axis.Axis** class on the instance or object of the **matplotlib.figure.Figure** class. Let's take a quick look at what figures and axis mean in Matplotlib.

The Matplotlib figure is the top-level container to draw all the plot elements, the figure can contain one or more axis, and axis is the added area on the figure used to plot the data, or we can say that axis is the individual plot on the figure.

Let's see the following example: use an object-oriented interface to plot the simple line we plotted using the previous pyplot interface.

```
#Object-Oriented Inteface
import matplotlib.pyplot as plt
fig = plt.figure()
ax = fig.add_axes([0.1,0.1,1,1]) # [left, bottom, width, height]
x= [1,2,3,4,5,6]
y=[2,3,4,5,6,7]
ax.plot(x,y)
plt.show()
```

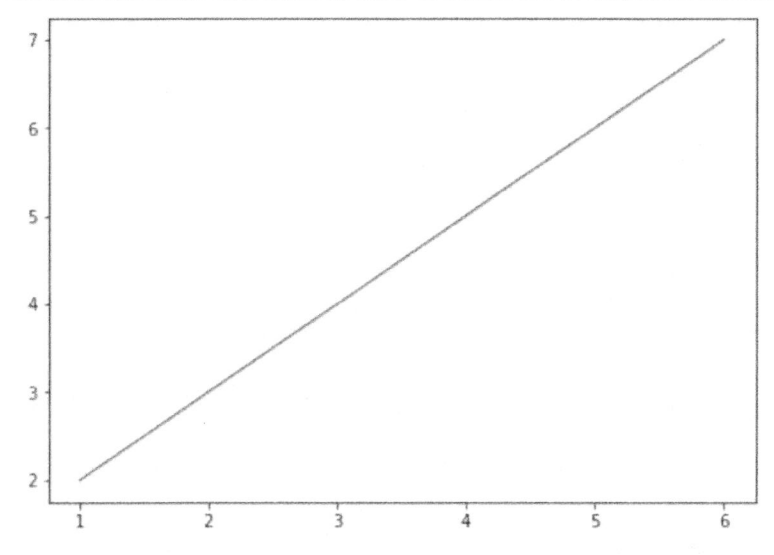

Figure 11.4: Simple line plot with figure and axis

Let's understand this Object-Oriented Interface example. In line #2, we have created an instance object fig of the figure.

In line#3, we added axis object with values 0.1,0.1,1,1, corresponding values for the axis or subplots left, bottom, width, and height. In lines #5 and #6, we have given the x-axis and y-axis values list.

In line#7, we called up the method **plot()** on axis ax passing the x and y-axis values, which plotted the corresponding plot in axis ax.

In line#8, we called the function **show()** to display the plot.

The subplot() function in matplotlib

Suppose we need to plot multiple plots in one figure in matplotlib, then we can use the **subplot()** function. This function takes a number of rows and a number of columns as arguments to generate the subplot.

The following is the coding example to understand the function **subplot()**:

Example#1 (1 by 2 subplot)

```
1  import matplotlib.pyplot as plt
2  fig,axes = plt.subplots(nrows=1,ncols=2)
3  fig.set_facecolor('lightgray') # setting the display color for figure
4  x= [1,2,3,4,5,6]
5  x_squre = [x*x for x in x]
6
7  axes[0].plot(x,y)
8  axes[1].plot(x,x_squre)
9
10 plt.show()
```

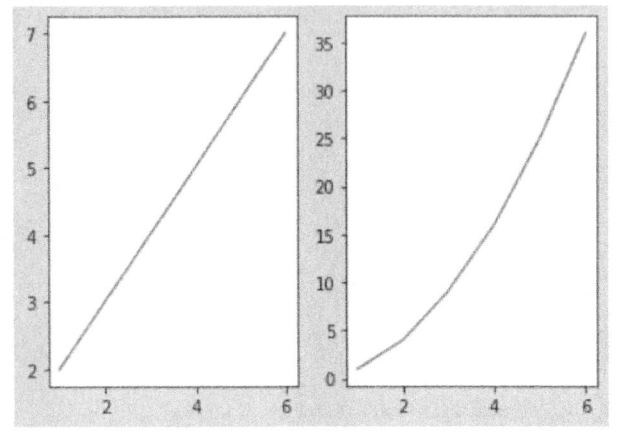

Figure 11.5: *The subplot() function -Example#1*

In this coding snippet, at line#2, we have invoked the function **subplot()**, with the arguments nrows=1 and ncols=2, meaning we want one row and two columns subplots grid. This will return the figure and array of axis.

We can access the subplots using indexes like axis[0], meaning the first subplot, and axis[1], meaning the 2nd subplot. It follows the simple array indexing concept to access the subplot object. Line#7 and #8 are instructed to pass the data to the plot on the subplots.

Example#2 (2 by 2 subplot)

Let's see the following code snippet, where we create a 2 by 2 subplot, meaning 4 subplots.

```
1  import matplotlib.pyplot as plt
2  fig,axes = plt.subplots(nrows=2,ncols=2)
3  fig.set_facecolor('lightgray') # setting the display color for figure
4  x= [1,2,3,4,5,6]
5  y=[2,3,4,5,6,7]
6  x_squre = [x*x for x in x]
7  y_squre = [y*y for y in y]
8
9  axes[0][0].plot(x,y)
10 axes[0][0].set_title("I") # setting the title of subplot
11 axes[0][1].plot(x,x_squre)
12 axes[0][1].set_title("II") # setting the title of subplot
13
14 axes[1][0].plot(y,y_squre)
15 axes[1][0].set_title("III") # setting the title of subplot
16
17 axes[1][1].plot(x_squre,y_squre)
18 axes[1][1].set_title("IV") # setting the title of subplot
19
20 plt.show()
```

Figure 11.6: The subplot() function -Example#2

In this example, we have created a two by two subplots grid on the figure. Also, we can see in line #9, and subsequent others, how we have used the indexing concept to access the specific subplot object.

Customizing the plot

We have a basic idea of creating a plot and subplots in Matplotlib. Let's learn more about customizing the plots, like setting titles, axis names, and other essential elements to create the plots according to your need. The following are some important settings to customize the plot.

- **Adding a title**

    To add the title of a subplot, we have the function `matplotlib.set_title()`; this function takes the title text and location of the tile as arguments.

    In the following coding snippet, we can see that in line#8, we used the function `set_titile ()` with the "Simple line plot" and loc='center' as arguments passed to this:

```
1  import matplotlib.pyplot as plt
2  fig = plt.figure()
3  ax = fig.add_axes([0.1,0.1,1,1])
4  x= [1,2,3,4,5,6]
5  y=[2,3,4,5,6,7]
6
7  # setting the Title
8  ax.set_title("Simple line Plot",loc='center')
9  ax.plot(x,y)
10
11 plt.show()
```

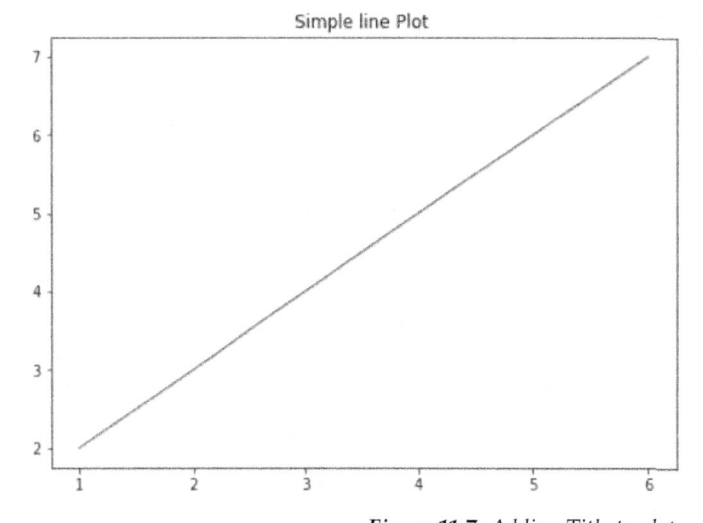

Figure 11.7: Adding Title to plot

- **Adding axis labels**

    We have **matplotlib.set_xlable()** and **matplotlib.set_ylable()** functions to set the axis lables. Let us see the following example to understand it better.

    In the following coding snippet, at lines #11 and #12, we passed the "X-Axis" as the label of the x-axis and "Y-Axis" as the label for the y-axis.

```
1   import matplotlib.pyplot as plt
2   fig = plt.figure()
3   ax = fig.add_axes([0.1,0.1,1,1])
4   x= [1,2,3,4,5,6]
5   y=[2,3,4,5,6,7]
6
7   # setting the Title
8   ax.set_title("Simple line Plot",loc='center')
9
10  #Setting the X and Y axis text
11  ax.set_xlabel("X-Axis")
12  ax.set_ylabel("Y-Axis")
13
14  ax.plot(x,y)
15
16  plt.show()
```

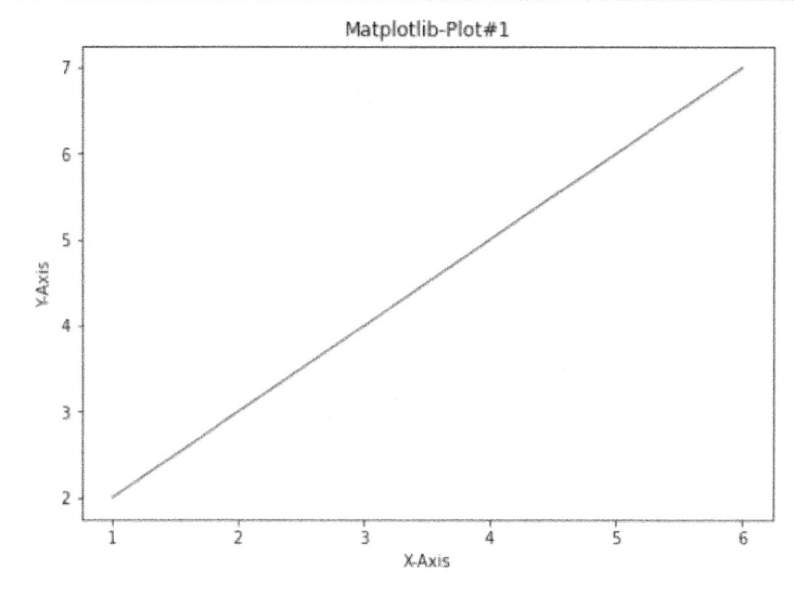

Figure 11.8: Adding axis labels

- **Adding text in plot**

    Sometimes, we have to add some text to the plot, so we have the function `matlotlib. text(<x-axis position>, <y-axis position> <text>)`. This function needs three arguments x-axis position, y-axis position, and the text which we want to put on the plot; see the following example to understand it better.

    In the following example, we added the text "Simple Line" at position (3,4), which means x-axis=3 and y-axis=4.

```
1  import matplotlib.pyplot as plt
2  fig = plt.figure()
3  ax = fig.add_axes([0.1,0.1,1,1])
4  x= [1,2,3,4,5,6]
5  y=[2,3,4,5,6,7]
6
7  # setting the Title
8  ax.set_title("Simple line Plot",loc='center') # adding the title
9
10 #Setting the X and Y axis text
11 ax.set_xlabel("X-Axis")  # adding the x-axis label
12 ax.set_ylabel("Y-Axis")  # adding the y-axis label
13
14
15 #Adding text to plot
16 plt.text(3,4,"Simple Line")
17
18 ax.plot(x,y)
19
20 plt.show()
```

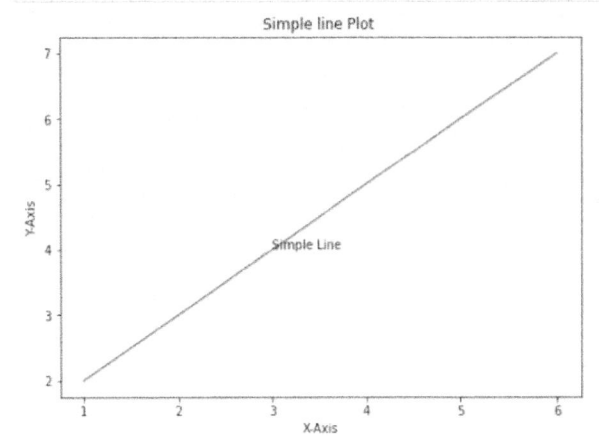

Figure 11.9: Adding text to plot

- **Adding markers**

    We can use the `plot()` function with the keyword argument marker to specify the (x,y) points on the plot with the specified symbol. In line#18, we set the plot with a circle using ax.plot(x,y, marker='o'), We can also use markers like marker='s', marker='v', and others mentioned in the following table:

```python
import matplotlib.pyplot as plt
fig = plt.figure()
ax = fig.add_axes([0.1,0.1,1,1])
x= [1,2,3,4,5,6]
y=[2,3,4,5,6,7]

# setting the Title
ax.set_title("Simple line Plot",loc='center') # adding the title

#Setting the X and Y axis text
ax.set_xlabel("X-Axis")  # adding the x-axis label
ax.set_ylabel("Y-Axis")  # adding the y-axis label


#Adding text to plot
plt.text(3,4,"Simple Line")

ax.plot(x,y,marker='o')  # setting the marker style to circle

plt.show()
```

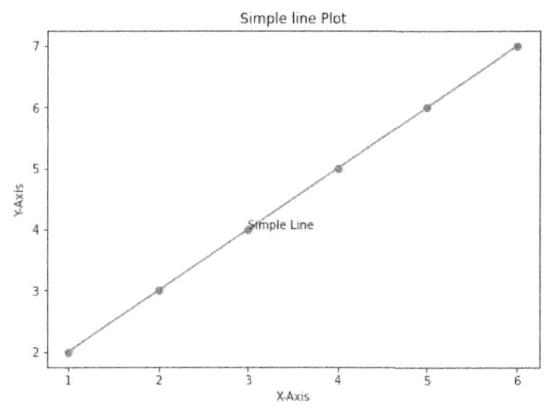

Figure 11.10: Adding markers

Marker values	Description
marker='o'	Circle
marker='*'	Star
marker='.'	Point
marker=','	Pixel
marker='x'	X
marker='X'	Filled X
marker='+'	Plus
marker='P'	Filled Plus
marker='s'	Square
marker='D'	Diamond

Marker values	Description
marker='d'	Thin Diamond
marker='p'	Pentagon
marker='H'	Hexagon
marker='h'	Hexagon
marker='v'	Downside triangle
marker='^'	Upside triangle
marker='<'	Left side triangle
'>'	Triangle right
'1'	Tri down
'2'	Tri up
'3'	Tri left
'4'	Tri right
'|'	Vline
'_'	Hline

- **Adding the line style, line color, and line width**

  To customize the plot's line style, we can pass the argument linestyle in the **plot()** function with the valid value like ':' for dotted line, '--' for the dashed line, and so on. Similarly, we can use the argument color and linewidth to set the color and width of the plotline.

  In the following example, we can see that in line #18, we have used argument linestyle="--" to set the plotline as a dashed line, color ='red' to set the line color Red, and linewidth='3' to set the width of line 3 pt:

```python
1  import matplotlib.pyplot as plt
2  fig = plt.figure()
3  ax = fig.add_axes([0.1,0.1,1,1])
4  x= [1,2,3,4,5,6]
5  y=[2,3,4,5,6,7]
6
7  # setting the Title
8  ax.set_title("Simple line Plot",loc='center') # adding the title
9
10 #Setting the X and Y axis text
11 ax.set_xlabel("X-Axis")  # adding the x-axis label
12 ax.set_ylabel("Y-Axis")  # adding the y-axis label
13
14
15 #Adding text to plot
16 plt.text(3,4,"Simple Line")
17
18 # setting the marker to circle and line as dashed line with red color and customised line width
19 ax.plot(x,y,marker='o',linestyle="--",color='red',linewidth='3')
20
21 plt.show()
```

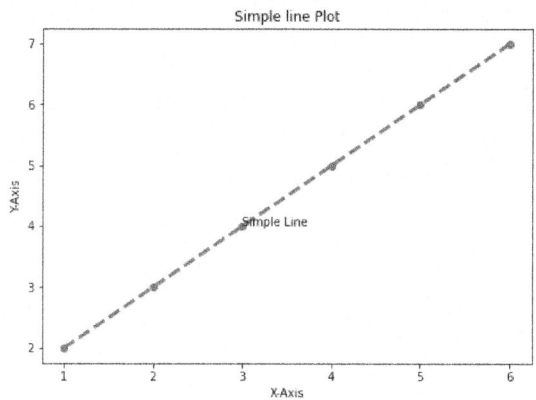

Figure 11.11: Line style, color, and width

We can also use '-' solid, ':' doted,'-.' dash-dot as linestyle values.

- **Adding gridlines**

    We can add the grid lines on the plot using the **grid()** function. Let's see the following example#1 where we have used the **ax. grid()** function at line #21 and added the x and y axis grid lines on the plot.

    We can also add the grid line specific to the axis; we can see that in example#2 and example#3, where we have added grid lines corresponding to the x and y-axis, respectively.

Example#1: grid()

```python
import matplotlib.pyplot as plt
fig = plt.figure()
ax = fig.add_axes([0.1,0.1,1,1])
x= [1,2,3,4,5,6]
y=[2,3,4,5,6,7]

# setting the Title
ax.set_title("Simple line Plot",loc='center') # adding the title

#Setting the X and Y axis text
ax.set_xlabel("X-Axis")   # adding the x-axis label
ax.set_ylabel("Y-Axis")   # adding the y-axis label


#Adding text to plot
plt.text(3,4,"Simple Line")

# setting the marker to circle and line as dashed line with red color and customised line width
ax.plot(x,y,marker='o',linestyle="--",color='red',linewidth='3')

ax.grid() # adding the grid lines to the plot

plt.show()
```

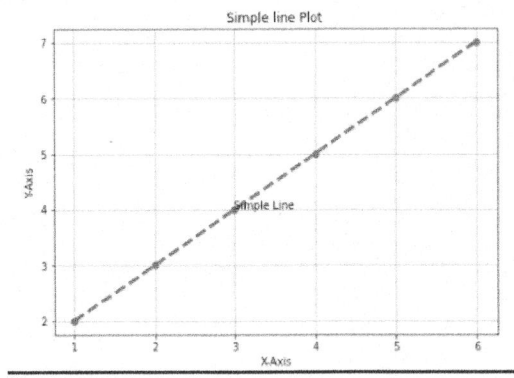

Figure 11.12: The grid() -example#1

Example# 2: grid(axis='x')

In the following example, we have used an **ax. grid(axis='x')** function to draw the gridline concerning the x-axis:

```python
import matplotlib.pyplot as plt
fig = plt.figure()
ax = fig.add_axes([0.1,0.1,1,1])
x= [1,2,3,4,5,6]
y=[2,3,4,5,6,7]

# setting the Title
ax.set_title("Simple line Plot",loc='center') # adding the title

#Setting the X and Y axis text
ax.set_xlabel("X-Axis")  # adding the x-axis label
ax.set_ylabel("Y-Axis")  # adding the y-axis label


#Adding text to plot
plt.text(3,4,"Simple Line")

# setting the marker to circle and line as dashed line with red color and customised line width
ax.plot(x,y,marker='o',linestyle="--",color='red',linewidth='3')

ax.grid(axis='x') # adding the grid lines to the plot for x-axis only

plt.show()
```

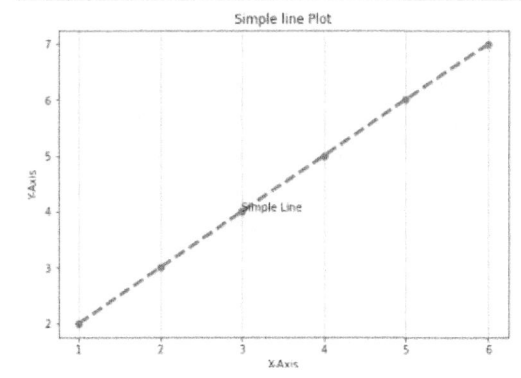

Figure 11.13: The grid() -example# 2

Example# 3: grid(axis='y')

In the following example, we have used an **ax.grid(axis='y')** function to draw the gridline concerning the y-axis:

```python
import matplotlib.pyplot as plt
fig = plt.figure()
ax = fig.add_axes([0.1,0.1,1,1])
x= [1,2,3,4,5,6]
y=[2,3,4,5,6,7]

# setting the Title
ax.set_title("Simple line Plot",loc='center') # adding the title

#Setting the X and Y axis text
ax.set_xlabel("X-Axis")  # adding the x-axis label
ax.set_ylabel("Y-Axis")  # adding the y-axis label


#Adding text to plot
plt.text(3,4,"Simple Line")

# setting the marker to circle and line as dashed line with red color and customised line width
ax.plot(x,y,marker='o',linestyle="--",color='red',linewidth='3')

ax.grid(axis='y') # adding the grid lines to the plot for y-axis only

plt.show()
```

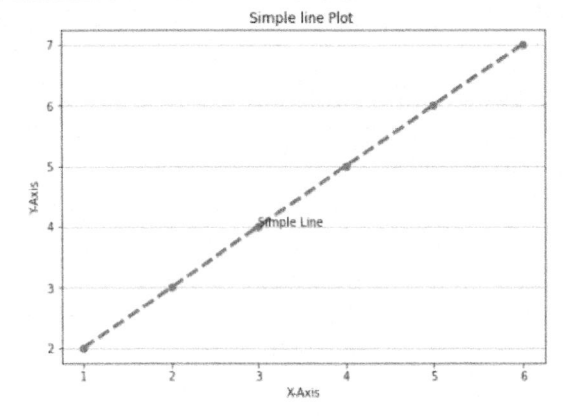

Figure 11.14:The grid() -example#3

- **Setting the axis limits**

    Though, Matplotlib automatically puts the minimum and maximum values which have been displayed among the axis (like x-axis or y-axis), it also provides the function like **set_xlim()** and **set_ylim()** functions to set the limit of the axis values.

```
import matplotlib.pyplot as plt
fig = plt.figure()
ax = fig.add_axes([0.1,0.1,1,1])
x= [1,2,3,4,5,6]
y=[2,3,4,5,6,7]

# setting the Title
ax.set_title("Simple line Plot",loc='center') # adding the title

#Setting the X and Y axis text
ax.set_xlabel("X-Axis")  # adding the x-axis label
ax.set_ylabel("Y-Axis")  # adding the y-axis label

ax.set_xlim(0,10) # settign the x-axis limit
ax.set_ylim(0,8) # settign the y-axis limit


#Adding text to plot
plt.text(3,4,"Simple Line")

# setting the marker to circle and line as dashed line with red color and customised line width
ax.plot(x,y,marker='o',linestyle="--",color='red',linewidth='3')

ax.grid() # adding the grid lines to the plot

plt.show()
```

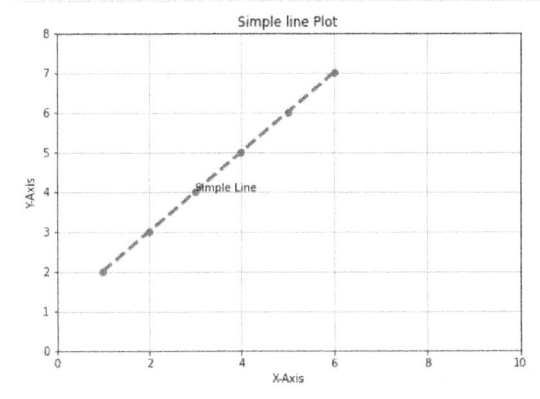

Figure 11.15: Setting axis limits

- **Adding the ticks and ticklables**

    Matplotlib provided the functions **set_xticks()**, **set_xticklables()**, **set_ytickes()** and **set_yticklables()** to set the ticks and tick lables along the x and y axis. Let's see the following example to understand this better:

Example#1 set_xticks() and set_xticklables()

In this example, we can see in the following coding snippet that in lines #15 and line #16, we set the ticks and tick labels for the x-axis:

```python
import matplotlib.pyplot as plt
fig = plt.figure()
ax = fig.add_axes([0.1,0.1,1,1])
x= [1,2,3,4,5,6]
y=[2,3,4,5,6,7]

# setting the Title
ax.set_title("Simple line Plot",loc='center') # adding the title
#Setting the X and Y axis text
ax.set_xlabel("X-Axis")  # adding the x-axis label
ax.set_ylabel("Y-Axis")  # adding the y-axis label
ax.set_xlim(0,10)  # settign the x-axis limit
ax.set_ylim(0,8) # settign the y-axis limit

ax.set_xticks([1,2,3,4,5,6,7,8,9,10]) # setting the x-axis ticks
ax.set_xticklabels(['one','two','three','four','five','six','seven','eight','nine','ten']) # setting the x-axis ticklables

#Adding text to plot
plt.text(3,4,"Simple Line")
# setting the marker to circle and line as dashed line with red color and customised line width
ax.plot(x,y,marker='o',linestyle="--",color='red',linewidth='3')
ax.grid() # adding the grid lines to the plot
plt.show()
```

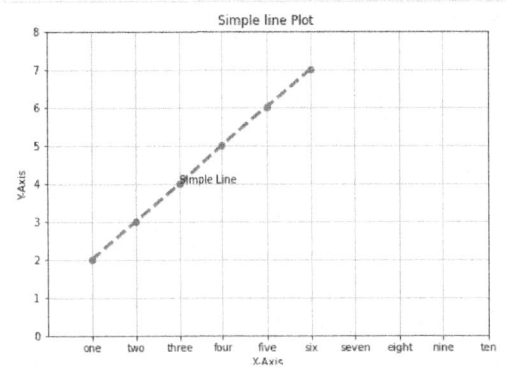

Figure 11.16: Adding Ticks and Ticklables -Example#1

Example#2 set_yticks() and set_yticklables()

In this example, we can see in the following coding snippet that in lines #15 and line #16, we set the ticks and tick labels for the y-axis:

```python
import matplotlib.pyplot as plt
fig = plt.figure()
ax = fig.add_axes([0.1,0.1,1,1])
x= [1,2,3,4,5,6]
y=[2,3,4,5,6,7]

# setting the Title
ax.set_title("Simple line Plot",loc='center') # adding the title
#Setting the X and Y axis text
ax.set_xlabel("X-Axis")  # adding the x-axis label
ax.set_ylabel("Y-Axis")  # adding the y-axis label
ax.set_xlim(0,10)  # settign the x-axis limit
ax.set_ylim(0,8) # settign the y-axis limit

ax.set_yticks([1,2,3,4,5,6,7,8,9,10]) # setting the y-axis ticks
ax.set_yticklabels(['one','two','three','four','five','six','seven','eight','nine','ten']) # setting the y-axis ticklables

#Adding text to plot
plt.text(3,4,"Simple Line")
# setting the marker to circle and line as dashed line with red color and customised line width
ax.plot(x,y,marker='o',linestyle="--",color='red',linewidth='3')
ax.grid() # adding the grid lines to the plot
plt.show()
```

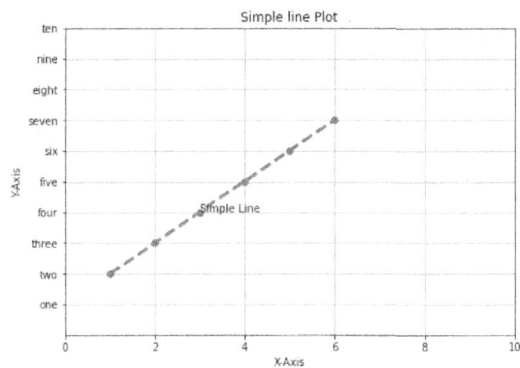

Figure 11.17: Adding ticks and ticklables -Example#1

Some basic types of plots in matplotlib

Matplotlib has various functions to plot multiple plots representing the data for specific purposes: bar graphs, histograms, and so on. Some of them we will discuss below:

- **Bar graph**

    A bar graph has been used to plot the categorical data. Matplotlib has the function **bar()** to plot the bar graph.

    ```
    import matplotlib.pyplot as plt
    course = ['Python','Java','Hadoop','Spark']   # x values
    students = [11,12,23,50]   # heights for the bars
    fig = plt.figure()
    ax = fig.add_axes([0,0,1,1])

    ax.bar(course,students,width=0.6,color=['b','r','g','y'])
    plt.show()
    ```

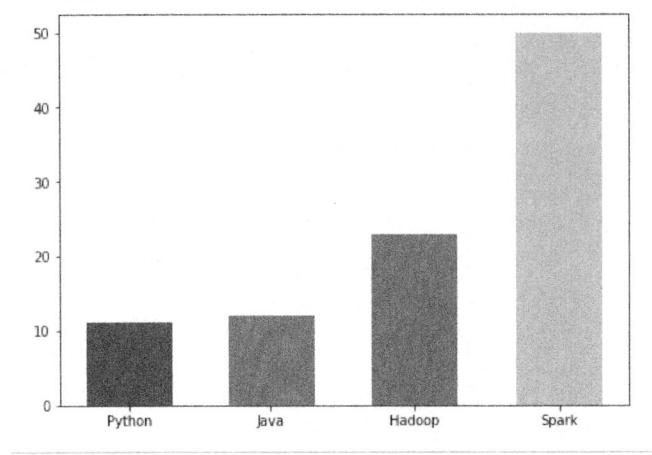

    Figure 11.18: Bar graph

- **Histograms**

    Histograms are good for showing the frequency distributions of numerical data. Matplotlib has the function **hist()** to plot the histogram. In the following coding snippet, we have plotted a histogram to see the range of employee salaries distributed among employees:

```
from matplotlib import pyplot as plt
import numpy as np
fig,ax = plt.subplots(1,1)
x = np.array([90,91,98,99,100,105,107,178,160,140,122,89,])
ax.hist(x, bins = [80,90,100,125,150,200])
ax.set_title("Emp Salary - Histogram")
ax.set_xticks([80,90,100,110,120,130,140,150,160,170])
ax.set_xlabel('Annual Salry in $')
ax.set_ylabel('no. of Employees')
plt.show()
```

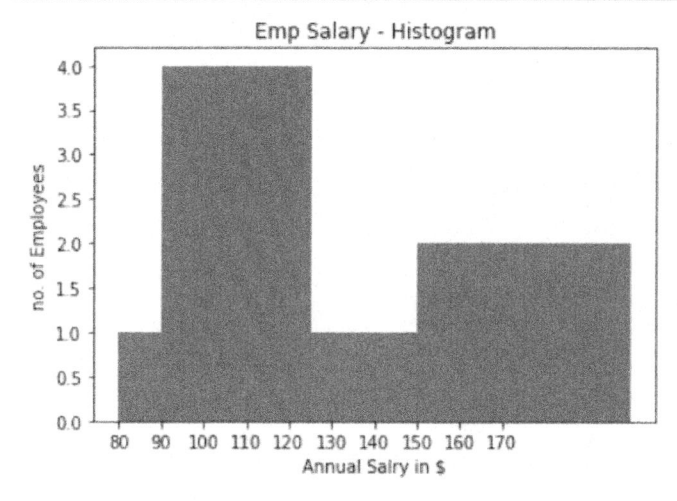

Figure 11.19: Histograms

- **Scatter plots**

    A scatter plot is used to compare the variables and also to compare how much one variable is affected by another. Matplotlib has the function **scatter()** to plot the scatter graph.

The following example is a scattered plot with scaled dots to see the profits among products:

```
import matplotlib.pyplot as plt

fig = plt.figure()
ax = fig.add_axes([0.1,0.1,1,1])

profit = [.2, .1, 0.0, .5, 1.2, .15]  # Profit
product = [1,2,3,4,5,6] # 6 differn product p1,p2,p3,p4,p5,p6

#profit*200 to scale-up the size of dot on plot
Scale=[p*200 for p in profit]

ax.scatter(x=product, y=profit,s=Scale)
ax.set_title("product-Profit")

ax.set_xlabel("Product id")
ax.set_ylabel("Profit")
plt.show()
```

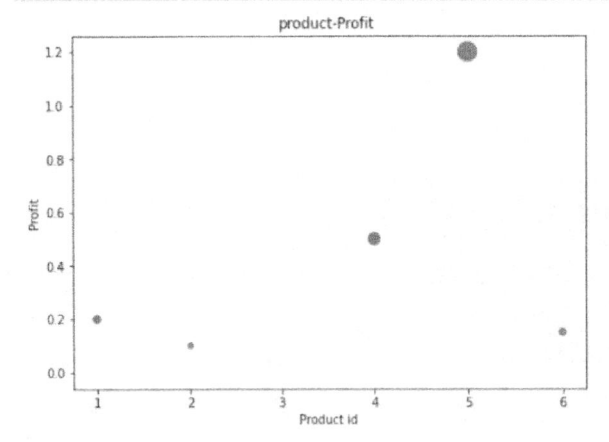

Figure 11.20: Scatter plot

- **Pie charts**

    Pie charts are suitable to represent the contribution of data. Matplotlib has the function **pie()** to plot the pie chart. In the following example, we planned a pie chart of the student numbers and enrollment in the different courses:

```
1  import matplotlib.pyplot as plt
2
3  fig = plt.figure()
4  ax = fig.add_axes([0.1,0.1,1,1])
5
6  no_of_students = np.array([35,30,25,45])
7  courses = ["Python", "Java", "Data Science", "Big-Data"]
8  ax.pie(no_of_students, labels = courses)
9
10 ax.set_title("Pi Chart")
11 plt.show()
```

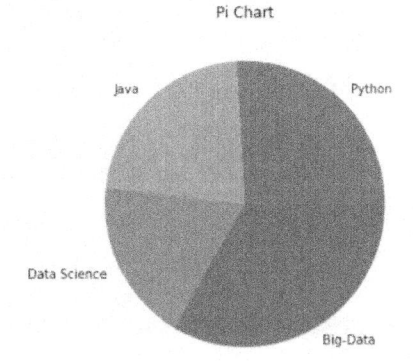

Figure 11.21: Pie Chart

Export the plot into a file

We can export the plot into a pdf file and a jpeg image file. Matplotlib has functions for both methods. Let's see the following examples:

- **Export the plot into a jpeg file**

    We can save the plot into a pdf file and a jpeg image file. Matplotlib has the function **savefig()**. In line #11, we save the fig (plotted pie chart) as a jpeg file in the following example:

```
1  import matplotlib.pyplot as plt
2
3  fig = plt.figure()
4  ax = fig.add_axes([0.1,0.1,1,1])
5
6  no_of_students = np.array([35,30,25,45])
7  courses = ["Python", "Java", "Data Science", "Big-Data"]
8  ax.pie(no_of_students, labels = courses)
9  ax.set_title("Pi Chart")
10
11 fig.savefig("data\out\myplot.jpeg",dpi=200)          # Saving the plot in myplot.jpeg file
```

Figure 11.22: Export to jpeg

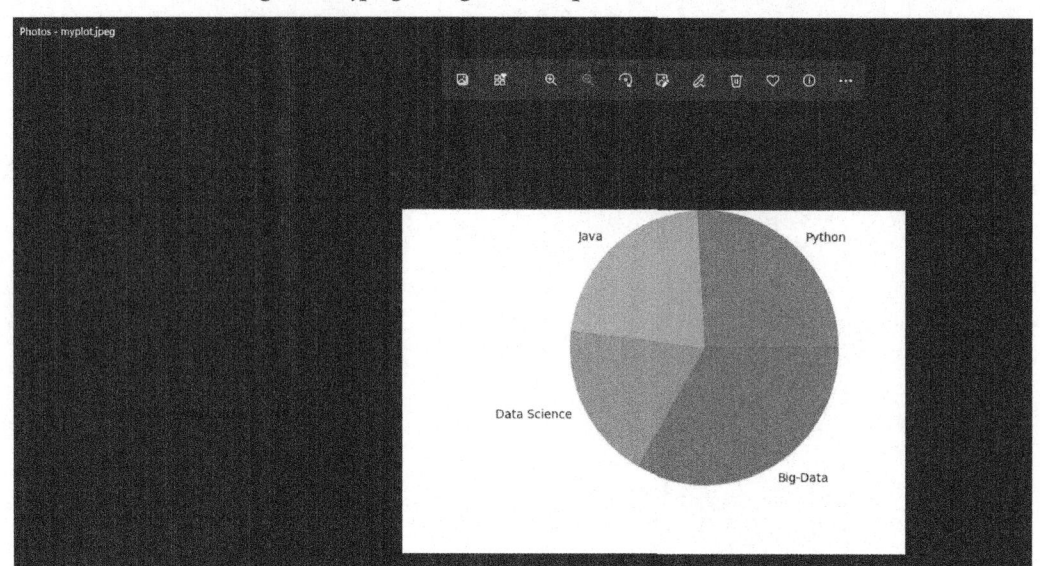

The following is the jpeg image of the plot that we have saved:

Figure 11.23: Exported plot into jpeg

- **Export the plot into a pdf file**

    Exporting the plot to a pdf file cannot be done directly; we will use the **savefig()** function, but to accomplish this, we need to take the help of the pdf pages module from **matplotlib.backend.backendpdf**. Let's understand the following example. In the following example, we have imported Pdf pages in line#2, then created the mypdf as an object using **Pdfpages()** in line #12 with the file name as an argument. After that, we executed the **savefig()** function by passing object **fig** as the argument value.

```
1  import matplotlib.pyplot as plt
2  from matplotlib.backends.backend_pdf import PdfPages
3
4  fig = plt.figure()
5  ax = fig.add_axes([0.1,0.1,1,1])
6
7  no_of_students = np.array([35,30,25,45])
8  courses = ["Python", "Java", "Data Science", "Big-Data"]
9  ax.pie(no_of_students, labels = courses)
10 ax.set_title("Pi Chart")
11
12 mypdf = PdfPages('data\out\myplotpdf.pdf')
13 mypdf.savefig(fig)                          # Saving the fig in mypdf.pdf file
14 mypdf.close()
```

Figure 11.24: Export to pdf

The following is the snippet of the pdf for the plot we have exported to the pdf file:

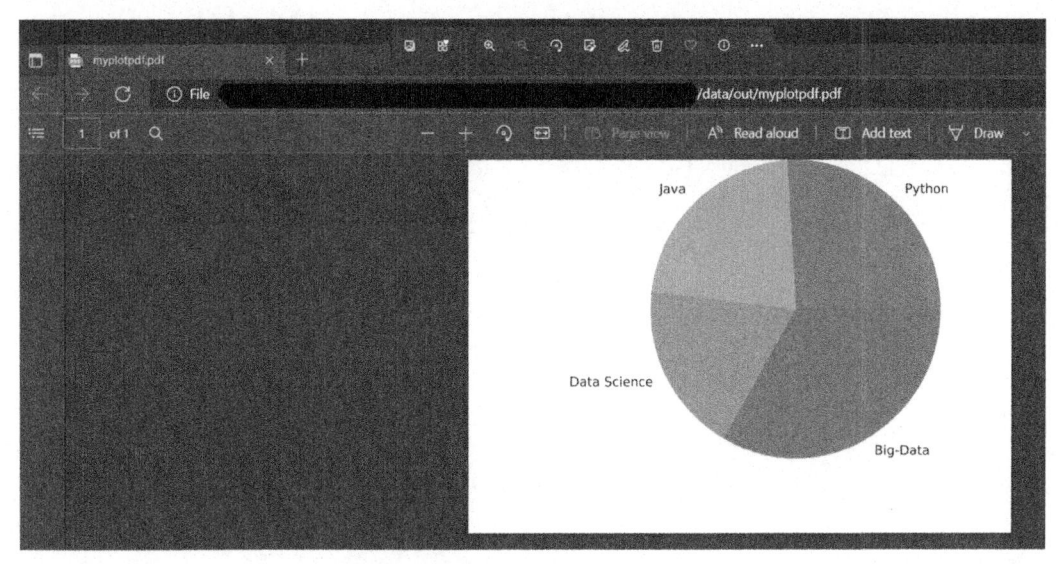

Figure 11.25: Exported plot in pdf

So, by using these approaches that we discussed earlier, we can export or save our plot into the files for future use.

Conclusion

In this chapter, we have learned about the various features and functions of the Matplotlib library. We understand and have good hands-on practice on Matplotlib, how to use that, and various other useful functions and methods that we need for data visualization.

We have covered all the essential basics of data analysis concepts, tools, and necessary Python libraries, which we need for data analysis. In the next chapter, we will connect all the pictures and solve a full-length data analysis task using our gathered knowledge.

Questions

1. What is Matplotlib, and why is it so popular?
2. What is the figure and axis in matplotlib?
3. Is object-oriented API available for plotting the data in matplotlib?
4. How can we plot a bar graph, histogram, scatter plot, and pie chart in matplotlib?
5. How to export the plot into a pdf and jpeg file?

Chapter 12
Connecting Dots – Step-by-step Data Analysis and Hands-on Use Case

We have covered the basic building block of Python programming language, the basics of data analysis, and some important Python libraries like Pandas, NumPy, and Matplotlib. So, to perform any basic data analysis task now, we are ready with all the necessary prerequisites.

In this chapter, we will discuss an end-to-end data analysis problem and perform an end–to–end data analysis task where we can utilize our past knowledge, which we have learned in previous chapters.

Structure

In this chapter, we will discuss the following topics:

- Understanding the data set
- Understanding the problem statement
- Importing the dataset into DataFrame
- Exploring, selecting, cleaning, and preparing the data
- Performing the data analysis and plotting the summary

Objectives

After studying this chapter, you should be able to:

- Understanding how to solve real-time data analysis problems
- Reading and analyzing the data from an external file
- Finding answers by analyzing the data and plotting the results

Understanding the Dataset

Our dataset will be taken from the World Bank (https://data.worldbank.org/). Youth Global Unemployment Rate information: unemployment is a significant indicator. This data set contains 267 countries' youth unemployment information from 1991 to 2021.

This dataset has the following columns:

'Country Name', 'Country Code', '1991', '1992', '1993', '1994', '1995',

'1996', '1997', '1998', '1999', '2000', '2001', '2002', '2003', '2004',

'2005', '2006', '2007', '2008', '2009', '2010', '2011', '2012', '2013',

'2014', '2015', '2016', '2017', '2018', '2019', '2020', '2021

Country Name column contains the name of the country, the **Country Code** has the three character country code, and the rest of the columns with year (like 1991,1992....2021) contain the unemployment rate for that particular year.

Problem statement

We need to analyze the youth global unemployment dataset for the last five years, from 2017 to 2021, to get the answers for the following points and plot the results:

- List all the countries where youth unemployment is greater than or equal to 25% in 2021.
- List all countries where youth unemployment is less than or equal to 1% in 2021.
- Top 10 countries that have an average high rate of youth unemployment from 2017 to 2021
- Top 10 countries that have an average low rate of youth unemployment from 2017 to 2021

- Top 10 countries that have a high COVID impact (for years 2019 and 2020)
- Top 10 countries that have a less COVID impact (for years 2019 and 2020)

Step by step example to perform the data analysis on a given dataset

Now, we have an idea about our dataset, and we also know about the problem statement and the points we need to analyze and get the information about those from the given dataset. The following is the step-by-step process for this:

1. Importing the dataset into DataFrame:

   The very first task is to import the required libraries. In this case, we need Pandas and Matplotlib, so you can see in the following coding snippet that we imported these libraries:

```
import pandas as pd
import matplotlib.pyplot as plt
data = pd.read_csv("./data/in/Word_UnemploymentData_91-21.csv")
```

Figure 12.1: Importing Data

Also, in line #3, we imported the dataset CSV into the pandas DataFrame.

2. Exploring, selecting, cleaning, and preparing the data:

   a) See the columns:

      We can use the **data.columns** to get all columns from the dataframe data.

```
data.columns
```
```
Index(['Country Name', 'Country Code', '1991', '1992', '1993', '1994', '1995',
       '1996', '1997', '1998', '1999', '2000', '2001', '2002', '2003', '2004',
       '2005', '2006', '2007', '2008', '2009', '2010', '2011', '2012', '2013',
       '2014', '2015', '2016', '2017', '2018', '2019', '2020', '2021'],
      dtype='object')
```

Figure 12.2: Display the columns

b) **Display the top 5 rows from the DataFrame data:**

In the following coding snippet, we used `data.head()` to display the top five rows of the DataFrame data:

Figure 12.3: head()

c) **Display the last five rows from the data frame data:**

In the following coding snippet, we used `data.tail()` to display the bottom five rows of the data frame data:

Figure 12.4: tail()

d) **Display the shape of the DataFrame (rows and columns):**

In the following coding snippet, we used `data.shape()` to display the shape of the DataFrame data; it has 266 rows and 33 columns.

```
1  data.shape
```

(266, 33)

Figure 12.5: Display the shape

e) **Selecting the subset of data from the given dataset:**

As mentioned in the problem statement, we need to do our data analysis for the given points from 2017 to 2021. So, it is better if we select only that subset of data. In the following coding snippet, we did the same:

As you see in the following coding snippet, we used the iloc function and passed the range of rows and subset of columns to slice the specific data from the DataFrame and created a new DataFrame **data_5yr**.

Data.iloc[:,[0,1,28,29,30,32,32]], here 0,1,28,29,30,31,32 are the corresponding column index for the columns: Country Name, Country Code, 2017, 2018, 2019, 2020 and 2021 of the DataFrame.

```
1  data_5yr = data.iloc[:,[0,1,28,29,30,31,32]].copy()
2  data_5yr
```

	Country Name	Country Code	2017	2018	2019	2020	2021
0	Aruba	ABW	NaN	NaN	NaN	NaN	NaN
1	Africa Eastern and Southern	AFE	6.714955	6.731163	6.914353	7.563187	8.111783
2	Afghanistan	AFG	11.180000	11.152000	11.217000	11.710000	13.283000
3	Africa Western and Central	AFW	6.019505	6.041092	6.063362	6.774914	6.839009
4	Angola	AGO	7.408000	7.421000	7.421000	8.333000	8.530000
...	...	...	...	...	...	...	...
261	Kosovo	XKX	NaN	NaN	NaN	NaN	NaN
262	Yemen, Rep.	YEM	13.297000	13.145000	13.056000	13.391000	13.574000
263	South Africa	ZAF	27.040001	26.910000	28.469999	29.219999	33.558998
264	Zambia	ZMB	11.630000	12.010000	12.520000	12.848000	13.026000
265	Zimbabwe	ZWE	4.785000	4.796000	4.833000	5.351000	5.174000

266 rows × 7 columns

Figure 12.6: Slicing the data

We can see the columns of the new DataFrame (**data_5yr**) by using **data_5yr.columns**.

```
1  data_5yr.columns
```
Index(['Country Name', 'Country Code', '2017', '2018', '2019', '2020', '2021'], dtype='object')

Figure 12.7: Display the columns

f) Check for null values.

We used the **isnull()** function to check the null values present in the data frame. In the following example, we can see that some columns have null values:

```
1  data_5yr.isnull().sum()
```

```
Country Name     0
Country Code     0
2017            31
2018            31
2019            31
2020            31
2021            31
dtype: int64
```

Figure 12.8: Checking for the nulls count

g) Dropping the rows with null values.

The following coding snippet contains the code to drop the rows that have null values in columns 2017, 2018, 2019,2020, and 2021; if any country does not have unemployment information, then it's better to drop that row. We did the same in the following coding snippet:

```
1  data_5yr.dropna(how='all',subset=['2017','2018','2019','2020','2021'],inplace=True)
2  data_5yr.isnull().sum()
```

```
Country Name    0
Country Code    0
2017            0
2018            0
2019            0
2020            0
2021            0
dtype: int64
```

Figure 12.9: Dropping null values

We can see no null present after dropping the null rows from the DataFrame.

h) Check for the duplicates:

In the following coding snippet, I have checked for duplicates and found that there is no duplicate data present:

```
1  data_5yr.duplicated().sum()
```

```
0
```

Figure 12.10: Checking for the duplicates

i) Checking the datatypes of the columns:

In the following coding snippet, we printed the data types for all columns in the DataFrame:

```
1  data_5yr.dtypes
```

```
Country Name     object
Country Code     object
2017             float64
2018             float64
2019             float64
2020             float64
2021             float64
dtype: object
```

Figure 12.11: Display the data types of columns

j) Sorting the DataFrame:

In the following coding snippet, we sorted the data frame on the column **Country Name**:

```
1  data_5yr.sort_values('Country Name')
```

	Country Name	Country Code	2017	2018	2019	2020	2021
2	Afghanistan	AFG	11.180000	11.152000	11.217000	11.710000	13.283000
1	Africa Eastern and Southern	AFE	6.714955	6.731163	6.914353	7.563187	8.111783
3	Africa Western and Central	AFW	6.019505	6.041092	6.063362	6.774914	6.839009
5	Albania	ALB	13.620000	12.300000	11.470000	13.329000	11.819000
60	Algeria	DZA	10.333000	10.420000	10.513000	12.550000	12.704000
...	...	...	...	...	...	...	...
196	West Bank and Gaza	PSE	25.680000	26.260000	25.340000	25.889999	24.903000
259	World	WLD	5.557731	5.389813	5.357086	6.573491	6.177190
262	Yemen, Rep.	YEM	13.297000	13.145000	13.056000	13.391000	13.574000
264	Zambia	ZMB	11.630000	12.010000	12.520000	12.848000	13.026000
265	Zimbabwe	ZWE	4.785000	4.796000	4.833000	5.351000	5.174000

235 rows × 7 columns

Figure 12.12: Sorting the data frame

k) Setting the index :

We set the **Country Code** column as an index in the following coding snippet:

```
1  data_5yr.set_index('Country Code',inplace=True)
2  data_5yr
```

	Country Name	2017	2018	2019	2020	2021
Country Code						
AFE	Africa Eastern and Southern	6.714955	6.731163	6.914353	7.563187	8.111783
AFG	Afghanistan	11.180000	11.152000	11.217000	11.710000	13.283000
AFW	Africa Western and Central	6.019505	6.041092	6.063362	6.774914	6.839009
AGO	Angola	7.408000	7.421000	7.421000	8.333000	8.530000
ALB	Albania	13.620000	12.300000	11.470000	13.329000	11.819000
...	...	...	...	...	...	...
WSM	Samoa	8.578000	8.686000	8.406000	9.149000	9.837000
YEM	Yemen, Rep.	13.297000	13.145000	13.056000	13.391000	13.574000
ZAF	South Africa	27.040001	26.910000	28.469999	29.219999	33.558998
ZMB	Zambia	11.630000	12.010000	12.520000	12.848000	13.026000
ZWE	Zimbabwe	4.785000	4.796000	4.833000	5.351000	5.174000

235 rows × 6 columns

Figure 12.13: Set the columns as an index

l) Adding two new columns, `5yrs_avg` and `covid_Yr_diff` :

To analyze some points, we need the latest five years (from 2017 to 2021) of average unemployment information. So for that, we have to calculate the average values using from 2017 to 2021 information and we need to store them in some columns in an existing data frame. In our case, we are using the column name `5yrs_avg`.

In the following coding, the snippet has the code for the same; in line #1, we took the subset of columns (2017, 2018, 2019, 2020, and 2021) and calculated the average row-wise (axis =1), then stored that in column `5yrs_avg`, in data frame `data_5r`.

In line #2, we displayed the same data frame with a new column `5yrs_avg`.

```
1  data_5yr['5yrs_avg'] = data_5yr[['2017','2018','2019','2020','2021']].mean(axis=1)
2  data_5yr
```

Country Code	Country Name	2017	2018	2019	2020	2021	5yrs_avg
AFE	Africa Eastern and Southern	6.714955	6.731163	6.914353	7.563187	8.111783	7.207088
AFG	Afghanistan	11.180000	11.152000	11.217000	11.710000	13.283000	11.708400
AFW	Africa Western and Central	6.019505	6.041092	6.063362	6.774914	6.839009	6.347576
AGO	Angola	7.408000	7.421000	7.421000	8.333000	8.530000	7.822600
ALB	Albania	13.620000	12.300000	11.470000	13.329000	11.819000	12.507600
...	...	...	...	...	...	...	...
WSM	Samoa	8.578000	8.686000	8.406000	9.149000	9.837000	8.931200
YEM	Yemen, Rep.	13.297000	13.145000	13.056000	13.391000	13.574000	13.292600
ZAF	South Africa	27.040001	26.910000	28.469999	29.219999	33.558998	29.039799
ZMB	Zambia	11.630000	12.010000	12.520000	12.848000	13.026000	12.406800
ZWE	Zimbabwe	4.785000	4.796000	4.833000	5.351000	5.174000	4.987800

235 rows × 7 columns

Figure 12.14: Adding column 5yrs_avg

Similarly, we need another column with the difference between 2019 and 2020 information to be used on the impact of the COVID situation on unemployment. Here, we have the assumption to ignore all other factors for a change in unemployment except COVID. The following is the coding snippet where we calculated a new column **covid_Yr_diff** in the existing DataFrame:

```
1  data_5yr['covid_Yr_diff'] = data_5yr['2020']-data_5yr['2019']
2  data_5yr
```

Country Code	Country Name	2017	2018	2019	2020	2021	5yrs_avg	covid_Yr_diff
AFE	Africa Eastern and Southern	6.714955	6.731163	6.914353	7.563187	8.111783	7.207088	0.648834
AFG	Afghanistan	11.180000	11.152000	11.217000	11.710000	13.283000	11.708400	0.493000
AFW	Africa Western and Central	6.019505	6.041092	6.063362	6.774914	6.839009	6.347576	0.711552
AGO	Angola	7.408000	7.421000	7.421000	8.333000	8.530000	7.822600	0.912000
ALB	Albania	13.620000	12.300000	11.470000	13.329000	11.819000	12.507600	1.859000
...	...	...	...	...	...	...	...	...
WSM	Samoa	8.578000	8.686000	8.406000	9.149000	9.837000	8.931200	0.743000
YEM	Yemen, Rep.	13.297000	13.145000	13.056000	13.391000	13.574000	13.292600	0.335000
ZAF	South Africa	27.040001	26.910000	28.469999	29.219999	33.558998	29.039799	0.750000
ZMB	Zambia	11.630000	12.010000	12.520000	12.848000	13.026000	12.406800	0.327999
ZWE	Zimbabwe	4.785000	4.796000	4.833000	5.351000	5.174000	4.987800	0.518000

235 rows × 8 columns

Figure 12.15: Adding column covid_Yr_diff

m) Plotting the **5yer_avg** unemployment data:

The following is the coding snippet and the plotted bar graph for the **5yer_avg** unemployment rate corresponding to all countries (x-axis: countries, y-axis: unemployment rate):

```
import matplotlib.pyplot as plt
avg5Yrs = data_5yr['5yrs_avg']   # x values
countries = list(data_5yr.index)  # heights for the bars
fig,ax = plt.subplots(nrows=1,ncols=1,figsize=(120,40))

ax.bar(countries,avg5Yrs,align='edge')

plt.xlabel('countries', fontsize=60)
plt.ylabel('5 Yrs Avg unemployment Rate', fontsize=60)
plt.xticks(rotation='vertical',fontsize=20)
plt.title("UNEMPLOYMENT AVG of Last 5 Yrs (2017 to 2021)",fontsize=80)

plt.show()
```

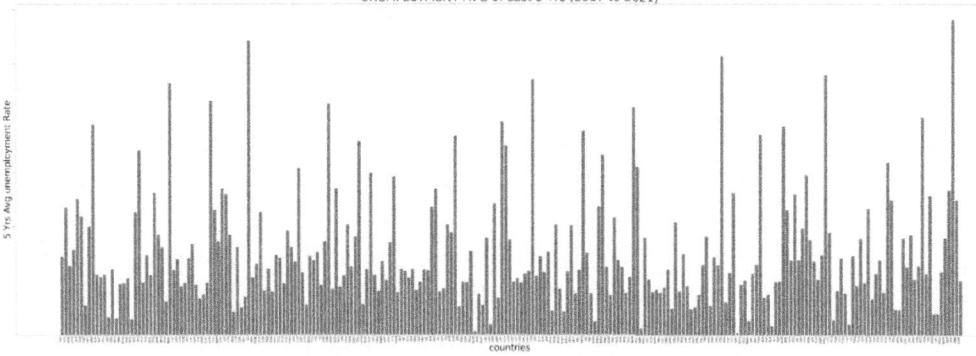

Figure 12.16: The 5yer_avg unemployment data plot

So, we have prepared a complete data frame for the following analysis task:

1. Performing the data analysis and plotting the summary of them:

   So, we have prepared a complete data frame ready for the subsequent analysis task.

   a) List all countries where youth unemployment is greater than or equal to 25% in 2021.

   In the following coding, we have tried to select all records with an unemployment rate of more than or equal to 25%: so we got three countries under this condition:

```
1  #list All Countries where Youth Unemployment is greater than or equal to 25% in 2021
2  data_5yr[data_5yr['2021']>=25.00][['Country Name','2021']]
```

Country Code	Country Name	2021
DJI	Djibouti	28.386000
SWZ	Eswatini	25.756001
ZAF	South Africa	33.558998

Figure 12.17: Unemployment >=25

2. List all countries where youth unemployment is less than or equal to 1% in 2021.

   In the following coding, we have tried to select all records with an unemployment rate less than or equal to 1 %: so we got three countries under this condition:

```
1  #list All Countries where Youth Unemployment is less than or equal to 1% in 2021
2  data_5yr[data_5yr['2021']<=1.00][['Country Name','2021']]
```

Country Code	Country Name	2021
KHM	Cambodia	0.612
NER	Niger	0.751
QAT	Qatar	0.258

Figure 12.18: unemployment <=1

3. Top 10 countries that have an average high rate of youth unemployment from 2017 to 2021.

   In the following coding snippet in line #1, we have the first sort of the data for column **5yr_avg** in descending order, which means the highest value at the top. We sliced the top ten rows from this, and this way, we got the top 10 countries with a high average youth unemployment rate from 2017 to 2021.

```
1  top_10_countries_high_uemp = data_5yr.sort_values('5yrs_avg',ascending =False)[0:10].copy()
2  top_10_countries_high_uemp
```

Country Code	Country Name	2017	2018	2019	2020	2021	5yrs_avg
ZAF	South Africa	27.040001	26.910000	28.469999	29.219999	33.558998	29.039799
DJI	Djibouti	26.059999	26.188999	26.357000	28.389999	28.386000	27.076400
PSE	West Bank and Gaza	25.680000	26.260000	25.340000	25.889999	24.903000	25.614600
SWZ	Eswatini	22.753000	22.792000	22.837000	25.509001	25.756001	23.929400
LSO	Lesotho	23.200001	22.813000	22.440001	24.563000	24.598000	23.522800
BWA	Botswana	21.566000	22.070999	22.610000	24.930000	24.722000	23.179800
COG	Congo, Rep.	20.559999	20.614000	20.622000	22.843000	23.011000	21.529800
GAB	Gabon	20.721001	20.749001	20.742001	21.972000	22.264999	21.289800
NAM	Namibia	21.639000	19.879999	19.988001	21.445999	21.677999	20.926200
VCT	St. Vincent and the Grenadines	19.181999	19.180000	19.280001	21.002001	21.618000	20.052400

Figure 12.19: *Top 10 countries that have an avg. high unemployment from 2017 to 2021*

In the following coding snippet, the plot of the top 10 countries with a high average youth unemployment rate from 2017 to 2021 is shown:

```
1   import matplotlib.pyplot as plt
2   uemp = top_10_countries_high_uemp['5yrs_avg']
3   # countries = top_10_countries_high_uemp['Country Name']
4   countries = list(top_10_countries_high_uemp.index)
5
6   fig,ax = plt.subplots(nrows=1,ncols=1)
7
8   ax.bar(countries,uemp)
9
10  plt.xlabel('Country Code', fontsize=12)
11  plt.ylabel('5 Yrs Avg unemployment Rate', fontsize=12)
12  plt.xticks(rotation='vertical',fontsize=15)
13  plt.title("Top 10 Countries with high Unemplyment Rate",fontsize=15)
14
15  ax.grid()
16  plt.show()
```

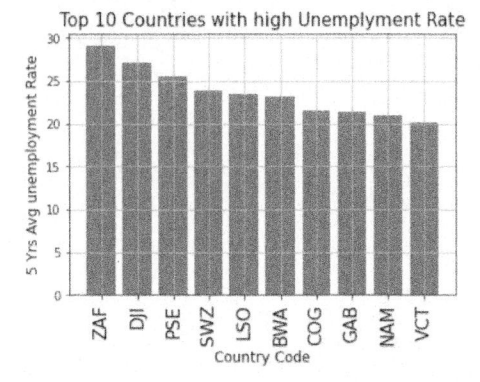

Figure 12.20: *Plot for the top 10 countries that have an avg high unemployment from 2017 to 2021*

4. Top 10 countries that have an average low rate of youth unemployment from 2017 to 2021.

   o In the following coding snippet in line #1, we have the first sort of the data for column **5yr_avg** in ascending order, which means the lowest value at the op. Then, we sliced the top ten rows from this, and this way, we have got the information about top ten countries that have an average low rate of youth unemployment from 2017 to 2021.

```
1  top_10_countries_low_uemp=data_5yr.sort_values('5yrs_avg')[0:10]
2  top_10_countries_low_uemp
```

Country Code	Country Name	2017	2018	2019	2020	2021	5yrs_avg
QAT	Qatar	0.140	0.110	0.100	0.214	0.258	0.1644
KHM	Cambodia	0.140	0.143	0.147	0.331	0.612	0.2746
NER	Niger	0.542	0.545	0.554	0.624	0.751	0.6032
SLB	Solomon Islands	0.707	0.724	0.755	0.916	1.029	0.8262
LAO	Lao PDR	0.805	0.827	0.852	1.034	1.258	0.9552
THA	Thailand	0.830	0.770	0.720	1.100	1.418	0.9676
MMR	Myanmar	1.560	0.870	0.500	1.058	2.173	1.2322
RWA	Rwanda	1.137	1.111	1.098	1.485	1.607	1.2876
TCD	Chad	1.119	1.130	1.123	1.742	1.882	1.3992
BHR	Bahrain	1.183	1.201	1.196	1.781	1.874	1.4470

Figure 12.21: Top 10 countries that have an Avg low unemployment from 2017 to 2021

In the following coding snippet, the plot of the top 10 countries with a low average youth unemployment rate from 2017 to 2021 is shown:

```
1   import matplotlib.pyplot as plt
2   uemp = top_10_countries_low_uemp['5yrs_avg']
3   # countries = top_10_countries_high_uemp['Country Name']
4   countries = list(top_10_countries_low_uemp.index)
5
6   fig,ax = plt.subplots(nrows=1,ncols=1)
7
8   ax.bar(countries,uemp)
9
10  plt.xlabel('Country Code', fontsize=12)
11  plt.ylabel('5 Yrs Avg unemployment Rate', fontsize=12)
12  plt.xticks(rotation='vertical',fontsize=15)
13  plt.title("Top 10 Countries with low Unemployment Rate",fontsize=15)
14
15  ax.grid()
16  plt.show()
```

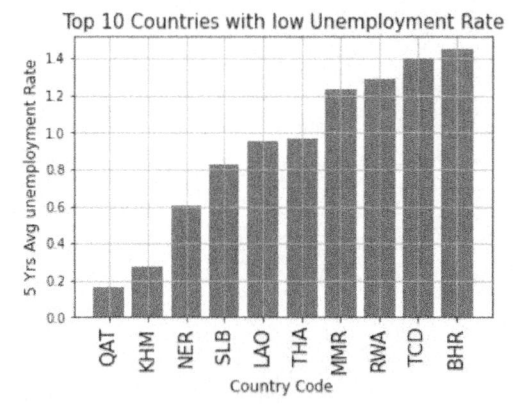

Figure 12.22: Plot for the Top 10 countries that have an Avg low unemployment from 2017 to 2021

5. Top 10 countries that have a high covid impact on the unemployment rate (for the immediate year 2019 and the covid year 2020).

In the following coding snippet in line #1, we have the first sort of the data for the column **covid_Yr_diff** (this column calculated as 2020 - 2019 values) in descending order, which means the highest value at the top. We sliced the top ten rows from this, and this way, we got the top 10 that have a high COVID impact (for the immediate year 2019 and the COVID year 2020).

```
1  high_impact_of_covid = data_5yr.sort_values('covid_Yr_diff',ascending=False)[0:10]
2  high_impact_of_covid
```

Country Code	Country Name	2017	2018	2019	2020	2021	5yrs_avg	covid_Yr_diff
PAN	Panama	3.859000	3.833000	4.726000	12.854000	12.088000	7.472000	8.128000
GEO	Georgia	13.940000	12.670000	11.570000	18.500000	10.659000	13.467800	6.930000
CRI	Costa Rica	8.140000	9.630000	11.490000	17.410000	17.954000	12.924800	5.920000
COL	Colombia	8.870000	9.110000	9.960000	15.040000	14.336000	11.463200	5.080000
USA	United States	4.360000	3.900000	3.670000	8.050000	5.464000	5.088800	4.380000
NAC	North America	4.578024	4.112751	3.891094	8.206108	5.695047	5.296605	4.315014
BOL	Bolivia	3.650000	3.520000	3.820000	7.900000	8.509000	5.479800	4.080000
CHL	Chile	6.960000	7.230000	7.290000	11.180000	9.128000	8.357600	3.890000
CAN	Canada	6.340000	5.830000	5.660000	9.460000	7.510000	6.960000	3.800000
PER	Peru	3.690000	3.490000	3.380000	7.180000	4.833000	4.514600	3.800000

Figure 12.23: Top 10 countries that have a high COVID impact on unemployment

The following is the coding snippet of the plot of the top ten countries with a high COVID impact (for the immediate year 2019 and the COVID year 2020):

```
1   import matplotlib.pyplot as plt
2   uemp = high_impact_of_covid['covid_Yr_diff']
3   # countries = top_10_countries_high_uemp['Country Name']
4   countries = high_impact_of_covid['Country Name']
5
6   fig,ax = plt.subplots(nrows=1,ncols=1)
7
8   ax.bar(countries,uemp)
9
10  plt.xlabel('Countries', fontsize=12)
11  plt.ylabel('imediate diff in uemp due to covid (2019 vs 2020)', fontsize=12)
12  plt.xticks(rotation='vertical',fontsize=15)
13  plt.title("Top 10 Countries with high impact of covid",fontsize=15)
14
15  ax.grid()
16  plt.show()
```

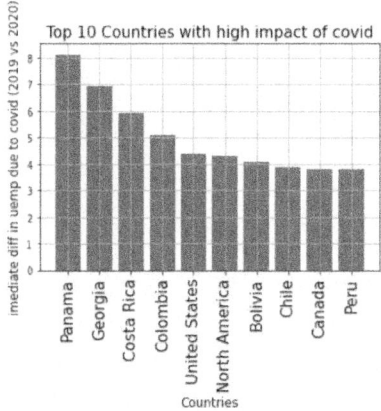

Figure 12.24: Plot for Top 10 countries that have a high COVID impact on unemployment

6. Top 10 countries that have a less COVID impact (for the immediate year 2019 and the COVID year 2020).

   In the following coding snippet in line #1, we have the first sort of the data for column **covid_Yr_diff** (this column is calculated as 2020 - 2019 for values) in ascending order, which means the highest value is at the top. We sliced the top ten rows from this, and this way, we got the top 10 that have a less COVID impact (for the immediate year 2019 and the COVID year 2020).

```
1  low_impact_of_covid = data_5yr.sort_values('covid_Yr_diff')[0:10]
2  low_impact_of_covid
```

Country Code	Country Name	2017	2018	2019	2020	2021	5yrs_avg	covid_Yr_diff
SRB	Serbia	13.480000	12.730000	10.390000	9.010000	11.807000	11.4834	-1.380000
MDA	Moldova	4.100000	4.110000	5.100000	3.820000	3.962000	4.2184	-1.280000
GRC	Greece	21.490000	19.290001	17.309999	16.299999	14.795000	17.8370	-1.010000
ITA	Italy	11.210000	10.610000	9.950000	9.160000	9.834000	10.1528	-0.790000
TUR	Turkey	10.820000	10.890000	13.670000	13.110000	13.386000	12.3752	-0.560000
BIH	Bosnia and Herzegovina	20.530001	18.400000	15.690000	15.265000	15.215000	17.0200	-0.424999
FRA	France	9.410000	9.020000	8.410000	8.010000	8.063000	8.5826	-0.400000
DOM	Dominican Republic	5.830000	5.860000	6.360000	6.130000	8.496000	6.5352	-0.230000
POL	Poland	4.890000	3.850000	3.280000	3.160000	3.368000	3.7096	-0.120000
MKD	North Macedonia	22.379999	20.740000	17.260000	17.200001	16.202999	18.7566	-0.059999

Figure 12.25: Top 10 countries that have a less COVID impact on unemployment

The following is the coding snippet to plot the top ten countries with less COVID impact (for the immediate year 2019 and the COVID year 2020):

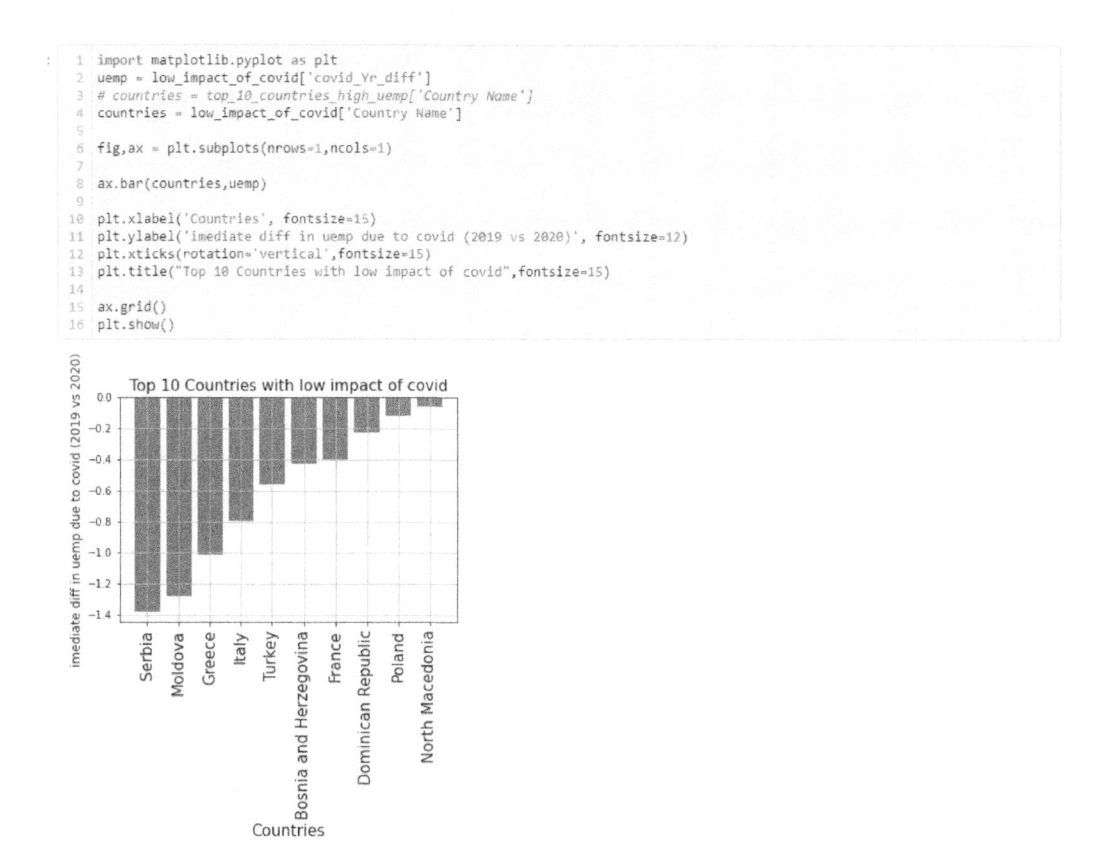

```python
import matplotlib.pyplot as plt
uemp = low_impact_of_covid['covid_Yr_diff']
# countries = top_10_countries_high_uemp['Country Name']
countries = low_impact_of_covid['Country Name']

fig,ax = plt.subplots(nrows=1,ncols=1)

ax.bar(countries,uemp)

plt.xlabel('Countries', fontsize=15)
plt.ylabel('imediate diff in uemp due to covid (2019 vs 2020)', fontsize=12)
plt.xticks(rotation='vertical',fontsize=15)
plt.title("Top 10 Countries with low impact of covid",fontsize=15)

ax.grid()
plt.show()
```

Figure 12.26:Plot for top 10 countries that have a less COVID impact on unemployment

Conclusion

In this chapter, we have solved a complete data analysis problem step by step. We perform various tasks importing the data into the DataFrame, exploring and understanding the nature of data, and cleaning and preparing the data according to the problem so that it can be used to answer the question by analyzing the data.

We completed a full hands-on example in this chapter. Also, we have plotted our results which we have got after doing data analysis.

If you have completed till here, you will now understand the Python basic blocks, data analysis, and some famous data analysis libraries. You will also have a good idea of solving real-time data analysis problems.

Index

A

aggregate function 142
Anaconda
  downloading 10
  installation, testing 17
  installing 10-16
AND/OR condition
  with if statements 69, 70
anonymous functions 88
append() function 146
arguments
  keyword arguments 86
  key-word variable-length arguments 88
  positional arguments 85, 86
  positional variable-length arguments 87
  variable-length/arbitrary arguments 86

arithmetic operators 24
  coding example 25
array() function 173
assignment operators 28
  coding examples 29

B

bar graph 228
bitwise operators
  coding examples 31
Bitwise operators 31
built-in data types 34
  dictionaries 57
  list 41
  numeric 34
  sets 52
  string 38
  tuples 48

C

Centrum Wiskunde & Informatica (CWI) 2
close() function 98
concat() function 154
conditional statements
   AND/OR condition, with if statements 69, 70
   if...else statement 65, 66
   if statement 64, 65
   nested if statement 67-69

D

data analysis 106
   data types 111
   descriptive data analysis 107
   diagnostic data analysis 108
   importance 107
   predictive data analysis 108
   prescriptive data analysis 108
   tools, using 111
   use case 237-250
   versus, data analytics 106, 107
data analysis process flow 108
   data analysis 110
   data cleaning 110
   data collection 109
   data interpretation and result summarization 110
   data preparation 110
   data visualization 110
   requirements, gathering and planning 109
DataFrame. *See* pandas DataFrame
DataFrame.columns 127
DataFrame.describe() 126
DataFrame.dtypes 127
DataFrame.head(n) 125
DataFrame.info() 126
DataFrame.replace() 140
DataFrame.shape 124
DataFrame.tail(n) 125
data structures, in Pandas
   DataFrame 117
   pandas series 117
data types, for data analysis
   semi-structured data 111
   structured data 111
   unstructured data 111
data types, in NumPy 181, 182
   examples 185
   float data type 184
   int examples 183
   structure data type 185, 186
data visualization 210, 211
default arguments 86
descriptive data analysis 107
diagnostic data analysis 108
dictionaries 57
   element membership, checking 59
   elements, adding 58
   item, removing 59
   items, accessing 58
   iterating 60
   key or value iterable, converting into 61
   list of keys, obtaining 60
   list of tuples, obtaining 60
   list of values, obtaining 60
   working with 58
drop_duplicates() function 133
drop() function 152
dropna() function 134

dropna(subset) 135
duplicated() function 132

E
else statement
  using, with loops 78, 79

F
file
  closing 97, 98
  content, reading 99-101
  content, writing 101, 102
  opening 96, 97
fillna() function 136
filter() function
  using 89
for loop 76
function
  arguments 85
  definition 84, 85
  parameters 85

G
groupby() function 141

H
histograms 228

I
identity operators 33
  code examples 33
if...else statement 65, 66
if statement 64, 65
indentation 64
IPython 111

J
join() function 162-165
Jupyter Notebook
  running 18-20
  testing 21

K
Key Performance Indicators (KPIs) 107
keyword argument 86
key-word variable-length arguments 88

L
lambda function
  using, with filter() 89
  using, with map() 89
  using, with reduce() 90
  writing 88
list 41
  concatenation 43
  element count 46
  element membership, checking 45
  elements, adding 42
  item, removing 44
  items, accessing 42
  items, sorting 45
  length 46
  repetition 43
  slicing 46
  string, converting into 47
  tuple, converting into 47
  updating 44
  working with 42
logical operators 30
  coding examples 30
loop control statements 79
  break 79
  continue 80
  pass 80
loops
  else statement, using with 78, 79
  for loop 76

nested loop 77
while loop 74, 75

M

map() function
  using 89
Matplotlib 112, 211
  object-oriented API 213, 214
  plot, customizing 216-227
  simple line plot 212
  subplot() function 214
  working with 211
membership operators 32
  coding examples 33
merge() function 157-161

N

nested if statement 67-69
nested loop 77
  for loop 77, 78
  while loop 77
numeric data types 34
  casting 36
  complex 35
  conversion 36
  float 35
  integers 34
numeric operations, in NumPy 199
  numpy.mod() 201
  numpy.power() 200
  numpy.reciprocal() 201, 202
Numpy
  numeric operations 199-202
  statistical functions 195-198
NumPy 112, 171, 172
  data, reading from files 206, 207
  data types 181
  data, writing into files 204-206
  sorting 202-204
numpy.append() 188
NumPy array 173
  creating 173-176
  creating, from numeric range series 177, 178
  creating, with list and tuple 176, 177
  elements, deleting 188-190
  elements, inserting 188-190
  indexing 178-180
  joining 191-195
  reshaping 186-188
  slicing 178-180
  splitting 191-194
numpy.concatenate() 191
numpy.hsplit() 194
numpy.hstack() 192
numpy.insert() 190
numpy.load() 206
numpy.loadtxt() 206, 207
numpy.save() 204
numpy.savetxt() 205
numpy.sort() function 202
numpy.split() 194
numpy.vstack() 193

O

object-oriented interface, in Matplotlib 213, 214
open() function 96
operators 24
  arithmetic operators 24, 25
  assignment operators 28, 29
  Bitwise operators 31
  identity operators 33
  logical operators 30

membership operators 32, 33
relational operators 26, 27

P

Pandas 111, 115
  data structure 117
pandas DataFrame
  aggregation 142, 143
  column, adding 148-151
  concatenating 154-156
  creating 117-119
  data cleaning 131-140
  data, exploring 124-127
  data, loading from CSV 119-121
  data, loading from Excel file 123
  data, loading from external files 119
  data, loading from JSON file 123, 124
  data, loading from pipe-delimited input file 122
  data, selecting from 128, 129
  data, selecting with multiple conditions 130
  grouping 141, 142
  merging/joining 157
  ranking 145, 146
  row, adding 146-148
  row/column, dropping 152, 153
  sorting 143-145
  writing, to external files 165-168
pandas library
  defining 115
  need for 115, 116
pandas series 117
  creating 117
pie chart 230
plot
  bar graph 228
  customizing 216-227
  exporting, into file 231-233
  histograms 228, 229
  pie charts 230
  scatter plot 229, 230
  types 227
positional arguments 85
positional variable-length argument 87
predictive data analysis 108
prescriptive data analysis 108
Python
  conditional statements 64
  features 3-5
  file, working with 96
  history 2
  indentation 64
  loop construct 74
  testing, in interactive shell 17, 18
  use cases 5
  versions 2
Python modules 91
  creating 91
  using 92-94

R

rank() function 145
read() function 99, 100
readline() function 100
readlines() function 101
reduce() function
  using 90
relational operators 26
  coding examples 27
replace() function 136

S

scatter plot 229
sets 52
   element membership, checking 54
   elements, adding 52
   items, accessing 52
   items, removing 53
   list, converting into 57
   operations 55
   string, converting into 57
   tuple, converting into 57
   working with 52
simple line plot
   creating 212
sort_index() function 143
sorting, in NumPy 202
   examples 203, 204
sort_value() function 143
statistical functions, in NumPy
   numPy.amaz() 195
   numPy.amin() 195
   numpy.average() 197
   numpy.mean() 196
   numPy.median() 197
   numpy.percentile() 198, 199
   numpy.std() 198
   numpy.var() 198
string 38
   built-in methods 40, 41
   components 39
   concatenation 40
   operations 40
subplot() function 214
   example 214, 215

T

tools, for data analysis
   IPython 111
   Matplotlib 112
   NumPy 112
   Pandas 111
tuple 48
   concatenation 49
   element membership, checking 50
   elements, adding 49
   items, accessing 48
   list, converting into 51
   repetition 49
   slicing 50
   string, converting into 51
   working with 48

U

use case
   data analysis, on dataset 237-250
   dataset 236
   problem statement 236
use cases, Python
   Artificial Intelligence and
      Machine Learning 6
   automation 5
   data analytics 6
   finance and banking 6
   healthcare 5
   web scraping 5

V

variable-length/arbitrary arguments 86
variables 24
   defining rules 24

W

while loop 74
   example 75
write() function 101

Printed in Great Britain
by Amazon